DEAF SPORT
The Impact of Sports
Within the Deaf Community

David A. Stewart

GALLAUDET UNIVERSITY PRESS
Washington, D.C.

Gallaudet University Press
Washington, DC 20002

Library of Congress Cataloging-in-Publication Data

Stewart, David Alan, 1954–
    Deaf sport : the impact of sports within the deaf
community / David A. Stewart.
      p. cm.
    Includes bibliographical references (p.) and index.
    ISBN 0–930323–74–2 (alk. paper)
    1. Deaf—United States. 2. Sports for the physically
handicapped—United States. I. Title.
HV2551.S74   1991
796′.087′2—dc20   91–2056
                                            CIP

Cover photographs by Rick Schoenberg, U.S. Team, World
Games for the Deaf Committee.

To My Mother and Father

CONTENTS

CHAPTER

PAGE

PREFACE — vii

INTRODUCTION — ix

1 DEAF SPORT
Portrait of a Deaf Community — 1

2 A LOOK AT DEAFNESS
Redefining Reality — 20

3 PSYCHOLOGICAL CONSIDERATIONS
for a Denied Minority — 44

4 PSYCHOLOGICAL IMPLICATIONS
of Deaf Sport — 64

5 DEAF IN A HEARING WORLD
A Quest for Equity — 86

6 SOCIALIZATION
in Deaf Sport — 111

7 THE EDUCATIONAL IMPLICATIONS
of Deaf Sport — 155

8 DEAF SPORT
as a Vehicle for Deaf Integration — 175

9 FUTURE DIRECTIONS
for Deaf Sport — 187

REFERENCES — 204

APPENDIX — 218

INDEX — 225

PREFACE

Sitting before my fellow CISS (Comité International des Sports des Sourds) executives at international meetings I am often awed by the sense of togetherness that we all share. We come from different countries and very different societies around the world. We bring to our meetings different sign languages, and we have had distinctly different social and educational upbringings. But tucked away in a hotel in the mountains of Austria or among the exotic animals of Australia, the bond of deafness overrides our differences. With this bond, our sense of who we are and where we are going is bred. In this book, David Stewart captures the spirit of kinship among all deaf people as he meticulously portrays the world of Deaf sport.

Deaf Sport provides a look at the games and events that Deaf people have organized for themselves. It is a look at the psychological forces that have influenced the development of cultural activities that are proudly by and for the Deaf community. Nowhere in the Deaf community is the sense of Deaf people taking charge of their own lives as strong as it is in Deaf sport. *Deaf Sport* gives us an analysis of the sociological forces that have combined to create a community open to all deaf people regardless of race, education, or social background. *Deaf Sport* takes us to the schools to illustrate the responsibility that all people, deaf and hearing, have in making sure that our young deaf children have access to all that Deaf sport has to offer.

As president of the CISS, I am constantly asked why deaf people have a separate international sport program. I am also asked why deaf people do not simply participate in games for the disabled. My first response is to say that deaf athletes are not disabled in any way when playing various sports; in fact, fair competition can be achieved only with other deaf people, with whom communication comes easily. But being deaf in a hearing world means much more than simply having separate sports, teams, games, and other social activities. David Stewart has helped us move far beyond a simple interpretation of the cultural activities of the Deaf community. Using Deaf sport as an example, he introduces us to many new insights about deafness and being part of the Deaf community that challenges the very way we think about deaf people.

Deaf athletes are neither fish nor fowl. On the one hand, they are medically disabled, which leads to the tendency of the hearing population to classify them with other disabled athletes. On the other hand, as far as sports are concerned, they are able-bodied. No adaptations to the rules of sports need be made. No new sport needs to be conceived to make participation of deaf persons possible. What deaf athletes do need is an environment that will meet their physical needs as well as their social needs. Where competition with able-bodied, hearing athletes provides ample opportunities to hone athletic skills, it often fails to satisfy basic social needs, like communication and getting to know fellow players on intimate terms. The research of David Stewart and his colleagues clearly identifies social gratification as a primary reason for why deaf people prefer to compete with one another, and this phenomenon is directly linked to the evolution of a socially dynamic Deaf community.

Thus, *Deaf Sport* is not simply a book about athletes. It is about Deaf people. David Stewart has done a masterful job at combining his experience as a Deaf athlete and a Deaf sport director with his professional knowledge of educational and cultural issues relating to the deaf population. Our task now is to take up the challenge of truly liberating the traditional mindset about deafness. *Deaf Sport* has pointed us in this direction.

Jerald M. Jordan
President, Comité International des Sports des Sourds

INTRODUCTION

My introduction to the Deaf community came one Saturday night more than fifteen years ago at an ice rink. Sitting on a bench, I paused from lacing my skates to gaze over the hundred or so Deaf people enjoying an evening of skating. At least that's what I thought. For me, an ice rink was always a place to skate, play games of speed and agility with friends, or play hockey. I reasoned that the presence of this large group of Deaf people was directly related to the pleasures of gliding over ice on two thin blades. I looked over the ice and I wondered at how similar they all looked. The explanation for the likeness was simple, too—they were all signing. Two decades of indoctrination of a societal mindset had had its effect on me. I was good at fitting people into a nice, clean mold. I did not see the lithe lady twirling in the corner. Or the middle-aged man struggling to gain his balance at center ice. All I could see was this group of Deaf people skating and signing.

Today, I keep this simple snapshot of a Deaf community having a night out on ice handily tucked in the folds of my grey matter. I pull it out from time to time as a reminder that too often in pursuit of understanding our fellow citizens we fall prey to our ignorance of the complex forces that shape our social lives.

This book is an exploration of how a multitude of forces have shaped the evolution of the Deaf community. The institution of Deaf sport is used as an example of how psychological, social, and educational factors have persuaded a large segment of the deaf population to form and preserve a way of life that is distinct from that of the hearing population.

In my analyses of the impact of sport in the Deaf community, deafness is the one criterion that all members of the Deaf community must have. This criterion distinguishes my perspective from those who subscribe to a broader definition of membership in the Deaf community that includes hearing people.

The presence of deafness, then, becomes the point of access that any deaf person has to all that Deaf sport and other aspects of the Deaf community have to offer. As an example, a person deafened at seventeen years of age who is only in the process of learning American Sign Language (ASL) can conceivably become president of a Deaf sport organization or participate in international competitions for deaf athletes. On the other hand, a hearing person who has Deaf parents, learned ASL as a native language, married a Deaf person, and works as a teacher of deaf children will at no time have a similar degree of access within the realm of Deaf sport.

In discussing the different aspects of the Deaf community, I have made a distinction in meaning between *Deaf* and *deaf.* When referring to individuals who are linked by, among other things, shared experiences of deafness and their use of ASL, I use the term *Deaf* (e.g., the Deaf community). Deaf is also capitalized when a reference is made to institutions or entities directly related to the Deaf community. Examples of such references are Deaf sport, Deaf culture, Deaf mainstream, and Deaf world. When I refer to anyone who has a significant hearing loss, then I use the term *deaf.*

Each chapter in this book deals with a specific aspect of Deaf sport. In chapter one, the various functions of Deaf sport are described. A rationale is provided to explain why Deaf sport is an excellent vehicle for understanding the forces that have shaped the evolution of the Deaf community and the dynamics of being a Deaf person. The psychological, social, educational, and political dimensions of Deaf sport are introduced. The implications of these dimensions are critical in understanding the impact that sport has in the Deaf community.

Chapter two provides a perspective on who deaf people are and what adjustments they make to living in the larger hearing society. To further explore the intricacies of deafness, the impact of communication technologies and the importance of using sign language are discussed. The chapter ends with soliloquies by two individuals who contrast greatly in their initiation into the world of Deaf sport.

The psychological effects of living in a hearing world is the focus of chapter three. The influence of the home environment on raising a deaf child is also examined because parental values often mirror societal values. Children learn about responding to others by first learning to respond to their parents. If parents do not accept their child's deafness, they risk having their deaf child viewing others outside of the family in a negative manner.

Chapter four examines ways in which deaf people reflect upon their roles and values in life. Deaf sport is a positive influence that helps deaf individuals interact in a Deaf world and in the larger hearing society. Four of the major issues discussed in this chapter are the adoption of community and cultural values, the discovery of self, the roles of Deaf athletes and Deaf coaches, and the roles of other participants in Deaf sport.

In chapter five the theoretical foundation of symbolic interactionism is applied to an analysis of symbols and meanings in Deaf sport. This analysis reveals that within the activities and structure of Deaf sport are embedded the symbolic representations of the power and security of self-determination. The issue of equity in a hearing world as a primary motivational factor for the growth and maintenance of Deaf sport and other cultural activities related to the Deaf community is also discussed.

How socialization processes in Deaf sport are helping all deaf people achieve equity is the theme of chapter six. Within the framework of Deaf sport, opportunities for involvement are created at the participant, administrative, and spectator levels, yet involvement in Deaf sport is affected in part by the social agents that socialize individuals into sport. The critical social agents discussed include the community, the family, peer groups, and schools.

Chapter seven looks at the relationship between educational institutions and programs for deaf students and sport. An examination of the division within the education field with respect to communication methodologies reveals that programs that emphasize signing are more likely to instill values that closely resemble those of the Deaf community than are oral education programs. The concluding remarks emphasize that it is incumbent upon all schools to ensure that deaf students are aware of the options they have in both Deaf and hearing communities.

The traditional mindset that there is just one mainstream for deaf individuals is challenged in chapter eight. It is suggested that interacting in an environment consisting mainly of

Deaf individuals is an example of being in a Deaf mainstream. Deaf sport is espoused as an excellent vehicle for integrating individuals into a Deaf mainstream.

The direction that Deaf sport might take in the future is the subject of the ninth, and final chapter. It is suggested that Deaf sport administrators strengthen their commitment to the deaf population and reach out to a larger proportion of this population. Deaf youngsters and deafened adults are identified as two groups that need special attention from the field of Deaf sport.

In writing this book I am indebted to many individuals. To Donalda Ammons, Martin Belsky, Donald McCarthy, Jerald Jordan, and Art Kruger, all stalwarts in the field of Deaf sport, I am grateful for their wisdom and interpretations of the purposes and directions of Deaf sport. I am deeply appreciative of the fascinating insights I received into what it is like to be Deaf in a hearing world (and how Deaf sport challenges societal views of the implications of deafness) from Thor Fridriksson, Wayne Goulet, Chris Hunter, Francine Lauer, Diane Little, Donald McCarthy, Lawson McNally, and Rohan Smith. I express my gratitude to reviewers of earlier versions of this book—Donalda Ammons, Walter Bazley, David Beaver, Martin Belsky, Wayne Bottlinger, Bryan Clarke, Diane Little, Gail Dummer, Francine Lauer, Chris Hunter, Jerald Jordan, Annelies Knoppers, Donald McCarthy, James Mosenthal, Jo-Anne Robinson, and David Updegraff—and to those who participated in a blind review. Many thanks to Ivey Pittle Wallace for helping me keep the book in focus and for providing encouragement throughout the long period of writing.

My warmest appreciation I extend to my loving wife, Elizabeth, whose optimism saw me through the entire process, and to my daughters, Rachel, Rebecca, and Jennifer, whose childhood innocence and playfulness provided me with much inspiration.

DEAF SPORT

CHAPTER 1

DEAF SPORT
Portrait of a Deaf Community

T here is something about being "Deaf" that is quietly comforting to those who have this identity. It has to do, in part, with American Sign Language (ASL), a language oblivious to the rambling operations of speech. It has to do with experiences among Deaf people that cannot be shared with hearing people. The resolve to be Deaf is steeped in hundreds of years of culture that has steadfastly evolved within a predominantly hearing society despite the interferences of educators, politicians, and a battalion of society's "do-gooders." Preservation of a Deaf identity is fueled by the reassuring presence of a community of Deaf individuals.

Deaf sport can be thought of as a vehicle for understanding the dynamics of being Deaf. It facilitates a social identification among Deaf people that is not easily obtained in other sociocultural contexts (Stewart 1986). It relies on a Deaf perspective to define its social patterns of behaviors, and it presents an orientation to deafness that is distinctly different from that endorsed by hearing institutions. Essentially, Deaf sport emphasizes the honor of being Deaf, whereas society tends to focus on the adversity of deafness.

A further advantage of using Deaf sport as a basis for talking about Deaf people is the fact that Deaf sport does not threaten the sport structure of society in general. Rather, Deaf sport demonstrates how a common interest in sport can be handled to the mutual satisfaction of two different groups of people without one group's infringing upon the realm of another. Hearing persons do not feel that they have to control Deaf sport, although they are in a position to exert considerable influence in sport and physical education for school-age deaf students. Indeed, other than in sport contests, the only friction between Deaf and hearing sport groups is economic. Deaf sport associations must compete for the use of facilities, federal support, private sponsorships, research funds, and spectators.

Social Dynamism through Deaf Sport

Deaf sport is a social institution within which Deaf people exercise their right to self-determination through organization, competition, and socialization surrounding Deaf sport activities. The magnitude and the complexity of Deaf sport reflects many of the dimensions of being Deaf in a hearing society. In this sense Deaf sport is a microcosm of the Deaf community.

The most prominent dimension of Deaf sport is its social sphere, which thrives in a Deaf environment that relies on signing for communication. Hence, a primary function of sporting events for deaf people is to serve as a catalyst for the socialization of a low-incidence and geographically dispersed population. Deaf sport brings deaf people together under nonthreatening social conditions that puts at a disadvantage anyone who must rely solely on hearing and speech for communication. For deaf adults who spend most of their days working and interacting in the absence of other deaf individuals and signers, Deaf sport is a niche well suited to their social and psychological needs. Furthermore, deafness is the main defining characteristic of participants in Deaf sport. Thus, as a whole, Deaf sport nurtures a healthy image of Deaf people and their relationship to society at large.

The psychological dimension of Deaf sport is embodied in its ability to provide deaf individuals with access to a social support system. The mere awareness of being able to tap into this support system can be psychologically beneficial (Gottlieb 1985). With this support, Deaf individuals are better able to develop their social and mental potential without constantly dealing with society's negative stereotypic images and misconceptions of deaf persons. No doubt, the Deaf community contains vestiges of the adverse effects of stereotyping. Not everyone in the Deaf community has come to accept the implications of deafness or has taken advantage of a Deaf environment. In a sense, optimizing the lifestyles of Deaf persons is what Deaf sport and other activities of the Deaf community are all about. Thus, all of these activities serve as dynamic blueprints for living as a Deaf person.

A third dimension of Deaf sport is education. This dimension is best revealed in schools for deaf students, which historically have had strong ties to the Deaf community. However, such schools are not necessarily supportive of the values of the Deaf community. This is illustrated by the fact that in these schools ASL, the language of the Deaf community, is rarely used for instructional purposes; decision-making processes are dominated by hearing persons; there are relatively few Deaf teachers and Deaf administrators; and most teachers and administrators are only slightly aware of the implications of the Deaf community for deaf children and youngsters. On the other hand, educators connected with education programs for deaf children located in neighborhood schools will tend to be even less cognizant of the activities of the Deaf community than their peers in schools for deaf students. Nevertheless, programs that pool deaf students in any kind of educational setting have the potential to introduce them to the values and actions of the Deaf community.

In this book only the social, psychological, and educational dimensions of Deaf sport are examined. Other dimensions need to be explored to expand our understanding of Deaf dynamics and of the numerous implications of deafness. It would be of interest to compare the ramifications of race as it appears in Deaf sport and in the general world of sport. In the United States sport clubs for Black Deaf persons can be a springboard for exploring the relationships that exist between majority and minority Deaf groups. Comparisons of the social behavior of Deaf French Canadians living in Quebec and the Maritimes with the rest of the Deaf population in Canada could be readily initiated because of the close ties between both of these groups through the Canadian Deaf Sports Association (CDSA).

The political dimension of the Deaf community has rarely been examined in any aspect. Observation of the control and organization of Deaf sport hints at some intriguing insights about the political culture of Deaf people. At the international level, the power structure is dominated by males and is therefore a recapitulation of the power structure of hearing sport. Female sport directors of high national status experience frustration in trying to increase their input in international Deaf sport matters. One plausible explanation is that national Deaf sport governing bodies also tend to be male dominated. Since it was first founded in 1945, the American Athletic Association of the Deaf (AAAD) has never had a female president. According to its 1987 letterhead, AAAD had no women in prominent positions in its complex administrative structure, which included a nine-member administrative board, eight regional presidents, five chief officers of standing committees, and four chairpersons of national tournament committees. Only in 1988 did the AAAD elect a Deaf woman to be secretary-treasurer.

There are also differences in the political structure between countries. In just over twenty years the CDSA has had one female president, and three of its then eight provincial affiliates (the Alberta Deaf Sports Association, the Manitoba Deaf Sports Association, and the Féderation Sportive des Sourds du Québec) had female presidents in 1986. In Canada female sport directors do not share the same concerns about making inroads in the power structure of Deaf sport with their counterparts in the United States, and it would be interesting to note how the presence of women affects perceptions of the role of national Deaf sport governing bodies. Political difference is also noted in the bylaws of the CDSA, which states that only deaf members have voting privileges, whereas in the AAAD bylaws such a direct exclusion of hearing persons is not addressed.

Another political aspect is found in the influence of matters pertaining to competition in hearing sports. The 1984 boycott of the Los Angeles Olympic games by Eastern Bloc countries led to a similar boycott by all of these countries except Hungary at the 1985 World Games for the Deaf, which were also held in Los Angeles. Romania, which did attend the 1984 Olympics, did not send a team to the 1985 World Games for the Deaf.

In Profile 1, Jerald M. Jordan, president of the Comité International des Sports des Sourds (CISS), points out the political differences in the approach to sports taken by Deaf sport, Olympic sport, and disabled sport groups. That Deaf sport has been the innovator in several aspects relating to international competition illustrates its independence from traditions that were established by a hearing-operated organization such as the International Olympic Committee. Jordan's clear separation of the focus of Deaf sport from disabled sport groups is timely, for it mirrors the political concerns the CISS has with the encroaching power of large disabled sport groups.

The dynamics of Deaf sport indicates a highly versatile social group that challenges negative representations of "socially isolated" and "socially deprived" deaf persons. In-depth investigations of the various dimensions of Deaf sport would help erase societal misconceptions that the lives of deaf persons are incontestably deprived when compared with those of their hearing counterparts. Moreover, such comparisons may be spurious because there is no viable alternative to a signing environment for meeting the communication needs of many Deaf people, and that environment therefore defines the primary population for social interactions.

The Attraction of Sport

At the macro level, sport can be described as a social institution with functions similar to institutions of education, science, family, religion, and politics. Eitzen and Sage (1982) have described institutions as "social arrangements that channel behavior in prescribed ways in the important areas of societal life" (p. 12). For sport these ways reflect the norms, values, and

Profile 1
Jerald M. Jordan
President
Comité International
des Sports des Sourds

Jerald M. Jordan is the current president of the Comité International des Sports des Sourds (CISS). Deafened at the age of seven years from spinal meningitis, he attended the Lutheran School for the Deaf, Michigan School for the Deaf, and Gallaudet University. He also spent part of his school years in a public high school. He has been a teacher and administrator at Gallaudet University for the past thirty years. His interest in sport has always been on the administrative side. After serving several terms as vice-president of the American Athletic Association of the Deaf (AAAD), he became chairman of the Xth World Games for the Deaf, which were held in Washington, D.C., in 1965. In 1967 he was elected to the executive committee of CISS and in 1971 was chosen president, a position he still holds.

Jordan draws from his extensive experience in the international scene of Deaf sport to share insights about the directions of the CISS and its importance to deaf people:

"The competition and spirit surrounding the World Games for the Deaf is far closer to the 'olympic' ideal than that associated with the Olympics as the public knows it. I am continuously reminded of this each time I watch the Olympics struggle with issues related to professionalism, doping, internal politics, and nationalism. In time, it may well be that the World Games for the Deaf will be one of the last remaining vestige of the true 'olympics.'

"Yet, the CISS shares the same goals as the International Olympic Committee (IOC). We believe that there is a need for athletes to compete with each other, and a need for a group of people with a commonality, deafness, to come together and share their experiences. International Deaf sport competition actively promotes the old ideal of the Olympics—the brotherhood of man through sports.

"However, it should be clear that CISS does not simply imitate the activities and philosophy of the IOC. In some ways, CISS has been the innovator, with the IOC following in our footsteps. CISS elected a woman to its executive committee before the IOC saw fit to do so. CISS has celebrated its summer and winter games two years apart since 1955. The IOC will begin that in the 1990s. Tennis and table tennis have been medal sports in the World Games for the Deaf for many years, whereas it was only in the 1980s that both of these sports were introduced into the Olympics.

"CISS also distinguishes itself from sports for disabled groups. In recent years there has been much pressure on Deaf sport groups to combine our games with those for the disabled. CISS, along with all national Deaf sport organizations, strongly resists this movement. In the Paralympics the primary focus is on classification of the disability and adaptation of a sport to each particular disability. This a necessary condition in order to maintain fairness. In Deaf sport there is only one classification—deaf. No modification to any sport occurs other than minor technical adjustments to make auditory cues visible.

"The programs sponsored by the CISS are critical for deaf athletes around the world. They allow top deaf athletes a chance to know the joys of international competition and the camaraderie that goes with competing with their own people. It is through international Deaf sport that the flame of idealism embedded in the 'olympic' dream continues to glow."

role expectations of the athletes, spectators, and all others encompassed by its broader sphere of activities. Snyder and Spreitzer (1978) suggested that the pervasiveness of sport allows it to "express some of the dominant values of a society" (p. 25). By extension, they argued that one justification for sport in schools is that it prepares children for playing the game of life. Thus, sport is a vital component contributing to the overall unity and stability of a society and ultimately to its survival (Eitzen and Sage 1986).

Sport is attractive to people because as a social institution it helps individuals meet certain needs. Eitzen and Sage (1982) reviewed other writers' work and identified several societal needs and the role of sport as follows:

> (1) Sport serves as a safety valve for both spectators and participants, dissipating excess energies, tensions, and hostile feelings in a socially acceptable way; (2) athletes serve as role models, possessing the proper mental and physical traits to be emulated by the other members of society; (3) sport is a secular, quasi-religious institution using ritual and ceremony to reinforce the values of society, and thereby regulating behavior to the channels prescribed by custom. (p. 13)

Sport also has its negative points. Alcohol and other drug abuse is a prime example of the negative social behaviors that can be induced by sport, and authoritarianism, racism, and sexism have been associated in the organization and playing of sport.

However, sport is also enjoyed for its physical fitness value and for the pure fun of participation. Hence, recreational leagues that place a premium on enjoyment while downplaying the competitive and skill-oriented side of sport are preferred by many people.

Sport draws a huge gathering among those who do not participate. For every sport, fans in attendance cheer their favorites, jeer the opposition, and, when called to the task, assume the role of armchair expert. For the organizers, among other responsibilities, there are the tasks of fund raising and publicity that operate according to principles common to all amateur sport organizations.

Finally, many people have argued that the "effects of involvement in physical activities extend beyond the immediate fun and excitement of the moment," although more research is needed to determine the nature of these effects (Sage 1986, 344). For now, it is fair to assume that sport is not immune to society's values, and in some instances it mirrors those values held to be important in a society (Leonard 1980). Hence, it should not be surprising that Deaf sport reflects the values of the Deaf community. Although to a certain degree Deaf sport falls under the rubric of sport as it is known by the general public, Deaf sport reinforces certain values that are not subscribed to by society in general. This is the primary reason for viewing Deaf sport as a separate sport institution existing within the confines of a Deaf community.

The Business of Deaf Sport

The business of Deaf sport is much like the business of hearing sport. Games are organized, supervised, and played as they are in any community. The type of sports played varies according to the desires of the community. These, in turn, are influenced by demographic and geographic factors. Small communities may focus on a sport that many can play and thereby increase the number of participants. Sports falling into this category are bowling, volleyball, and slo-pitch. Larger communities are obviously able to offer a greater selection of sports. The Greater Vancouver Association of the Deaf at one time offered its members curling, soccer, slo-pitch, basketball, volleyball, badminton, tennis, table tennis, skiing, and hockey (Stewart 1987). In these larger communities there are few times of the year when there are no sports available. Sport is also influenced by geographical considerations, as some communities take advantage of their environment to meet the desires of their population. Thus, in the Pacific Northwest, downhill skiing and four-wheel drive clubs represent regional options in sport.

In addition, the technical rules associated with Deaf sport are not unique in any respect. When changes are made in specific sports, they always reflect adaptations to the communication needs of deaf persons (Robinson and Stewart 1987). Common adaptations are lights to start swimming and track races, flags to signal calls in soccer and volleyball, flashing lights and flags to signal calls in basketball, and the use of manual signs by umpires in slo-pitch, basketball, and volleyball. These adaptations do not in any way change the rules of the games. Basketball, hockey, football, baseball, wrestling, and other sports are played following the same rules used by high school, college, and professional players. A player who misses a referee's call to halt play and then commits an infraction will not be penalized unless the infraction was uncalled for or intended to inflict pain. In these instances referees use the same judgment they would with hearing players. Thus, Deaf sport does not represent a unique way of playing sports or a new kind of game.

Adaptations, however, can lead to some creative strategies on the part of players hoping to gain an edge in playing. For example, sprinters rely on visual information such as a strobe light to indicate the start of a race. However, some sprinters have been known to watch the trigger finger of the starter for the first sign of trigger release. This way, they will be able to start the take-off motion before the starting gun or light actually goes off. Hearing sprinters do not normally attempt this strategy because the ideal starting position requires them to keep their eyes down and head pointed straight ahead (Bressler 1990).

The continuity of Deaf sport is ensured by the very mechanisms that have fostered its development. For deaf individuals, assimilation into the hearing mainstream of society is not readily accomplished. Furthermore, assimilation depends upon the indoctrination of social ideals through a common language. For any given community, language is one of the identifying cultural characteristics (Hoijer 1948), and the United States, for example, demands that its citizens and inhabitants speak English. Facing physical constraints in meeting this demand, deaf persons look elsewhere for social compatibility and cultural gratification. Deaf sport activities, in contrast, offer an accessible mainstream to all deaf persons.

The many dimensions of Deaf sport provide a rationale for keeping its purposes and values intact. At a personal level, Deaf sport is a physical oasis for the body. It attracts athletes and recreation seekers and encourages them to exercise and keep fit. Intellectually, Deaf sport challenges athletes to meet the strategic demands of sports, the organizers to handle the complexities of planning and overseeing sporting events, and spectators to assess the outcomes of games and skills of players. Emotionally, Deaf sport events provide a means for relieving anxieties and a source of inspiration for the victorious and disappointment for the losers. At a political level, competitions between Deaf teams help forge relationships between rival clubs, communities, states, and nations. In education, Deaf sport is a source of inspiration for many youngsters who wish to compete beyond their school years. Finally, in the area of socialization, Deaf sport serves as a unifying force for members of the Deaf community.

Ultimately, Deaf sport is more than a vehicle for direct and indirect participation in sporting activities. Deaf sport is a social institution that allows Deaf people to negotiate their own evolutionary pathway that is to a large extent unfettered by the demands of a hearing society. Deaf sport induces its constituents to come to terms with their deafness and establish realistic social goals with respect to interpersonal interactions, communication, language, and social mobility.

The Organization of Deaf Sport

At the highest level of organization many countries have a national sport governing body that coordinates and promotes the development of Deaf athletes. In the United States the national body is the AAAD, and in Canada it is the CDSA. Both the AAAD and the CDSA are nonprofit organizations that rely upon the services of Deaf volunteers. When hearing people are involved, their roles are typically related to public relations, liaison between the Deaf sport organizations and other sport organizations, fund raising, coaching, officiating, and interpreting.

The AAAD and CDSA do receive federal support to cover some of the costs of administration, transportation for athletes and sport directors, dissemination of information, and various programs such as the development of athletic skills and coaching credentials. They also rely on the support of local Deaf communities and the public to send athletes to national and international competitions. Public awareness of their many activities is facilitated through the *AAAD Bulletin* and the CDSA's *Competitor,* newsletters of the regional and local Deaf sport associations, and word of mouth.

To promote the development of Deaf athletes, the AAAD and CDSA formed the North American Deaf Sports Association (NADSA), which allows teams and athletes from the United States and Canada to compete against each other on a regular basis. The NADSA gives both countries the opportunity to expose their athletes to international competition before going to the World Games for the Deaf. The structure and affiliations of AAAD and CDSA are different; a brief description of each follows.

Originally called the American Athletic Union of the Deaf when it was founded in 1945, the AAAD is "the first national group among deaf persons to eliminate and prohibit discrimination because of a person's race or creed" (Kruger 1986, 17). The AAAD is a parent body of the following eight regional athletic associations, each of which consists of a number of states (Ammons 1984, 1986): Northeast Athletic Association for the Deaf, Eastern Athletic Association for the Deaf, Southeast Athletic Association for the Deaf, Central Athletic Association for the Deaf, Midwest Athletic Association for the Deaf, Farwest Athletic Association for the Deaf, Southwest Athletic Association for the Deaf, and Northwest Athletic Association for the Deaf. The AAAD strives to "foster and regulate athletic competition among member clubs to develop uniform rules governing interclub competition, and to provide adequate competition for those members primarily interested in interclub athletics" (Ammons 1986, 69). It is most active at the national level through its sponsorship of annual basketball and softball tournaments. The AAAD uses the sites of these tournaments to hold its board meetings. The board helps the AAAD to keep in touch with grassroots organizations and provide leadership support to organizations sponsoring tournaments. These meetings provide a "blend of sports, business meetings, and social gatherings" (Kruger 1986, 18).

The regional associations of AAAD help to coordinate and regulate sporting activities among Deaf sport clubs. They rely on local clubs to provide teams for annual regional tournaments in basketball and softball, the winners of which represent the regions at national tournaments (Kruger 1986). Local clubs may be involved in one or more sports (for example, basketball, bowling, golf, and slo-pitch). Local clubs are also the most critical building block in a Deaf sport network. They provide the foundation for recruiting and developing athletes and sport directors. Regional and national tournaments are used to select and prepare athletes for representing the national team.

Members of the national team compete at international competitions and most notably at the World Games for the Deaf. Preparations for international competitions in sports played at the World Games are undertaken by the United States World Games for the Deaf Team Committee. This committee holds tryouts at least one year before the summer and winter World Games to select the members of the U.S. team, and it conducts training camps just before each World Games for the Deaf.

The AAAD has twice hosted the World Summer Games for the Deaf, first in Washington, D.C., in 1965 and then in Los Angeles in 1985. It also hosted the World Winter Games for the Deaf in Lake Placid, New York, in 1975.

In Canada the CDSA is the parent organization of the following ten provincial Deaf sport associations: British Columbia Deaf Sports Federation, Alberta Deaf Sports Association, Saskatchewan Deaf Sports Association, Manitoba Deaf Sports Association, Ontario Deaf Sports Association, Féderation Sportive des Sourds du Québec, New Brunswick Deaf Sports Association, Prince Edward Island Deaf Sports Association, Nova Scotia Deaf Sports Association, and Newfoundland Deaf Sports Association. Each of the provincial associations is responsible for coordinating sporting activities within its own jurisdiction. In addition, each selects and prepares athletes and teams for competition at regional (for instance, the Central Canada Deaf Summer Games) and national tournaments.

The CDSA was incorporated in 1964 under its previous name, the Federation of Silent Sports of Canada. The general function of the CDSA is to promote and facilitate the "practice of fitness, amateur sports and recreation among deaf people of all ages in Canada" (CDSA promotional flyer, 1988). Canada has a geographically dispersed population, and the CDSA Board of Directors, like its American counterpart, holds its meetings in different cities around the country in an effort to promote the development of Deaf sport at the local and provincial levels. Currently, the CDSA sponsors national tournaments in curling and slo-pitch. Future plans include national tournaments for bowling and darts.

To oversee the operations of different sport activities, the CDSA has two standing committees. The Non-Olympic Sports Committee encourages participation in all sports not included in the World Games for the Deaf. Its major focus is in assisting local Deaf sport associations as they host national events in curling and slo-pitch. The World Games for the Deaf Organizing Committee recruits and trains athletes for regional, national, and international competitions. Regional and national competitions such as the Canadian Deaf Badminton and Table Tennis Championships are used to select athletes for the Canadian Deaf Team. In 1991 the CDSA hosted the XIIth World Winter Games for the Deaf in Banff, Alberta.

In accordance with Canada's commitment to multiculturalism, the CDSA recognizes English and French as the official languages for all of its documentation. It also maintains a French-speaking director on its board to facilitate the coordination of Deaf sport between the CDSA and Deaf sport organizations in Quebec and New Brunswick.

Hearing People in Transition

In view of our current understanding of the dynamics of being Deaf, it becomes obvious that in order for Deaf and hearing people to coexist, their respective communities must be accorded equal social status. For far too long the implications of deafness from the Deaf community's perspective received little attention from educators and other professionals as they attempted to understand what it was like to be deaf in a hearing society. Today, the Deaf community and some of its more prominent features such as ASL are slowly working their way into society's mainstream of common knowledge. Even for those who choose to deny the significance of these aspects of deafness, it is no longer professionally acceptable for them to belittle these aspects.

With Deaf people more openly asserting their Deaf status and gaining respect for their beliefs and actions, it is incumbent upon hearing persons to adjust their perspectives accordingly. They must undergo a change in their own thinking and come to view deaf persons not in terms of their deviations from hearing norms but as a group of individuals who have the right to follow their own standards of social behavior. It is hard to avoid the ethnocentric notion that the capacity to hear is conducive to a superior lifestyle. How individuals feel about their own lifestyles and others' is a personal matter. However, ethnocentrism translates into oppressive dogmatism when one group uses it to justify their intrusion into the rights of another group.

Thus, a critical issue is the ways the hearing population can refrain from intruding in the lives of the deaf population. To accomplish this, a change in their perspective of all types of deaf people is necessary, because only with such a transition in thinking will deaf and hearing persons become equal citizens in an equal society. Hearing professionals and parents interacting with deaf persons should not be asking what is needed to synchronize the lives of deaf people with that of hearing persons. Rather, society needs to demonstrate its respect for the communication and social needs of Deaf persons within their own institutions (for example, educational, political, economic, sport, religious, and family). This change in outlook also needs to take into account the way Deaf people view themselves and their desire to seize control of their own lives.

In some ways a change in perspective may already be occurring. A number of books written by deaf individuals serve to ease hearing individuals through this transition by discussing societal attitudes toward deafness or illustrating the experiences and implications of being Deaf (for example, Bowe 1986; Gannon 1981; Hairston and Smith 1983; Holcomb 1985; Jacobs 1974; Padden and Humphries 1988; Robinson and Stewart 1987). Still other books also describe deaf experiences (for example, Batson and Bergman 1985; Holcomb and Wood 1988;

Ogden and Lipsett 1982; Panara and Panara 1983). Accompanying the English print medium are videotaped productions on American Deaf culture that use the medium of signs (Bienvenu and Colonomos 1985, 1986). There are also many excellent books and articles by other authors discussing the educational, sociological, and psychological implications of deafness.

Assistance for this transition can also be found in courses on Deaf culture offered at some postsecondary institutions, in increasingly positive mass media attention as witnessed during the strike by Gallaudet University students for a Deaf president, in the addition of ASL to the foreign-language programs at the high school level in several states (for instance, Maine, Texas, Arizona, Michigan, California), in a proliferation of sign language courses across Canada and the United States, in newspaper coverage of Deaf sport events and Deaf athletes, in touring Deaf theatrical groups, and through public television programs such as "The Deaf Mosaic." What these examples and others illustrate is the robustness of the values and traditions of Deaf people. Deaf sport is not an institutional aberration. It will continue to exist as long as there are Deaf people who use sign language as their primary means of communication.

Direct interactions with Deaf people is another option for learning about the social implications of deafness. For those who do not already have access to this form of interaction, gaining it may present some problems. Some Deaf people may resent hearing people who intrude into their social affairs for the purpose of "learning about the Deaf" or because "they are fascinated with ASL." The Deaf community is not a fishbowl. However, receptiveness to those who wish to meet and socialize with Deaf people does vary from community to community. The size and location of a Deaf community, the type and frequency of its social activities, and its members' past involvement with hearing persons are some factors possibly influencing general receptiveness. Personal contact with a member of a Deaf community is perhaps the best means of introduction to other members of that community.

In lieu of a contact person, Deaf sport is a suitable way to introduce deaf newcomers and hearing individuals to one type of social environment that exists within the Deaf community. Attending tournaments has its advantages in that it allows a person to be unobtrusive while observing a large number of people interact, to be casual while making an introduction, and to leave at any time. Information can easily be obtained from national organizations such as the AAAD and CDSA, from regional or provincial affiliations of these national sport governing bodies, from local Deaf associations, and from schools for deaf students. In addition, interested players on hearing sport teams could take the initiative and invite a Deaf team to participate in their league or to play exhibition games against them. The hearing athletes' lack of signing skills will obviously be a handicap; however, in such a situation other means of communication such as the use of pencil and paper or interpreters should be explored.

Another option for interacting with Deaf people is to participate in the activities of the World Recreation Association of the Deaf (WRAD). The WRAD was created to "enlarge the scope of recreational, social, and other leisure activities in the deaf community; to educate the deaf community on issues of general community interest; and to educate the hearing community on the needs of the deaf . . . for full participation . . . in the community at large" (Gross 1987, 1). The integration of deaf and hearing persons is accomplished through a variety of activities including beach parties, air balloon rides, snow skiing, volleyball, bicycling, hiking, and tours to educational and cultural lectures. Interpreters are always on hand to convey information to both deaf and hearing participants. WRAD is especially interested in improving the recreational opportunities for deaf students who do not live in residential schools for deaf students (Schuetz 1988) and who therefore may lack social contacts with other deaf individuals.

In spite of suggestions like these for ways a hearing person can establish informal relationships with Deaf persons, it should be noted that even extensive contact does not guarantee that a person will come to recognize and accept Deaf people as they are. Support for this observation comes from a history of hearing professionals who have had extensive interactions with Deaf individuals in various fields and who still do not understand or accept many of the values, traditions, and actions of the Deaf. A chapter on the coming of age of the Deaf in Canada and the United States cannot yet be written.

Footnotes to Deaf Integration

There are two guiding principles that should be adhered to by those wishing to interact with deaf people whether in a professional capacity or as casual acquaintances. First, associating or working with deaf people is not a mission. Deaf people should not be at the mercy of zealots; they need equal opportunities to succeed. They do not need to be helped any more than hearing persons do. The key benefit of interpreters, captioned television, message-relay centers, and hearing aids is not that they "help" individuals overcome their deafness, because they do not. Rather, *they are tools for accessing auditory information and in this respect they contribute to the dynamics of being Deaf.* Watching captioned television and using interpreters are like using sign language and participating in the Deaf community; they are a way of living, not a battle with deafness.

The second principle is that the existence of a deaf population is the only justification needed for the values, sign language, social cohesiveness, sport, culture, and heritage of Deaf people. Society must refrain from putting Deaf people on the defensive for the things they believe in and the way they live. The Deaf community is seeking awareness, not approval from society.

Conclusion

As the end of the twentieth century draws near, we may be witnessing a new era of improved understanding between deaf and hearing individuals. It will be interesting to see how our educational institutions react to the increasingly strong presence of the Deaf community. Will cultural pluralism come to mean more than just deceptive rhetoric in the education of deaf students? Will ASL assume a more prominent role as a language of instruction in the classroom? Will Deaf individuals become a more influential force in the education of deaf students? For now, while hearing people continue to hold the majority of top administrative positions in education programs for deaf children and youths, the Deaf community will remain as the primary focal point of the social lives of these individuals during their adulthood.

Deaf sport provides strong institutional support for members of the Deaf community. It integrates deaf individuals into the mainstream of the Deaf community. It facilitates a greater sense of understanding and respect between the Deaf and hearing populations. It does not exclude the participation of hearing individuals in a number of ways, but it does ensure that the values of the Deaf community are not threatened by their involvement. Deaf sport also engenders a sense of pride and provides the flavor of self-determination among its participants. These and other dimensions of Deaf sport reflect the dynamics of being Deaf.

Among the many dimensions of Deaf sport, perhaps the most powerful one is the message that Deaf people cannot deny the fact that they are deaf and, therefore, they tend to favor social environments consisting mainly or entirely of Deaf people. Clearly, participation in sport brings with it much enjoyment and physical satisfaction. However, Deaf sport has social consequences that extend beyond the game itself. It is a primary vehicle for the socialization of deaf individuals who use sign language for communication. In its emphasis on socialization processes, Deaf sport does more than just promote an "it's all right to be deaf" attitude. In the face of a dominating and hegemonic hearing society, Deaf sport aims to assert being Deaf as the status quo.

CHAPTER 2

A LOOK AT DEAFNESS
Redefining Reality

From a cultural perspective, the Deaf population consists of a group of people who have a hearing loss, use signs to communicate, and interact in the Deaf community. The primary sign language of the Deaf community in the United States and most of Canada is ASL, which is symbolic of the linguistic minority status of this group (Padden and Humphries 1988). This definition gives a sociological and anthropological perspective of the unifying characteristics of Deaf persons. It contrasts with others that are clinically or pathologically oriented and that define deafness in terms of deviation from norms based on and established by hearing persons. These latter definitions tend to focus on what society perceives to be normal.

There are many misconceptions about deafness and how it affects individuals. These misconceptions are not confined to the general public; professionals are suspected of misrepresenting, intentionally or not, the characteristics of deaf people (Carver 1987; Lane 1988). Indeed, there is a danger in any attempt to portray deaf people as possessing common traits because the heterogeneity of the deaf population defies simple and convenient categorization of behaviors: deaf individuals do not respond to their deafness in a prescribed manner. On the other hand, there are some commonalities that are worth exploring, and Deaf sport can be used as a backdrop for framing these commonalities. An examination of the intricacies of hearing loss, the impact of communication technologies, sign language, and socialization patterns is crucial to an understanding of the psychological and sociological aspects of deafness.

The Intricacies of Deafness

Deafness is not a prescription for a certain lifestyle, set of mores and beliefs, or even communication preferences. All deaf individuals make unique adjustments to living that take into account their degree of deafness and their reactions to different social environments. These adjustments are influenced by many factors, including families and their acceptance of deafness, educational placement (for example, in a school for deaf students or a general education classroom), linguistic proficiency (for example, in ASL, English), educational programming (for instance, total communication and oral education methodologies), contact with other deaf individuals, ability to communicate in various modalities, etiology, age at onset of deafness, hearing status of parents and siblings, extent to which residual hearing can be used with or without a hearing aid, and use of technical devices to assist in various aspects of living. Intrinsic personal characteristics such as self-esteem, ambitiousness, and physical and intellectual capacities to fulfill goals are also critical in determining the ecological and social niche that deaf persons eventually come to inhabit.

There is no intention here to discuss the audiological effects of a hearing impairment. Typically, these effects are delineated from the perspective of a hearing population, and their portrayal results in a list of things that deaf people are either unable to do or are able to do but to a lesser extent than their hearing counterparts. They do not illustrate the dynamics of being Deaf; rather, they accentuate the so-called difficulties of not being hearing.

Hearing Loss
and Deaf Sport

The CISS requires that an athlete must have at least a 55 decibel (dB) hearing loss in the better ear to compete in national and international levels of Deaf sport. Athletes must show proof of deafness as measured in a hearing test, and the responsibility for ensuring that athletes meet the qualifying standard for hearing loss rests with the national Deaf sport governing body (for example, the United States World Games for the Deaf Team Committee). To provide partial verification of evidence provided by the national associations, officials at the World Games for the Deaf randomly select athletes for hearing tests.

Athletes whose hearing loss is not severe enough to allow them to compete at the international level are still able, in most instances, to compete at local, state, provincial, or regional levels, depending on the respective regulations governing eligibility. There are at least three important reasons for this difference in hearing-loss requirement between higher and lower levels of competition. First, there is much cost and time involved in having an individual's ears tested. Even on a one-time basis, the enforcement of such a requirement may discourage some from participating in sports. Second, deaf people constitute a low-incidence population. Games require participants, and in some communities it may be difficult to find enough players to form a team. Thus, by expanding the pool of potential players to include those with lesser degrees of hearing losses, a Deaf sport association can expand the number of sports and teams that it can organize.

The third explanation is that most if not all Deaf communities have an interest in expanding their membership. Relaxed entry requirements at lower levels of competition allows non-signing deaf athletes and those who can sign but have less than a 55 dB hearing loss to sample a Deaf lifestyle. How well a person hears is not a factor at this level of participation, although it is a time-honored agreement in Deaf sport that proof of deafness (to whatever degree) lies with each individual.

Still, suspicion does arise as to how much a new person can hear and whether a hearing loss is severe enough to warrant the individual's participation at a local and possibly noncompetitive level of Deaf sport. These suspicions can usually be resolved when a member of the Deaf community vouches for another person's deafness. The need for such assurances is rare, and the issue is not considered serious. When the need does occur, it is a subtle reminder of the bond that deafness has for members of the Deaf community. For some newcomers to Deaf sport, the declaration of one's deafness is the first step toward full initiation into the activities of the Deaf community.

At one time the CISS debated the feasibility of using the condition "socially Deaf" as a criterion for competition. However, such a criterion would have led to much confusion, given that whether or not a person is socially Deaf could not be independently verified. Hence, an audiological criterion that offered a high degree of objectivity was agreed upon.

There have also been attempts by some members of the CISS to change the criterion from 55 dB to 70 dB in the better ear. This would narrow the population from which deaf athletes could be drawn. Proponents for this change argued that a greater degree of hearing loss would eliminate participation by athletes who are able to benefit from the use of their hearing even without hearing aids. They noted that the resulting corps of deaf athletes would consist to a large extent of those who would be labeled Deaf or "socially Deaf." Those opposing this change believed that population size and degree of hearing loss were the critical issues. They feared that a reduced pool of athletes might result in less financial support from governments as well as a less competitive field of athletes. The CISS Congress at the 1985 World Games for the Deaf in Los Angeles defeated a motion to change eligibility requirements to 70 dB.

However, the concern of some CISS members over the degree of hearing loss that should be considered for determining the eligibility of competitors remains. At the 1989 World Games for the Deaf in New Zealand, it was obvious that a few athletes were able to use their hearing well enough that they stood out from the typical Deaf athletes. Particularly noticeable were those athletes who were able to carry on a spoken conversation without hearing aids and with relative ease. I asked one Deaf sport director what he was thinking about while he observed a track athlete talk to a spectator who was at least forty feet away.

He responded that he could not believe that this athlete had at least a 55 dB hearing loss and was convinced that some cheating during a hearing examination had taken place.

The choice of 55 dB hearing loss in the better ear as the standard is significant because at this level the perception of speech through audition alone and without the use of a hearing aid is severely impaired (Northern and Downs 1984). Thus, at international games such as the World Games for the Deaf, athletes are not allowed to wear hearing aids during competition, and it is then believed that whatever players can hear, it will not be advantageous to their performance. This requirement is also significant in that it meets the spirit of the CISS motto—Equal through Sports.

The fact that hearing aids are not permitted during competition is a crucial cornerstone in Deaf sport. On a practical note, hearing aids may be damaged in sport or may cause damage to the ear during play. At a social level the use of a hearing aid represents a symbolic adaptation of a deaf person to the hearing and speaking world. It is a hearing person's answer to deafness. It is a panacea for some, who view deafness merely as an impairment of the hearing mechanism. For those who perceive deafness as an abnormal state of being, then a deaf person who wears a hearing aid is somehow "more normal" than those who choose not to.

But deafness is a complicated trait that defies simple mechanical attempts to compensate for the loss of hearing. A hearing aid may offer little or no benefit to many severely and profoundly deaf people. For these people it does not amplify or clarify speech signals to the point that they become meaningful.

Although Deaf people in general do not scorn or discourage the use of hearing aids at a social level, they do recognize its symbolic link to the hearing world. Hearing aids are a beacon from the hearing world that deafness can be overcome and that helping deaf people hear sounds is a commendable goal. To hearing persons, a hearing aid signals the willingness of a deaf person to comply with this goal. Indeed, there are some severely and profoundly deaf people who do benefit from the use of hearing aids. However, these benefits are not translated within the Deaf community.

Thus, Deaf sport sends a strong message to members of the Deaf community that *on the playing field deaf athletes compete on equal terms*. Since hearing-aid usage affects individuals differently and unpredictably, its exclusion from the playing field is, in part, a symbolic gesture of deafness and fairness. Yet Deaf sport is the only part of the Deaf community where it is acceptable to ban the use of hearing aids. In this respect, Deaf sport reflects the natural evolution of competition among Deaf peers.

Networking within the Deaf Sport Community: Communication Technologies

Perhaps the most important impact of modern technology has been to give Deaf persons direct control over the management of all of their sports and related events. This accomplishment symbolizes Deaf persons' appetite for establishing their own place in a communication-dominated world while maintaining an ecological kinship with the hearing population.

Important technical devices and systems range from telecommunication devices that allow deaf persons to converse on a telephone to signal devices that alert them to sound-induced stimuli in the environment. They are crucial in bridging the gaps that a hearing world has created for deaf persons. The knock on a door, the cry of a baby, the dialogue of television programs, and the beeping of a pager are all accessible to deaf persons through various devices. Likewise, technical systems have been instrumental in making the telephone system in many regions a convenient medium through which deaf persons may converse with hearing persons. An understanding of some of these technological innovations is necessary if one is to gain a better picture of the social behaviors of deaf persons.

Telecommunication devices for deaf people (TDD) translate the characters on a keyboard resembling that of a typewriter to signals that can then be relayed over regular telephone lines using normal telephone handsets. At the other end of the line these signals are converted by compatible TDDs to print on paper, to lighted print resembling that on a calculator, or both (Freeman, Carbin, and Boese 1981). A TDD allows deaf persons to converse with anyone else who has one. Some TDDs are also equipped with an answering machine. Before TDDs became widely available, deaf people relied mainly on personal contacts to pass on messages. In the case of sport events, there were no convenient means for informing athletes and others about last-minute game cancellations, changes of sites, or other changes in plans.

In addition, from an administrative standpoint TDDs have many other uses in handling the demands of Deaf sport. For example, complications arising from international competitions can be dealt with more effectively, as onsite sport directors can seek advice from officials of the national Deaf sport governing body back home. In the past such problems might have been handled through hearing persons who would relay messages over the phone on behalf of a Deaf sport director. In effect, for many Deaf sporting events the necessity of having hearing persons present to relay messages in times of urgency has either been diminished or completely eliminated by the advent of TDDs.

Further self-reliance on the part of deaf persons is encouraged with the availability of TDDs at many service-oriented agencies, including police stations, transportation companies, hospitals, government departments, schools, credit card offices, airlines, offices of elected government officials, and hotels (Freeman, Carbin, and Boese 1981). TDD services expand the environment to which Deaf persons have direct contact and make it easier for them to manage their sport and other cultural activities.

The popularity of TDDs led to the creation of *message-relay centers.* Such a system allows a person with a TDD to talk to another person who does not possess a TDD. This is accomplished through a third party who has both a TDD and a telephone handset and who converts TDD messages to voice and vice versa. Thus, a deaf or hearing person calls the message-relay center, where someone dials the appropriate number and establishes contact with the desired party and then simultaneously maintains contact with both. In Deaf sport this system has especially been useful in helping Deaf athletes establish a more intimate relationship with their hearing coaches and other sport agencies.

Among Deaf sport directors a technological tool that is quickly gaining support is *computer networking.* Computer networking is a means by which information can be shared via elec-

tronic mail, interactive messages, bulletin boards, or file transfer. One such system is BITnet, which is the acronym for
Because It's Time Network. BITnet is a network of computers
linked by high-speed telephone lines and is mainly used by professionals working in research institutions, colleges, and universities. BITnet is an extensive computer network with connections in many countries all over the world. DEAFTEK is a
computer network that specializes in providing information on
deafness. The Disability Information Services of Canada (DISC)
is a popular computer network that is commonly used by many
of the directors of the CDSA. My own introduction to computer
networking came from constant prodding from my Canadian
and American associates in Deaf sport. Like many computer
network users, my associates despair of the frustrations and
costs involved in making lengthy long-distance TDD calls and
of the time involved in using the postal services and so find
networking a good alternative.

Another major technological innovation is the *telecaption
adapter* or *television decoder*. Many television programs are captioned, and viewers are able to read these captions with the use
of decoders that convert special television signals into print.
Sport programs that are usually captioned include the National
Hockey League Stanley Cup finals, ABC Monday Night Football, ESPN Sunday Night Football, the National Basketball Association playoffs, and the Olympics. Videotapes can also be captioned, which opens up a new medium for the dissemination of
information about Deaf sport activities and events.

FAX machines are quickly becoming a necessary tool in the
administrative duties of Deaf sport directors. The American
and Canadian teams relied on FAX machines to relay home
daily results from the 1989 World Games for the Deaf in Christchurch, New Zealand. FAX transmissions are especially useful
in coordinating grant applications and other types of paper-
work between Deaf sport directors who live far apart.

Other technical devices that are beneficial to deaf con-
sumers include hearing aids, pagers, and alerting devices that
identify sounds (DiPietro, Williams, and Kaplan 1987). Each
technical device and system is a potential contributor to a deaf
person's mastery of the environment. Obviously, how they are
used and the extent to which they are used are influenced by
the personal traits of each deaf individual. In general, TDDs,

message relay centers, and decoders have a greater impact on the lives of deaf persons than do hearing aids in that their benefits are more readily accessed by all deaf persons. It is important to note that the use of technical aids and systems is determined by each deaf individual according to his or her needs.

American Sign Language

ASL is the primary language of the Deaf community in the United States and most parts of Canada. It has a grammar and a lexicon that differs from that of English or any other spoken language. It operates in a visual-gestural medium and is totally independent of the speech and auditory mechanism. Hands, fingers, body, and facial features are used to transmit linguistic information. Signs refer to the lexical items conveyed by the hands and are analogous to spoken words and phrases. Just as spoken languages use voice intonations and intensities to convey messages, ASL uses nonmanual features such as facial expressions, eye gazes, and body movements to indicate inflection, semantic, and other linguistic characteristics. ASL includes the use of fingerspelling, which is also known as the manual alphabet.

Within the multicultural makeup of Canada other sign languages are commonly used. La Langue des Signes Québécois, or LSQ (Bourcier and Roy 1985), is used in Quebec and parts of New Brunswick; Maritimes Sign Language (MSL) is found mainly in Nova Scotia but also in the other three Atlantic provinces; and Eskimo Sign Language is found among the natives in Yukon and the Northwest Territories (Bailey in press). In recognition of the distinctiveness of the culture and language of French Canadians, the CDSA has a French-speaking director on its Board of Directors, and CDSA meetings rely on Deaf interpreters to translate LSQ to ASL and vice versa. LSQ and other sign languages are not as well studied as ASL; however, much of what we know about the cultural value of ASL can be applied to them.

Although ASL is the dominant language of the Deaf community in the United States and Canada, some members of the sign community do not know or use it. Newcomers to the community, adults deafened at a later age, and those who simply find it a hard language to learn in their adult years belong to this group. However, the signing behavior of these members is not static, and over time many of them do learn ASL. Padden (1980) described one of the bonding characteristics of ASL:

> While not all Deaf people are equally competent in ASL, many of them respect and accept ASL. . . . For Deaf people who prefer to use ASL, the language serves as a visible means of displaying one of their unique characteristics. While use of ASL sets the Deaf person apart from the majority English-speaking culture, it also belongs to Deaf people. (p. 96)

Thus, lack of competence in ASL does not prevent participation in the Deaf community.

Society's fascination with ASL is a relatively recent phenomenon, and there is still much to learn about its linguistic and cultural features. The many misconceptions about ASL prevent some people from fully appreciating it. Some of the more global qualities of sign languages in general and ASL specifically are as follows: sign languages are not universal but are specific to each country, and variations within a single country do occur; some signs are iconic, but a vast majority of signs are not; ASL is capable of expressing both abstract and concrete thoughts; ASL grammar is distinctive and not related to spoken English, although there are some similarities between the two grammars; and ASL signs are not ideographic (Markowicz 1977). To this list one might add that although the production of individual signs does not pose a problem, ASL is as difficult to learn as any other language.

I will not attempt to describe the linguistic nature of ASL. Readers are referred to other sources that provide discussions of this complex visual-gestural language (for example, Baker and Padden 1978; Hoemann 1986; Klima and Bellugi 1979; Lane and Grosjean 1980; Stokoe 1978; Stokoe, Casterline, and Croneberg 1976; Wilbur 1987). However, awareness of the social and psychological values of ASL to Deaf persons contributes to a greater understanding of how Deaf sport nurtures these values. These values are illustrated through an examination of those factors that motivate Deaf individuals to learn and use ASL, and through an overview of the denial and acceptance of ASL in society.

Why Deaf Individuals Use American Sign Language

Among those who wish to interact in the Deaf community, motivation to learn ASL comes from several sources, all of which reinforce ASL as the language of the Deaf community. An explanation of five of these motivations follows.

ASL is perceived as a strong tool for socialization. Within the Deaf community knowledge of ASL widens the circle of acquaintances with whom an individual can interact. Although many deaf adults are bilingually fluent in ASL and English, there are some, like in other ethnic and linguistic minority communities, who have limited proficiency in English.

Deaf people who use ASL signal to others their acceptance of a value specific to Deaf culture. This value (Padden 1980) stems in part from the fact that ASL is only rarely recognized as a language of instruction in the classroom, which creates a schism between community and school-based languages. Except for deaf children of Deaf parents, most deaf children in schools learn ASL from deaf peers, a situation that is not paralleled in the hearing community. Moreover, relatively few hearing people ever acquire fluency in the use of ASL. Hence, acceptance of ASL as a community-based language is a critical cultural value of Deaf persons.

Acceptance of ASL also signals an acceptance of being Deaf. For a Deaf person, there is no need to justify one's use of a language. Only in a hearing environment is the use of ASL and the reality of being Deaf called into question. Many authors feel the need to point out that ASL is a language just like any other language. Granted that awareness of ASL is relatively new in our society, there is no need to justify its use. I do not ask native speakers of foreign languages to justify their speech codes as representing a "true" language. It is disconcerting that thirty years after ASL had been designated as a sign language of the Deaf community that individuals continue to justify it.

In their attempts to justify the use of ASL, these authors may unintentionally be reinforcing negative stereotypes of Deaf people. In April 1988 I appeared before a committee examining the question whether ASL could be used to meet the foreign-language requirements of a midwestern university. A committee member asked me if ASL could express abstract concepts. My response was to place the onus on him to demonstrate that ASL could not express abstract concepts. In other words, I was not about to face my peers at the university and be forced to proclaim that one of the languages I use is in fact as functional as the one they use.

ASL gives its users a means for distinguishing themselves from those who have little or no knowledge of it (Markowicz and Woodward 1978; Padden 1980; Padden and Humphries 1988). Cultural distinctiveness is also enhanced by the fact that ASL does not currently have a socially viable written form. This makes ASL a face-to-face language conducive to the learning of social behaviors that facilitate its use (Hoemann 1986). These social behaviors include specialized eye gazing and frequent use of rhetorical questions (Hoemann 1986).

At a psychological level, the use of ASL is so particular to the Deaf community that one wonders if there is a self-regulating monitoring system that prevents many Deaf persons from using it freely with hearing individuals. In the 1970s several authors observed that Deaf people rarely, if ever, use ASL with their hearing associates and that many Deaf people see ASL as a means of keeping hearing people out of their affairs. Today, there are some strong demands for ASL to be implemented in the education of deaf students, and ASL courses are rapidly increasing in Canada and the United States. The increased number of courses is designed to meet the demands of hearing people to learn ASL. Yet, it is not certain whether Deaf people feel more open about using ASL with their hearing friends and other associates. A Deaf ASL instructor at a university once confided to me that he expected his students to attain only a basic knowledge of ASL skills so that this skill would transfer to their more English-like signing behavior. He neither foresaw nor desired a time when a large number of hearing people would be fluent in ASL. He also stated that he rarely uses ASL with his close hearing associates.

This Deaf ASL instructor is not alone in his feelings. ASL is a primary distinguishing feature of the Deaf community. Thus, it is only reasonable that members of the Deaf community would feel that hearing peoples' success in using ASL would detract from the linguistic and cultural identity of their community.

On the other hand, Padden and Humphries (1988) noted that members of the Deaf community are becoming more self-conscious about the way they think about their sign language. This is evident in the way reflections on ASL are being incorporated in poetry, songs, plays, and story-telling. These instances of ASL usage appear to indicate a willingness of the Deaf community to express the idiosyncracies of ASL to its own members as well as the general population. It still remains unclear if a significant proportion of the Deaf community truly desires hearing people to become fluent in the use of ASL.

In Deaf sport, social and administrative structures help preserve the distinctiveness of ASL. The overwhelming majority of those attending Deaf sport events are Deaf individuals. Even if a large number of hearing people were to learn ASL, it is unlikely that they would become the dominant users of ASL at any Deaf sport events. At the administrative level, directors of Deaf sport in Canada and the United States are Deaf persons. I am not aware of any instance where a hearing person currently occupies a prominent role in a Deaf sport association. There have been times when hearing persons contributed to the founding and running of Deaf sport organizations, and in some countries hearing people continue to exert considerable power in the decision-making process. Nevertheless, the trend is toward complete domination of Deaf sport activities by Deaf persons.

Of all the communication modalities and languages available for deaf persons, ASL is the most efficient and aesthetically pleasing. This is not surprising, because ASL evolved within the Deaf community to meet the social needs of Deaf people. Reliance on non-manual communicative features such as facial expressions and body language add to ASL's vibrancy. ASL is steeped in Deaf folklore and poetry. The popularity of ASL is readily seen at any Deaf sport events where it is used by fans, athletes, and sport directors alike.

Historically, ASL evolved as a combination of signs taken from French Sign Language (FSL) and signs that have long been used in the United States (Woodward 1978). The influence of FSL occurred when an American, Thomas Hopkins Gallaudet, and a deaf teacher from France, Laurent Clerc, introduced it in the first school for deaf people in 1817 (Gannon 1981; Lane 1984). There is little documentation on the development of ASL syntax, although there are indications that ASL does share some similarities with both French and English grammar, and some of its initialized signs are derived from French words (for example, OTHER / AUTRE, T. Kluwin, personal communication, 1989) and English words (for example, FAMILY, GREEN).

The dynamics of producing ASL have not been compromised in order to accommodate the characteristics of a spoken language. Such accommodations are handled through the use of manually coded English systems, or MCE (Bornstein 1973) and pidgin signing. Manually coded English systems provide a means for coding English and have little function in the Deaf community. Pidgin signing, also known as Pidgin Sign English, has been described as a mixture of ASL and English (Woodward 1973) and is seen by many as a useful medium for bridging the communication gap between deaf and hearing individuals. *However, as a language, ASL has no substitute in the Deaf community.*

Deaf persons are better able to learn about Deaf culture and share their experiences with one another through ASL. This observation (Baker and Padden 1978) underscores a major implication of the Deaf community: it is the only community in which many Deaf individuals are able to socialize free of communication considerations. Because language plays a critical role in socialization processes, the value of learning ASL is linked to the quality of life of many Deaf people.

Indeed, until a deaf person acquires ASL skills, he or she might not have complete access to the mores and beliefs of a Deaf community. An example of how ASL can lead to greater access is shown in the following comment by Diane, a deaf teacher of deaf students in a public school and a Deaf sport director:

> Until I became involved with a committee for a Deaf sport association, I was never in a position to link into the Deaf community. I had always been a weak ASL signer, and my discussions with Deaf adults never led to keen discussions about being Deaf. This all changed after I assumed my position as a sport director. My fellow directors slowly began to accept my efforts to learn ASL and became more intimate in the knowledge about being Deaf that they shared with me. I have a long way to go before I will be fluent in ASL, but I can see that it will lead to more intimate relationships with other Deaf people.

The interesting point about Diane's account is that as a teacher of deaf students in a public school she was never motivated to become acculturated into the Deaf community. Deaf sport and ASL opened the door for her in this direction.

Knowledge of ASL also makes it easier to learn about the culture and experiences of Deaf people from other countries. Sign languages are not universal, but the skills of expressing and receiving information using a visual-gestural medium can be used to help understand other sign languages. At international Deaf sport competitions it is readily apparent that experienced sign-language users are much better able to communicate with their Deaf counterparts from other countries than are those who rely on spoken language communication.

Motivational factors like those discussed here clearly indicate the value of ASL to Deaf persons. For many, communication not restricted by the demands of interacting in a speech-oriented environment is the essence of the Deaf community.

The Oppression and Acceptance of American Sign Language

For most of the twentieth century ASL has experienced little use as a functional language outside of the Deaf community. Until recently, educators have been under the false impression that signing hindered the acquisition of speech and was a major obstacle in their attempts to integrate deaf children into the hearing world (Lane 1980, 1984). Therefore, signing of any type was rarely used for instructional purposes, and parents were advised not to allow their deaf children to learn signing. Because ASL has always managed to flourish within the Deaf community, opponents of signing denigrated this community as consisting of inferior deaf adults. To its opponents signing came to symbolize a failing of a deaf person, and opponents used this false notion to create a "fear of signing and a distaste for the Deaf community" (Stewart and Akamatsu 1988, 242). Despite many attempts by Deaf persons over the years to refute these claims (Gannon 1981), the will of hearing educators and parents could not be easily overridden. Even today, there are

professionals and parents who continue to accept these erro-
neous allegations.

But a language that has evolved specifically to meet the
communication needs of Deaf people and that is their most
effective tool for socialization does not easily bend to outside
social forces. Indeed, marriages between Deaf individuals, the
Deaf community's cultural distinctiveness, and the indisput-
able value of signing as a communication medium provide ASL
with a fail-safe mechanism for survival: there are no better
alternatives.

Today, after three decades of research and a widening circle of supporters, ASL is beginning to enjoy public recognition
as the language of the Deaf community. Although schools in
general pay only lip service to its potential benefit in the classroom, public interest in learning ASL has soared. Currently, several states allow high school students, hearing or deaf, to take
ASL for foreign-language credits. (Ironically, in these same
states ASL has little support for its use as an instructional tool
in the education of deaf children.) Some universities and colleges offer ASL as part of their foreign-language programs.
There is also an increasing number of sign-language instructional materials and books related to deafness available at many
bookstores.

Perhaps the greatest significance of this increased support
for ASL is the spillover effect of recognition of Deaf cultural
activities. Many adult education sign-language programs require their students to learn about the Deaf community and
its cultural activities as a prerequisite for or as a part of their
coursework in ASL. The greater interest in signing has pro-
duced a large number of hearing people who have achieved at
least a minimum level of sign skills. For example, Cokely (1986)
estimated that in the United States there were 772 colleges and
universities offering sign language or some other form of sign
communication. To this number we can add the number of
people who have taken sign courses offered by high schools and
community agencies.

Interestingly, many of these hearing people choose to sign
not because they know someone who is Deaf but because of
their curiosity about a different form of communication. Even
among nonsigners, awareness of deafness has increased as hear-

ing signers share with their acquaintances their experiences from learning to sign and interacting with Deaf people.

Deaf sport has been able to use this increase in public awareness of deafness to its advantage. Fund raising, recruiting qualified coaches, finding volunteers for sporting events, and booking of sport facilities have all been facilitated through greater understanding of Deaf people and their lifestyles. An example of an outcome of this improved awareness is seen in the preparation for the XIIth World Winter Games for the Deaf in Banff, Alberta, 1991. More than five hundred volunteers were needed to run the games, and a majority of those who volunteered were hearing individuals who were selected mainly because of their technical knowledge of sports and technological expertise (for example, in relaying information between game sites). Some of the facilities used for the 1988 Winter Olympics were used for the 1991 World Games, including the speedskating arena and Canmore's Nordic facilities. This display of community support for a sporting event that is for Deaf athletes alone is indicative of society's acceptance and support for Deaf people and their cultural activities.

A Word about
Other Sign Systems

As mentioned previously, there are other sign communication systems in addition to ASL. The most common one is pidgin signing or Pidgin Sign English. Pidgin signing is a mixture of ASL and English in that it puts signs in English word order while deleting and altering various grammatical features (Woodward 1973). It has also been described as a specific way of using two languages in certain situations (Cokely 1983; Hymes 1971). People learning to sign often go through several variations of pidgin signs before they gain fluency, for example, in ASL. The other common form of sign communication is manually coded English systems, which visually code English and are not referred to as sign languages per se.

Neither pidgin signing nor MCE is an identifying characteristic of the Deaf community. Their use may indicate the background of a deaf person (for instance, revealing that someone is still learning to sign) or the educational history of a person (for example, indicating that deaf persons who use some English characteristics in their signing might have been exposed to MCE in their schooling). The major contributions of these other systems are in the interactions of deaf with hearing individuals and in the education of deaf children. Within the Deaf community ASL continues to be the dominant and the preferred language of communication.

Being Deaf in Deaf Sport

Deaf sport plays an important role in the induction of deaf individuals into the Deaf community. Sport offers deaf athletes an opportunity to test the social environment of the Deaf community without fully adapting to its social and communicative demands. Handball players wishing to try out for a regional or a national team will not be excluded if they do not possess signing skills or have no previous experience in interacting with Deaf adults. All players are judged for their handball skills and their potential ability to contribute to the performance of the team. Following their initial venture into Deaf sport, players likely start weighing the benefits of their new experiences in an environment of Deaf signers and Deaf culture to determine their willingness to pursue further involvement in the Deaf community.

For deaf children of Deaf parents and for those who have attended a school for deaf students, the opportunities available in Deaf sport are likely already known. Some may choose to limit their participation in Deaf sport because of a lack of interest in sports or a greater interest in activities related to other aspects of the Deaf community. All deaf persons have access to information about Deaf sport through national general publications such as *The Deaf American, The NAD Broadcaster,* and *Silent News.*

Two Deaf Soliloquies

Two Deaf individuals who are heavily involved in Deaf sport here present their own accounts, which summarize the various points about being Deaf that are expressed in this chapter. The first is my own account.

Training to be a teacher of deaf children marked my first step into the Deaf community. To learn more about deaf children, I became a big brother to an eleven-year-old deaf boy named Kevin. He was my first introduction to the Deaf world. With Kevin, my education about being "Deaf" began quickly, as I learned about Deaf signs, captioned TV, and TDDs.

Teaching in a school for deaf persons was another step into the Deaf community. Up to that time I had relatively little association with Deaf adults. At the school my interest in sport got me around, and soon I was coaching volleyball and basketball, and driving students around for their tennis competitions. Several Deaf staff members entertained me with insights about being Deaf. It seemed that all of the Deaf staff had some kind of ongoing involvement in Deaf sport. They played curling, slo-pitch, soccer, tennis, basketball, and volleyball, and they held positions in Deaf sport clubs and organizations. It was through these Deaf adults that I learned about an irresistible opportunity to play hockey for a Deaf team. The Deaf hockey team gave me my first taste of in-depth participation in Deaf sport. The competition was not as intense as I had remembered as a minor league hockey player, but the camaraderie, closeness, and sensitivity that we each felt for one another was unequaled in any of my other social experiences. From this point on I was hooked on the Deaf community.

One thing I learned quickly about Deaf sport was that it was not something people gave up easily. Deaf sport was growing then, as it is now, and there were always more sports, more tournaments, more committees, and more travel opportunities. I became a Deaf sport fanatic. I taught deaf children, I coached them, and in the evenings and weekends I attended meetings of Deaf sport directors, tournaments for the Deaf, or played in a Deaf sport league. Eventually, my own signing took on the flavor of ASL, and it was more than one Deaf adult who commented that it was nice to see me finally talking in Deaf language. Although Deaf adults had always been kind and open to me with their opinions, I found that as I became more fluent in ASL, the intensity of our conversations increased and the intimacy of our discussions grew.

Attending regional and national tournaments for the Deaf was a whole new challenging experience. On out-of-town trips I picked up many little tricks to make life comfortable: signal devices to wake me up in the morning as I fought with jet lag, toting a TDD with me everywhere, booking into hotels that offered decoding devices, and checking up on local events in the Deaf community before going to a city.

I have found that the hearing people I meet through Deaf sport are a different breed than those in the field of education. They are often very naive about interacting with deaf people, but they aren't afraid of learning. Even when some of them never learn to sign, they are tolerated. This may be because the bottom line of their participation is the sport itself and not economic self-interest or even the socializing that Deaf people enjoy so much.

As a true Deaf sport fanatic I associate in other Deaf cultural activities but only for pleasure and to meet friends. I usually turn down requests to become involved in working with other Deaf community groups because Deaf sport keeps me too busy.

The hearing world? I still very much enjoy my contact with hearing people through my family, friends, and coworkers. Finding my niche in the Deaf world helped me in my interaction in the hearing world. I now recognize that my strength as a Deaf person will reflect the extent to which I am able to realize my potential in both the Deaf and hearing communities.

I am not your typical Deaf athlete, but the essentials of my entering the Deaf community via Deaf sport could easily be related by many others.

The next soliloquy is from Donald McCarthy, current executive director of the Canadian Deaf Sports Association.

Playing sports on Deaf teams is all I have ever done. A playing field has a special appeal to deaf people. It is an opportunity to learn athletic skills and experience the thrill of competition. It is also a doorway to the Deaf community. Because I am a player, it's the thrill of the game that has kept me actively involved. The chance to pull people out of their homes and into the community is a major source of my motivation as a sport director. I love to win, but more than that I love to see deaf people involved in sports and to help all deaf athletes reach their potential. But even in defeat, games and tournaments have much to offer deaf people.

I can remember my first adventure into sports as a child attending the Halifax School for the Deaf (HSD). The school had no gym, and a low ceiling in the basement barred any attempts to play indoor sports such as basketball and volleyball. So two outdoor sports, soccer and baseball, and less frequently, hockey (whenever the outdoor ice rink froze over) provided the entertainment for many generations of deaf youngsters at HSD.

The best impression of my involvement in sports back then is the simplicity with which the games were played and the spirit of togetherness that playing soccer and baseball developed. A Deaf dormitory supervisor supervised the soccer. He would bring out just one soccer ball, then allow us to play without direct supervision. All of us treasured the time spent kicking that one ball around day in and day out and through the winter. From such a simple activity we learned much about the pleasures of doing an activity together. Later, when I was 9 years old, I transferred to a new Interprovincial School for the Deaf (ISD), which had a gym. This gave all of the students a wider range of sport options.

My second impression of playing sports in a school for the Deaf is the fact that no one ever told us about the World Games for the Deaf. I learned about that when I was at Gallaudet University and saw a U.S. team training on campus. I couldn't understand why a group of Deaf soccer players had jerseys with USA on them. I had always thought only hearing teams participated at the international level of sports. When I found out that these players were aiming for gold at the 1969 World Games for the Deaf (WGD) in Belgrade, Yugoslavia, I was immediately sold on the idea of getting to the WGD and helping others get there too. Back in 1969 it was too late for me to get together a Canadian basketball team, but I resolved to aim for the 1973 WGD.

In 1973 Canada didn't have enough good players to send a basketball team to the Sweden WGD, but I was successful in getting the ISD to send a girl's volleyball team. The team walked away with a bronze medal. I continued to play sports at Gallaudet: basketball, hockey, soccer, and baseball. I also got my start as a sport director by coordinating the scheduling of intramural sports at Gallaudet. There, I had made a promise that future generations of deaf children will not miss out on learning about opportunities in Deaf sport during their school years.

That, in itself, was probably the most important reason why I became a physical education (PE) teacher. But I knew right off that just being a PE teacher at a school for the Deaf was not enough. I had to get involved with the community. I started at the grass roots, playing for the Greater Vancouver Association of the Deaf (GVAD) fastball team. It was obvious that fastball had little appeal to many Deaf adults because of the high level of skills required. Earlier, I had been to a Southeast American Athletic Association of the Deaf slo-pitch tournament and had seen many athletes playing who would never have had a chance in fastball. This led me to suggest that GVAD switch from fastball to slo-pitch, which would then be a way of pulling more Deaf players out of their homes and into the community.

You see, it is important that Deaf sport always emphasize the social aspects of sport participation. Without that, many potential athletes would just sit around at home. Luckily, with the Deaf, socializing during and after a sport event comes naturally. That is why I try hard to convince Deaf sport clubs and associations to sponsor a wide range of sports.

From my connections with sports at a local level I worked my way up to become president of the British Columbia Deaf Sports Federation, president of the Canadian Deaf Sports Association, and chairperson of the CDSA-WGD Organizing Committee.

Today, I am a full-time executive director of the CDSA. The hours of work and the time on the road are hard, but the feeling I get from helping others enjoy sports makes it well worth it.

Donald and I share a common interest: a love for Deaf sport. We also devote a large amount of our time to organizing and participating in various Deaf sport activities. We have a common goal, to actively promote the benefits of being involved in sports with Deaf people. What makes our soliloquies interesting is the different ways we arrived at the same goal. Donald went to a residential school for deaf students and then to Gallaudet University. He was a PE teacher at a school for deaf students for fourteen years and then became a full-time executive director for the CDSA. He is married to a Deaf woman and has two deaf children.

I, on the other hand, attended a hearing school for all of my education and was never in a classroom with a deaf person until I went to university. I played sports with and against hearing players all through elementary and high school and did not find out about Deaf sport until I was in university. I have a hearing wife and three hearing children.

Despite our different backgrounds, our commitment to Deaf sport and our ideas about the value of Deaf sport are identical. Deaf sport has been an equalizer for us. It provided the framework through which Donald could get people involved in the Deaf community. It provided the template for me to assimilate the values of the Deaf community.

Donald never mentioned sign language during his thoughts about Deaf sport. For him, signing was the natural way to communicate, and it needed no special attention. As for myself, sign language came later in life, and the insights into living that it provided me made signing an important part of my initial involvement in Deaf sport.

Conclusion

There is no typical Deaf person. Yet Deaf persons share many commonalities. Sign language, shared experience relating to deafness, similar culture, Deaf sport, and pride in the accomplishments of the Deaf community strengthen the bonds that ensure the continuity and growth of the Deaf community. It may well be that the reality of being Deaf can never fully be understood by nondeaf individuals. But empathy can be achieved between Deaf and other groups of people. The key to empathy is acceptance of the tenet that being Deaf cannot be compromised by imposing standards on Deaf persons derived from a hearing and speaking society.

CHAPTER 3

PSYCHOLOGICAL CONSIDERATIONS
for a Denied Minority

Deaf people use ASL to express their thoughts, TDDs to make phone calls, decoders to watch closed-captioned television and videos, and signal devices to translate the sound of the doorbell to a visual or tactile medium. All of these tools are seen as accommodations to living in a world that is dominated by the needs of a hearing majority. These accommodations illustrate the dynamic versatility of deaf people as they negotiate day-to-day interactions. Yet, perceived indications of inability define the way society typically assesses the overall capacity of a deaf person to experience life. Inability to hear correctly or speak clearly carries with it social overtones of some hypothetical incapacity to function "normally" in the social mainstream. Consequently, the culture and social behaviors of Deaf people are denied a status that is equal to that of hearing people.

To understand the impact of Deaf sport on the lives of deaf people, it is first necessary to explore some of the ways in which their psychological well-being is affected in a hearing society. Through this exploration the reader will gain an insight into the "psychology of the Deaf." Discussions of the psychological implications of deafness have typically resulted in negative comparisons of deaf individuals with their hearing peers. Such studies often examined deaf persons as being socially deviant in a predictable fashion and portrayed deaf persons as being incapable of fully enjoying life simply because they were unable to do some of the things that hearing individuals take for granted. Every attempt is made here not to perpetuate this false notion.

Instead, a more realistic perspective on deafness would examine *what deaf individuals get from life rather than what they supposedly miss.* Wherever the approach is to talk about psychological barriers to living that deaf people face in society and their oppression by a hearing population, the danger is that these barriers are presented as being problematic. Living in a hearing world is not a problem; it is a reality. Alternatively, a better understanding of the psychology of the deaf person might be gained through a discussion of the environmental forces that foster the integration of deaf individuals into and within the Deaf community. These forces are psychological, social, or physical and arise within all types of sociocultural settings.

In examining some of these forces, it is useful to begin with the home environment because it is in the home that most deaf children obtain their first experience of the accommodations that they must make in a hearing society. In particular, my examination focuses on those environments in which the parents are hearing. Although they are well-intentioned, some hearing parents may unwittingly foment conditions and attitudes associated with stereotypic images of deaf people.

I further explore environmental forces through a brief look at the 1988 rebellion at Gallaudet University. In 1988 students at the only liberal arts university for deaf people in the world staged a rebellion to force the university to appoint a deaf president, a rebellion that succeeded. Particular aspects of the rebellion provide a framework for examining psychosocial forces that influence the lives of deaf people.

The Home Environment: Oppressive or Misinformed Parenting?

The steadfast control of fields related to deafness that hearing people maintain has indirectly promoted the evolution of the Deaf community. The social behavior of Deaf individuals, in part, reflects their adjustments to deafness as well as their response to the psychosocial forces they face in society. This pattern of response has nurtured the growth of the Deaf community, and therefore of Deaf sport and other Deaf social institutions. Indeed, it may be that all Deaf cultural activities are a response to the conditions Deaf people face outside of the Deaf community. For deaf children of hearing parents, this response pattern begins in the home.

The birth of a deaf child is a challenge for parents to experience a different kind of childrearing. It is an opportunity for parents to reach beyond the confines of a world insulated with sound and into one that is nourished by a cultural identity that transcends ethnic and geographical boundaries. Just as a deaf child takes pleasure in a multitude of visual stimuli in the environment, parents must likewise learn to accentuate this form of pleasure in their everyday interactions with their child.

A deaf child is not born into a world without sound. Instead, sound for a deaf child takes on an entirely different meaning. It could mean a light flashing when a doorbell rings, the vibrations on a dance floor, or a force that guides thousands of heads to turn when a low-flying airplane is about to pass over a football stadium. It will mean many different things to each deaf individual. Deaf children do not react to a soundless world; they react to the activity they see in their immediate environment. Therefore, parents must raise a deaf child unshackled by the expectations of the hearing and instead primed for keen perception of visual stimuli.

Hearing parents of a new-born deaf infant must come to understand that deafness is a force that shapes a way of living and experiences to which they will never have full access. How parents react to their child's deafness influences the directions taken by this force. Thus, knowledge of the impact of deafness on a parent-child relationship is crucial to an understanding of the psychology of the deaf person. Literature on the impact of deafness on the family is sparse (Moores 1987); nevertheless, it is helpful to examine how parents react to a child's deafness, the effects of language development on parent-child relationships, and strategies for enhancing parent-child relationships.

Research in the Home Environment

Summarizing research (for example, Allen and Allen 1979; Freeman, Carbin, and Boese 1981; Freeman, Malkin, and Hastings 1975; Gregory 1976; Kampfe 1989; Leigh 1987; Schlesinger and Meadow 1972) on ways that parents react to their child's deafness, Vernon and Andrews (1990) identified denial, guilt, searching for many opinions and cures, feelings of impotence, questioning the reason for their child's deafness, isolation of affect, turning to religion for support, blaming the doctor, blaming other parents, fearing the future, complete overreaction, pregnancy, absorbing medical literature, increased motor activity, reacting positively, and grief and depression as common behaviors. It appears that parents generally tend to experience some level of psychological trauma during the course of raising a deaf child.

Vernon and Andrews (1990) also noted that some parents are upbeat and appear to look forward to being the parent of a deaf child. They stated that "polyanna-like, euphoric perceptions are a form of whistling in the dark that thinly veil true feelings and stand in the way of rehabilitation" (Vernon and Andrews 1990, 131). However, they neglected to account for the fact that there are many Deaf parents who might prefer to have a deaf child rather than a hearing one. In addition, they failed to note the resulting positive or negative effects of those parents (deaf or hearing) who maintain a positive outlook throughout the years they raise a deaf child.

Society should not expect all parents to experience psychological trauma when they discover a child's deafness. If trauma does occur, then support for the parents should be available. However, support is also needed for those parents who think positively about deafness and the prospects of raising a deaf child. The fact that psychological trauma does occur in some parents is a strong indictment of the negative attitudes about deafness that are widespread in our society. Thus, Vernon and Andrews (1990) are not alone in their position (for example, Kampfe 1989; Luterman 1979), and for some deaf persons the first psychological effect of being deaf is to have parents who question the very pleasure of raising a deaf child.

Another important area of study is the effect on language development and parent-child interaction of the various communication methods used in the homes (Brasel and Quigley 1977; Greenberg 1980; Maestas y Moores 1980; McCartney 1986; Meadow et al. 1981; Paul and Quigley 1990; Stuckless and Birch 1966). In a brief review, Paul and Quigley (1990) concluded that "parental acceptance and adequate communicative competence are important in familial interactions as well as for educational and vocational success" (p. 85). The literature does not define what "adequate communication" means, nor does it relate communication to a specific use of a language (that is, to ASL or English). Still, the importance of communication is obvious when we consider that most parents of deaf children do not themselves learn to sign. Thus, for deaf children who use signs as a primary means of communication, having parents who do not sign defines another important parameter in the psychology of being deaf.

Other authors have written about strategies for enhancing parent-child relationships (for example, Crowley, Keane, and Needham 1982; Freeman, Carbin, and Boese 1981; Somers 1987; Vernon and Andrews 1990). Freeman, Carbin, and Boese (1981) identified effective communication at an early age as a critical goal in developing strong parent-child relationships. Vernon and Andrews (1990) suggested that participation in self-help groups consisting of other parents of deaf children and of Deaf adults is an effective therapeutic approach that can help strengthen parents' relationships with their deaf children. However, parents must recognize their reasons for attending self-help group sessions. While these groups promote better understanding of deafness and provide parents with support, parents must not use them as a crutch to avoid taking on full responsibility for raising their deaf child.

In sum, the general thrust of the literature on family and deafness is on the psychological effects of deafness on parents and some of the coping strategies that parents use. The implication throughout the literature is that the cause of any difficulty that parents might have as they raise their deaf children stems principally from deafness. However, all parents experience difficulty in raising a child, deaf or hearing, at one time or another. The fact that a child is deaf adds a new dimension to childrearing. Moreover, a major difficulty in raising a deaf child does not stem from deafness per se. Rather, developing an effective parent-child bond and effective communication skills, in whatever modality, are crucial tasks for parents and child.

Finally, nowhere in the literature is there mention about the psychological effects of hearing parents on their deaf children. For example, what should deaf children do to enhance their relationship with their parents? My personal experience with deaf children and youngsters suggests that deaf children can benefit from their own self-help groups and especially from talking to Deaf role models. Some issues for deaf children include "what to do at the dinner table when no one else knows how to sign," "getting along with hearing siblings," and "teaching your parents about deafness." In lieu of formally establishing self-help groups for deaf youngsters, a dialogue can be initiated wherever deaf youngsters are already in groups. Such natural groupings can be found in educational programs for deaf children, churches for deaf persons, Deaf sport teams, and other settings where deaf peers gather together.

Sport, in particular, offers a relaxed setting in which deaf children and youths might be more comfortable in expressing concerns about their family, school, social life, and other personal matters. As a teacher and a coach in a school for deaf students, I often came across situations out on the playing field when players provided me with insights into how they felt about their parents that I never came across in class. Such diverse comments as "My parents are hearing, they don't need to come and watch me play" and "Hearing players are rude" helped me develop a better understanding of my players. Often, players would indicate that hearing people's lack of understanding about deafness and its implications and their difficulty in communicating with close hearing associates fueled these feelings. It became apparent that participation in Deaf sport offered players an outlet for their frustrations in dealing with a hearing world.

The Role of Communication and Language in the Home Environment

The role of communication in the home environment deserves further explanation. Deaf children begin their lives like all other children; they have no language and rely on the linguistic activities of those in their immediate environment in order to learn a language. For hearing children, the first year of life and of learning a language begins with attending to the underlying features of speech signals and mastering voluntary voicing (Streng, Kretschmer, and Kretschmer 1978). During the second year of life they learn to use voicing patterns to communicate. Especially crucial at this stage are the intonation patterns of mothers and other primary care-givers. Parents rely heavily on their speech not only to foster the development of language but also to establish a verbal relationship with their infant. Time spent talking to a child is also a time for child and parent to learn about each other.

The attention given to speech sounds varies for each deaf infant. For most deaf infants, acquisition of a spoken language proceeds at a significantly slower rate than it does for hearing infants. Intonations from the mother are not perceived or are not as readily perceptible. In a review of studies examining mother-child relationships, Paul and Quigley (1990) noted that hearing mothers who used speech with their deaf children tended to be "less flexible and creative and to provide fewer instances of approval for their children's behavior" (p. 84) when compared with hearing mothers of hearing children. They also noted that hearing mothers of deaf children tended to be "more controlling, directing, didactic, and intrusive, and less responsive to their children's need" (p. 84), while their children were not as likely as their hearing associates to participate in spontaneous communication or in independent play.

With respect to mothers who used signs with their deaf children, Greenberg (1980) and Greenberg and Marvin (1979) found that they were more responsive to their children's needs and were more likely to participate in longer and more complex verbal interactions than those mothers who used speech to communicate with their deaf children.

But the connection between communication and the development of a parent-child relationship is not clear. The research described above shows that hearing parents tend to interact with deaf children in a manner that differs from the way they would interact with hearing children. Wood et al. (1986) noted that whereas "adults interacting with hearing babies often make what they say and do contingent upon their interpretation of what the child is seeing or thinking, when hearing adults interact with deaf babies they often demand that the deaf baby attends to them and the baby has to work out what they mean" (p. 23). Although it is not known how deaf children differ from hearing children in developing a relationship with their parents, it seems reasonable to assume that because deaf children of parents who do not use signs probably do not absorb as much language during the early years as do hearing infants, it may be more difficult for their parents to impart values and beliefs to them during this period.

Thus another psychological effect of being deaf in a hearing family is that the child, in dealing with a different set of communication methods and skills, may confront altered conventions by which to assimilate the values of parents and society. Even those parents who have learned to sign are rarely fluent enough to facilitate communication comparable to that which can be expected between deaf children and deaf parents. Thus, the extent to which hearing parents are able to instill a set of mores and beliefs in their deaf children is likely below that which can be expected of deaf parents of deaf children or hearing parents of hearing children.

Even when parents use signs or when deaf children are able to speechread at a fairly high level of competency, communication between child and parent may be accompanied by a certain degree of uncertainty and shallowness (Mindel and Vernon 1971; Wood et al. 1986). There is much criticism of the superficiality of the conversations that many parents have with their deaf children. Commenting on this topic, Jacobs (1974) stated that "the most crippling effect of deafness is the fact that many parents and educators fail to realize the critical need for 'full communication.' This means an open, facile communication where meaningful responses are the rule, not mere monosyllabic utterances such as 'Yes,' 'No,' 'Mommy'" (p. 13). Add to this low level of communication competency the fact that deaf children and their parents might not share a common language. This situation might occur when younger deaf children develop ASL skills through conversations with their ASL signing deaf peers. Their parents, on the other hand, will likely only know English or another spoken language. Unless deaf children are able to understand English at some meaningful level, the discrepancy in language might add to the complexity of an already difficult communication situation.

But communication problems are not limited to hearing parent–deaf child relationships. At one time or another, all parents may experience communication problems with their children. However, in a society where much of a culture is transmitted through interpersonal communication, the low level of effective communication that typically exists between hearing parents and deaf children also creates a dual cultural handicap. Parents are not only faced with the task of transmitting their own culture but most are disadvantaged when it comes to exposing their children to Deaf culture. Thus, the deaf child's acculturation of Deaf culture typically occurs outside of the family.

The accumulation of years of interacting at a low level may lead to deaf persons' harboring disappointment toward their parents (Evans and Falk 1986). Benderly (1980) stated that the years spent in frustrated attempts to communicate creates an emotional barrier to further communication efforts. More explicitly, this low level of parent-child communication creates a stressful situation that is often handled by keeping the amount of parent-child interactions to a minimum while accepting the superficiality that such interactions create. The following comment of a Deaf woman, Francine, illustrates this problem:

> Growing up at home meant sitting at the dinner table and staring at the trees outside of the window. Every now and again through facial expressions I would catch the excitement of a conversation that the rest of the family was having. Then I would ask what they were talking about. The response was always just a few words, and I would have to ask a thousand other questions to tease out more information from them. The same thing would happen when I would watch TV. If I never asked questions, they would never pass on any information. Basically, I had to initiate all of the conversations with my family. This I endured until I was eight years old and was sent to the California School for the Deaf in Berkeley. The impact of learning to sign and having so many people to talk to was felt immediately. When I went home for Christmas four months later I then realized how important it was to have people to talk to. For those two weeks of Christmas I missed my deaf friends, my dormitory supervisor, and just about everyone else I had met who knew how to sign. That was when I first blew up at my parents. I wanted to know why they didn't sign. I wanted to know how come I had to be deaf and not my sister. Later, when I would go home from school, I dreaded the lack of communication at home so much that I started bringing a deaf friend with me so that I would have someone to talk to.

Francine went on to relate that when she became an adult, her mother started learning to sign. Then, when she married a hearing man, her mother stopped learning to sign and would rely on the husband to interpret conversations between the two of them. After Francine got a divorce, her mother once again tried learning to sign, a move that stirred bitter resentment in Francine. Simply stated, this mother, as do many other parents, never accepted her daughter's need for sign language. She was unwilling to relinquish the use of speech as her means of communication. Her weak effort to learn to sign was a last-ditch attempt to mend years of frustration and failed communications between herself and her daughter. However, communication at any level of fluency without acceptance of what deafness entails is an insufficient compromise.

Parents are not entirely unaware of the need to consider signing as a viable communication modality. Over the past decade much progress has been made in encouraging parents to establish effective communication with their deaf children from the time of diagnosis of their children's hearing loss (Freeman, Carbin, and Boese 1981). Still, many parents lack access to communication guidelines and strategies for dealing with children for whom signing is the preferred mode of communication. Further, their task of learning to sign is made difficult because appropriate sign language instruction may not be available, and hearing individuals in general tend to experience difficulty in learning to sign fluently.

Finally, parents must also contend with the conflicting opinions that they receive from professionals. There are many professionals who advocate that, at least for younger deaf children, speech and speechreading skills should be the only communication modalities used in the home and at school. The main rationale for this position, known as the oral approach, sees deaf children as living in a hearing and speaking society where they must learn to function like hearing people. For the first seventy years of this century, the oral approach dominated the field. Yet, the Deaf community contains many of the end products of this approach, people who are unable to use effective speech skills. This population of "oral graduates" vouches for the necessity of having signing as a communication option for deaf children at an early age.

The frustrations that parents feel in their effort to communicate with their deaf children contributes to an already strained parent-child relationship derived from the child's being deaf and not hearing. Until professionals are better able to accommodate parents' need for unbiased information and adequate support services in their efforts to raise deaf children, many parents will continue to feel inadequate in their communication with their deaf children and then do little to improve the situation. Inevitably, deaf children who rely on sign language for communication become the victims of their parent's frustrations. They are left in an uncompromising situation where they are unable to communicate in the language and modality of their parents, and unable to dictate to their parents the need to learn signs—a situation that parallels their interactions with other hearing members of society. In the home, as in society, the onus is usually on deaf persons to accommodate to the communication needs of hearing persons.

Acceptance: The Bottom Line in Any Environment

Another important psychological force from the home environment is the degree to which parents accept their deaf children as deaf individuals. Most Deaf parents have gone through the experiences that their deaf children have inherited. For these parents, sign language is the preferred means of communication, and the Deaf community is a major source of socialization opportunities. Deaf culture defines much of their day-to-day activities, and Deaf sport is an oasis of sport, recreational, and social opportunities. Further, Deaf parents have endured the stigmatization and negative stereotypes imposed on them by society. They have also experienced the education system that their deaf children will pass through. In short, Deaf parents embody the very responses to the psychosocial forces that can be expected of their children.

Thus, Deaf parents accept their deaf children for what they are and do not seek to raise them according to a model based on hearing children (Jacobs 1974; Levine 1981). Speech and listening skills, and full social and educational integration with hearing children are not typical parenting goals of Deaf parents of deaf children. Instead, they desire that their deaf children learn to sign, assimilate the values of the Deaf community, and acquire a sense of Deaf pride. In addition, Deaf parents want their deaf children to adopt communication strategies that will allow them to interact comfortably with hearing and speaking members of society in whatever modality (for example, speech, speechreading, gestures, pen and paper) their children find convenient.

In contrast, hearing parents have never had the experience of being deaf. Most have never engaged in Deaf cultural activities or have never used ASL. They do not have the security of being able to fall back on a history or a family tradition of raising deaf children. Their personal evolution has not prepared them for the challenges they must face with their deaf children. And a prejudiced society has served mainly to complicate these challenges.

Much has been written about the reaction of parents to news that their child is deaf and the typical manner in which they eventually respond to their parental responsibilities (for instance, Freeman, Carbin, and Boese 1981; Greenberg 1983; Levine 1981; Mindel and Vernon 1971; Moores 1987; Schlesinger and Meadow 1972; Spradley and Spradley 1978). Negative response behaviors can be fairly attributed to parents' lack of acceptance of their children's deafness.

Thus, for hearing parents, the task of raising a child is typically guided by a philosophical orientation that seeks to "normalize" the deaf child in the mold of a hearing child. Communication techniques that emphasize speech and listening skills are of higher priority than those that include signing. Likewise, interactions with hearing peers inside and outside of school are more desirable than associations with deaf peers. Faced with these decisions, the deaf children are then put to the test: Will *they* succeed in fulfilling their parent's dreams?

Most deaf children do not meet their parent's expectations, and realization of this inevitably dawns on the parents. This realization often marks a parent's first step toward accepting a child as a deaf individual whose primary communication and cultural identities may be derived from outside of the family. Unfortunately, except for personal accounts written by parents, there is little information about and no research that has examined the experiences of parents who have finally accepted that their child will be Deaf.

Likely, few parents fully accept their child as a Deaf person. The experience of Chris, a Deaf adult, shows how his father had only partially accepted his deafness and had always harbored a desire for Chris to be like a hearing person. The father accepted that signing was Chris's major means of communication and that Chris's attendance at Gallaudet University meant that he was surrounded by Deaf individuals; he also knew that within this signing environment there may not have been reason to rely on speech and listening skills to communicate. However, the father's total acceptance of Chris's deafness was not signaled by his agreeing to Chris's attendance at Gallaudet. As Chris relates in the following account, his father always maintained some hope that Chris would be able to hear.

> When I had just finished my junior year at Gallaudet my father approached me to discuss my future. He wanted to know how I was going to be able to work in a world where everyone could hear and speak. He was worried if I couldn't hear then I would not be able to do well in my career. I told him that I planned to teach deaf children and work in a school for the deaf where I will communicate with most of my coworkers in signs. This wasn't important to him. He advised me to see an audiologist and get a hearing aid. I was 22 years old at the time and I had already experienced hearing aids when I was younger. They did not help then, and I did not wish to pursue my father's wishes. Still, for his sake I did see an audiologist, who wrote a lengthy report stating that I could benefit from using a hearing aid. I kept the report until after I graduated and then threw it away. My father still wanted me to experience life as a hearing person. He would send me newspaper clippings, brochures, and other information about how the deaf can be helped by marvelous new medical procedures that supposedly cure deafness.

The lack of full acceptance of deafness will always be a source of stress in the relationship between Chris and his father. Deaf persons, especially adults, do not appreciate the advice of hearing people when it insinuates that there is something amiss simply because they are deaf. What Chris's father had failed to accept was that for his son, deafness and not hearing is the standard by which Chris will chart his destiny in life.

Communication in the sign modality, primary association with Deaf peers, and the desire to be a Deaf person rather than a defective clone of a hearing person signify a Deaf person's severing of the umbilical cord to the hearing world. For parents unable to come to terms with this disposition of Deaf individuals to determine their own place in society, the road to self-actualization assumed by their deaf children demands a painful reconceptualization of parenthood.

More specifically, the mere presence of a deaf child challenges the symbolic meanings that parents attach to the raising
of a family. Levine (1981) described some of the parental values
that are threatened in a hearing parent–deaf child relationship
as follows:

> Children often have a deep symbolic meaning to
> parents. . . . they may symbolize virility, an extension of
> the ego, the means of attaining status, the ideal self, an
> outlet for "the things I couldn't do or have when I was
> a child." These values are derived from the parents'
> own early experiences and are therefore deeply
> rooted. When a deaf child is born to nondeaf parents,
> the emotional reaction is apt to derive its charge as
> much from the symbolic meaning of an impaired child
> as from the implications of deafness. (pp. 57–58)

Perhaps, when notions of parenthood are challenged, action is
taken that is unconsciously aimed at reasserting the original values held by parents. Having experienced life only as hearing
persons, parents instinctively use this background to judge their
deaf children. Moreover, lacking knowledge about how to rede-
fine their values in terms meaningful to a deaf child, these parents may succeed only in prolonging their disappointment in
their deaf children.

Parents' lack of acceptance of the implications of deafness
do not go unnoticed by Deaf individuals. Lack of parental acceptance is a strong psychosocial force facing Deaf individuals
who have few alternatives in responding to it. Unable to hear
and often unable to speak effectively, they must resort to other
communication methods and, ultimately, to the Deaf community to ensure that they are able to fulfill their emotional and
intellectual needs. This response is a condition that invariably
assists them in their educational, career, social, and recreational
endeavors. Hence, the disappointment experienced by parents
is mutual, as many Deaf individuals are likewise disappointed
in the way their parents have treated them. At times, a Deaf
person's disappointment may not be strong enough to override
the value orientations of the parents. This is evidenced in
Chris's submission to his father's request that he receive counseling from an audiologist although Chris knew that his lifestyle
and beliefs did not warrant such action. The disappointment
on the part of Deaf persons, however, is tempered by their

knowledge that society's bias will continue to fuel the development of the "Deaf way."

The Gallaudet Rebellion

On March 6, 1988, Gallaudet University gained national attention for hiring a hearing person to become its president. Located in Washington, D.C., Gallaudet University is the only liberal arts university for deaf persons in the world. With its announcement of a new president, Gallaudet maintained a 124-year tradition of never appointing a deaf person to its premier leadership position. Over the next seven days Gallaudet students closed down the university and demanded that the board of trustees reverse its decision and hire a deaf president. They also demanded that the chair of the board resign, that the board have a 51-percent majority of deaf members (at that time just four of seventeen on the board were deaf), and that there be no reprisals against the students for striking. The strike made national news and had overwhelming support from all corners of the nation, as well as the support of the faculty and staff, both hearing and deaf, of Gallaudet University. On March 10 the appointed president, Dr. Elisabeth Zinser, tendered her resignation. On March 13 Dr. I. King Jordan was selected as Gallaudet's first deaf president, and all of the other students' demands were agreed to by the board.

The Gallaudet rebellion provides several examples that illustrate psychosocial forces stemming from the interactions of deaf and hearing persons. Of particular interest were the ways in which the strike reasserted the value of signing to the Deaf community, revealed attitudes of some hearing persons who work alongside deaf individuals, and restated society's negative stereotyping of the deaf individual's capabilities.

For hearing persons interacting with Deaf individuals, signing is the language of empathy; it is symbolic of their attempt to accommodate the communication needs of a minority group. From the stories and actions that occurred during the strike, it was obvious that there was a great deal of resentment against those people who had ongoing involvement with Gallaudet but who possessed minimal or no degree of signing skills (for example, see Levesque 1988). This was readily apparent in the ridicule of the chair of the board of trustees, who had a scant knowledge of signs although she had been on the board for seven years.

There is no question that individuals who know how to sign are able to develop more intimacy with Deaf people than those who do not. Conversely, hearing individuals who have ongoing contact with Deaf people but do not learn to sign succeed primarily in maintaining a communication barrier that can be divisive in the interactions of Deaf and hearing individuals.

A second highlight of the student rebellion at Gallaudet University was that it accentuated the overwhelming and, perhaps, overburdening presence of hearing individuals in the education of deaf people. To some, this presence is described as indicating a paternalistic approach that hearing persons use in their work with deaf persons. Within the Deaf community the behavior of many hearing professionals is often described as being arrogant. Whatever term is used, the presence of hearing professionals poses a dilemma for Deaf individuals. Nearly all aspects of Deaf persons' lives outside of the adult Deaf community are controlled by hearing professionals. Thus, it is not surprising that Deaf individuals point to hearing people as their greatest handicap (Falberg 1971).

The overwhelming pervasiveness of hearing professionals and hearing persons in general causes resentment among those who feel that self-determination begins with Deaf leadership in positions of influence, especially within educational institutions for deaf persons. This resentment is a response to the psychosocial forces stemming from the hearing community, and one outlet for this response is to continue the development of Deaf community activities that emphasize complete control by Deaf individuals.

Still, the idea of interacting with Deaf individuals and using signs to communicate seem to have an enticing effect on those who decide to focus their careers on deafness. This is illustrated by the action of Dr. Zinser, who with no experience in the field of deafness still applied to become president of a Deaf university. In many ways Dr. Zinser's application and eventual selection for the presidency position is typical of many professionals working with deaf persons. It is not unusual to find professors with no background in deaf education training teachers of deaf persons; teachers with little skill in signing teaching in educational programs where signs are used; professionals with no experience in teaching deaf students jumping on bandwagons rallying against current educational practices in the field; and always, few Deaf individuals involved in decision-making processes at any level.

The frightening aspect of this armchair-expert mentality is that experience in one field allows a person to be an expert on all matters related to deafness. It is not unusual to find speech and language pathologists, psychologists, linguists, and even interpreters assuming prominent roles in the education of the deaf. Their arrogance is indicated by their willingness to serve in a role that may be beyond their level of expertise.

Arrogance and paternalism on the part of hearing people is not always obvious, nor is it always intentional. Oliver Sacks, in an article printed in the *New York Review of Books* on June 2, 1988, reviewed the events of the Gallaudet student rebellion. In the article, Sacks described Deaf persons as, "far from being childlike or incompetent, as they were 'supposed' to be (and as so often they supposed themselves to be)" (Sacks 1988, 27), which is a naive and misleading assessment of Deaf persons. Deaf people do not see themselves as being incompetent, and to suggest that they might "suppose" themselves to be childlike is derogatory. Thus, in this one passage Sacks reinforced society's negative stereotype of deafness. Contrary to what some may believe, the most consistent source of incompetence in deafness-related fields may well be the inaccuracies with which hearing individuals portray deafness.

It might be argued that working with deaf people creates a dilemma for hearing professionals—how do they attain the necessary background experience in the first place? As in any other field, professionals must recognize their limitations and be sensitive to their shortcomings when venturing outside their areas of expertise. Although this is not an unreasonable request, the prevailing message remains all too clear—hearing individuals are society's major spokespersons for deaf people. Through mere affiliations with deaf individuals, hearing persons become experts on deafness—as if knowledge itself is a product of osmosis.

In summary, the Gallaudet rebellion revealed the discord that the Deaf community experiences when their lives are impeded by hearing individuals. In a community whose lifeblood is ASL, it is only reasonable to expect that people wishing to affiliate themselves either through friendship, work, sport, or other means take the time to learn to communicate through signs. Such a gesture from hearing individuals reciprocates the efforts of deaf children, who spend many years of their childhood learning to use English as a communication tool. However, learning to sign should not be taken to signify that a person is consonant with the values of the Deaf community. Hearing persons must recognize their limitations in a field as complex as deafness. Their hearing status and direct association with the dominant group in society is not, by itself, a mark of expertise on deafness.

Conclusion

The psychosocial forces that Deaf persons face kindle the drive to construct social avenues that cater to the interest of the Deaf community. Yet the negative stereotyping of all deaf individuals must be confronted. Goffman (1974) mentioned that those who "are not required to share the individual's stigma or spend much time exerting tact and care in regard to it find it easier to accept him ... than do those who are obliged to be in full-time contact with him" (p. 53). This may be one of the reasons why Deaf sport serves as a good facilitator of integration between deaf and hearing persons. The contact that hearing coaches and athletes have with Deaf persons is often temporary, and rarely does any such person's livelihood depend on maintaining this contact. Professionals in the field of deafness, on the other hand, have their careers and financial status staked on their interactions with Deaf people. They may feel that they have much to lose if Deaf individuals are allowed to exert more control in their field.

The psychosocial forces that the deaf population has inherited as part of their minority and physical status within the family structure and within society provide a strong impetus for Deaf persons to design and control their own cultural activities. Deaf sport is one such response of the Deaf community to these psychosocial forces. It is in this spirit of self-determination that the psychology of deaf people is most fully realized: How Deaf persons feel about themselves and the social and linguistic creations that they have designed for themselves are symbolic of the very dynamics of being Deaf.

CHAPTER 4

PSYCHOLOGICAL IMPLICATIONS
of Deaf Sport

The array of opportunities offered in Deaf sport allows deaf individuals to reflect upon their own roles and values in life. The challenge of physical activities, competitive and non-competitive sports, socialization opportunities, involvement in organizational activities, sign language, immersion in environments where there are few or no hearing persons, and many other aspects of Deaf sport provide a set of conditions within which these self-reflections can be made. Thoughts and behaviors are shaped through self-reflection. Over many generations the influence of Deaf sport on Deaf individuals and the Deaf community has become institutionalized.

The activities of Deaf sport create a social environment that, among other things, positively influences the way individuals come to think about their own deafness and their place in society and the Deaf community. The extent of the impact is found in a wide range of opportunities in Deaf sport in such areas as athletics, politics (that is, the control and organizing of sport activities), spectatorship, and social interaction. In its entirety, then, Deaf sport provides a social context for a look at those considerations that affect the psychological well-being of deaf persons.

As discussed in the previous chapter, family and social environments pressure deaf individuals to seek social activities that minimize the chances that they will be judged as society's failures because they do not conform to the behavior of the so-called normal hearing person. It seems only natural that as a social institution Deaf sport creates an environment that meets the social, physical, and psychological needs of Deaf people. In doing this, Deaf sport gives its participants greater opportunity to divest themselves of concerns relating to a hearing world.

In this chapter the psychological implications of Deaf sport are delineated in relation to the following four issues: the adoption of community and cultural values, the discovery of self, the roles of Deaf athletes and Deaf coaches, and the role of other participants in Deaf sport.

The Adoption of Community and Cultural Values

Deaf individuals face the social behaviors of a hearing world in their work, family relationships, schooling, shopping expeditions, traveling, and other day-to-day activities. When these individuals participate in Deaf sport, they are given the opportunity to realign their social behaviors to conform with those normally expected in the Deaf community. Communication, educational background (whether, for instance, in a school for deaf students or public school), educational experiences (for example, one's successes and frustrations), pride in being Deaf, and other factors contribute to this realignment. This transformation of social behaviors requires that Deaf individuals reconceptualize the roles they play within the two communities. For example, in hearing sport the low incidence of deaf athletes and communication considerations may place a constraint on the interactions of deaf individuals. On the other hand, Deaf sport offers a relief from these constraints through the overwhelming presence of Deaf persons and the primary use of sign language for communication.

Beyond these constraints, interpersonal interactions reveal a set of Deaf actions and beliefs that Nash and Nash (1981) refer to as "the Deaf consciousness." Deaf consciousness includes the belief that there are many sign variations, that deaf people, in general, feel less able to succeed because they sense a lack of chances for success in a hearing society, that deaf people can aspire to the "impossible dream" or accept a scaled-down version of cultural goals established in society, and that strengths can be derived from communal grief and story telling (Nash and Nash 1981). To this list can be added awareness of Deaf pride and Deaf power, resentment of negative interference of hearing cultural values (for example, denial of the right to communicate in different modalities), empathy and moral support for other deaf individuals, intrinsic motivation to elaborate upon a Deaf culture that is separate from other cultures, and a drive to control their own destiny.

One major impact of Deaf consciousness is that it provides the drive that makes the Deaf community a breeding ground for its own set of values, many of which conflict with the values of a hearing society. Examples of these values are signing as the primary form of communication, ASL and not English as the preferred language of communication, mainstreaming from a Deaf perspective that views the Deaf community as a desirable mainstream, Deaf pride, the promotion of cultural and sport events designed specifically to benefit Deaf participants, a sense of togetherness that spans geographical barriers, and a desire to support the interests of other deaf people and their families.

Some values of a hearing society are transformed to satisfy the unique needs of Deaf persons. Endogamous marriage is an example of a value that is transformed within the Deaf community. Although statistics are not available, deaf individuals apparently tend to marry other deaf persons. Another example is evident in international sports, where despite differences in national sign languages, Deaf athletes from different countries use an international form of signing to communicate directly with one another. Hence, unlike spoken languages, sign language is not a barrier to international interaction. Fewer barriers to communication also help these athletes fulfill a basic need to socialize.

Given the greater flexibility in communication, it appears that the value of maintaining a competitive edge in sports is not allowed to interfere with the interactions of Deaf athletes from competing countries. This social behavior at international Deaf games contrasts to the practice noticed in some sports among hearing athletes, who may be coached not to become too sociable with their opponents before competing with them. The extent to which the Deaf community adopts sports' values or transforms them requires more investigation.

The adoption of a set of values implies a fundamental conceptualization of how a person thinks about his or her place in the Deaf and hearing mainstreams of life. Here, the role of ASL becomes critical. As the leading language of communication among Deaf people in Canada and the United States, ASL is a means of establishing and maintaining cultural boundaries. Sharing the language of the Deaf community is important in the assimilation of Deaf cultural values. At the same time, lack of knowledge of ASL does not necessarily prevent a deaf person from assimilating Deaf cultural values. There are many deaf individuals who enter Deaf sport without knowledge of ASL. While they go through a social process of acquiring ASL, their interactions with others are likely to proceed in some form of English (for example, signs, speechreading, print). Later, as they become more proficient in ASL, their reliance on these other methods of communication decreases and the intimacy of their interaction with Deaf people increases. Thus, in Deaf sport the emphasis on the playing of a game allows newcomers with little or no knowledge of ASL the opportunity to absorb the importance of ASL while still being an active participant in the game (that is, as an athlete or a spectator).

Although ASL is of great value to the Deaf community, it is not the foundation of Deaf culture. The foundation of Deaf culture is the experience of being Deaf. ASL is the means by which this experience may be conveyed and transformed into cultural entities.

ASL is a culturally distinctive language that promotes recognition of Deaf persons as a linguistic minority (Kannapell 1982; Markowicz and Woodward 1978; Vernon and Makowsky 1969; Woodward 1982). However, in a society that is becoming increasingly more communication oriented—as demonstrated, for example, in the expanding use of computers, technical terminology, and the increasing proliferation of mass media—the value of English literacy skills may be exerting pressure on Deaf people to incorporate English lexicon and, possibly, grammatical features into ASL. Fingerspelling (a manual code for English) is an example of how English lexicon is adopted by ASL.

Initialized signs such as CONCEPT, REASON, and ASSOCIATION are another example of the influence of English on ASL.

As with other languages, it can be expected that ASL will continue to evolve, and the influence of English cannot and perhaps, should not be avoided. It is not unusual for languages to borrow vocabulary or grammatical features from other languages (Claiborne 1983). The fact that ASL has already done so might be an indication of an evolutionary enrichment or the creolization of a language in a fast-changing world. However, even as ASL undergoes changes, its unique visual-gestural characteristics, syntax, and articulation mechanism should be sufficient to maintain its cultural distinctiveness.

Furthermore, the mechanics of ASL forces its users to diversify their own use of signs, depending on the context of a conversation. In general, during sporting events the use of ASL by Deaf athletes and other participants proceeds unhindered by other communication demands. However, because ASL does not as yet have a viable written form, code switching tends to occur more often during administrative meetings, when participants switch from ASL to more English-like signing as they discuss matters such as the specifics of a motion and the wording of a bylaw.

Another Deaf cultural value indicated in Deaf sport is the sense of togetherness and belonging that it instills in Deaf people. In general, there are few restrictions for involvement in Deaf sport. In most of Canada factors such as race, educational background, socioeconomic status, or religious beliefs do not affect participation, although various cities do have Deaf social clubs based on some of these factors. This is one of the ways in which Deaf sport differs from sport in general. Segregation or discrimination as it is practiced in the broader world of sport (Eitzen and Sage 1982) is simply not prevalent in most of Canadian Deaf sport. Only in Quebec and New Brunswick, where there are a substantial number of Deaf French Canadians, are separate sport clubs established that recognize the linguistic differences between Deaf French Canadians and their Deaf counterparts who use ASL. These observations support the notion that Deaf sport is a favorable institution for mainstreaming Deaf individuals. At least in Canada the Deaf mainstream bypasses or diminishes the effects of the social constructs of discrimination and stigmatization. Deaf sport thus encourages a sense of equity among its Deaf participants. Given its multicultural nature in Canada, Deaf sport appears to be a viable vehicle for social integration among all ethnic groups, a function that should not be overlooked.

Assertions about equity among all participants in sport are likely not as readily applicable to Deaf communities in the United States. As late as the 1970s there were still segregated schools for deaf children in the United States, and although there is no Black sign language (Hairston and Smith 1983), there are distinctive dialectal variations between the signs of whites and Blacks (Woodward 1976; Woodward and Erting 1975). Also, Black Deaf people are active in clubs they have established in various urban areas across the United States (Hairston and Smith 1983), and their sense of belonging is likely strengthened by the commonality of race in addition to deafness.

Research into the role of race, gender, education, and religion in Deaf sport is needed and could provide information about divisions within Deaf sport and, to a lesser extent, within the Deaf community. One way of doing such research would be to look at biodemographic information concerning deaf athletes and Deaf sport directors. The information could address issues such as the empowerment of race and gender in Deaf sport and the role of educational settings in introducing deaf individuals to Deaf sport (see, for example, Stern 1989; Stewart, McCarthy, and Robinson 1988; Stewart, Robinson, and McCarthy in press).

Rohan Smith, a Black Deaf Canadian sprinter and winner of two silver medals at the World Summer Games for the Deaf, has this to say about the influence of race on equity and identity in a Deaf world:

> Where I grew up in Jamaica I always saw myself as a deaf person because there were so many Black people living there. Later, when I moved to Canada, I began to see that I am a Black person, which was how I identified myself. This is because there are a lot of white people living in Canada. Now that I am at Gallaudet University, I see myself as a Black Deaf person. But I had never experienced racism until I attended Gallaudet. Racism in the United States is much higher than in Canada.

Also, in Canada, I feel that I am treated just like any other white athlete, deaf or hearing. However, my coach tends to treat me better than other athletes because I am a highly skilled sprinter. But overall, I feel that I am treated as an equal among white sprinters. At Gallaudet (University) where I have been captain of the track team for three years, there are four assistant Black coaches. Because there are so many Black people, it is hard to judge whether I am treated equally with white athletes.

Rohan's reflections on his identity within different sociocultural settings are not unique, as many Black Deaf persons feel that they are victims of cultural neglect. In analyzing the demographic makeup of the leadership in the Deaf community, Dunn (1990) noticed that white Deaf persons were far more prevalent than Black Deaf persons. Dunn (1990) noted that "Black Deaf youth see themselves as Black first because they know that racism exists" (p. 26). However, in sports, such as basketball within the AAAD, Black Deaf people have been able to make their mark (Dunn 1990). Research in this area might explore whether sport serves as an equalizer among Black and white deaf athletes.

To date, the impact of educational setting has received the most attention. There appears to be a trend toward an increasing proportion of athletes who have been educated in a public school setting in national Deaf sport teams, which contrasts with the past, when teams consisted mainly of athletes who had attended a school for deaf students (Stewart, Robinson, and McCarthy in press).

Also, it would be of interest to know if the integration of deaf individuals among themselves is facilitated in Deaf sport to a greater extent than in other community activities; to know what the options are for integration in Deaf sport in a community that only has three or four Black Deaf youngsters or adults; and to know if Black Deaf athletes tend to compete in a more limited range of sports and positions, a finding that would parallel the participation of their hearing counterparts.

Deaf sport provides access to the news and events of the Deaf community at local, regional, and national levels. This is an important way through which an individual's Deaf consciousness expands. The Deaf grapevine comes close to being an institution in itself. By way of TDD calls, newsletters, computer networking, and face-to-face contacts, information travels quickly. Because the number of Deaf people is small, each individual is able to maintain contact with a relatively large percentage of a Deaf community. In a smaller Deaf community (less than 1,000) it is not unusual that some Deaf persons know at least by face if not by name nearly all of the members of that community. The efficiency of the Deaf grapevine is also aided by the fact that a high proportion of deaf persons marry other deaf persons; the rate has been estimated to be 90 percent for adults deafened early in life (Schein 1987) or as high as 95 percent for deaf people in general (Jacobs 1980). Communication about Deaf sport events relies heavily on this grapevine.

Another factor that has a strong impact on Deaf people's perception of their place in society is the power that they exert in running Deaf sport affairs. In Canada Deaf people control all aspects of Deaf sport in the community through the CDSA and its ten provincial affiliates. There are no hearing people on any of the national or provincial boards of directors. To the best of my knowledge, this absence of hearing people also holds for all local Deaf sport clubs in Canada. Indeed, the bylaws of the CDSA clearly state that hearing persons can be only associate or social members, but they cannot hold office or have any voting privileges. The only part of the association where a hearing person can come close to holding a position of power is on marketing committees established to raise funds for Deaf sport associations. Although they are crucial for their contributions to the financial status of the CDSA, the members of these committees deal strictly with fund-raising events and solicitations of donations from corporate sponsors. They have no say in Deaf sport associations' decision-making processes.

The AAAD has eight regional affiliates and close to two hundred member clubs throughout the United States. There are no hearing persons on the AAAD Board of Directors, although its bylaws do not specifically exclude them from holding an executive position. Regional and local Deaf sport clubs in the United States are also mostly, if not entirely, controlled by Deaf individuals. The United States World Games for the Deaf Team Committee oversees the selection, preparation, and competition of athletes in national and international sport competitions. Although this committee does allow hearing persons to participate in executive positions, efforts are made to fill all positions with qualified and experienced Deaf adults.

The deliberate exclusion of hearing people from positions of power within the administrative structure of the CDSA and AAAD is a cultural value of Deaf sport. Although, some might think that exclusion is another form of segregation, a more accurate assessment would be that it is a means by which Deaf people empower themselves to control their own cultural activities.

Coming as they do from a hearing society where the power or even the access to positions of power of deaf individuals may well be negligible, deaf people find the display of Deaf power in Deaf sport an illuminating experience. Exposure to Deaf power and with it to Deaf role models helps convey the importance of success, a critical value in society that is not as readily attained by deaf persons in interaction with their hearing peers. Deaf empowerment opens up a whole new world of aspirations and gratifications, and it challenges newcomers to adopt values such as the social desirability of associating with Deaf people and using ASL, values that allow them to pursue direct participation in the planning of Deaf sport.

My own appreciation of this unassuming display of Deaf power came long before I became a Deaf sport director. It was mentally refreshing to participate in activities in the knowledge that they had been organized by Deaf people and for Deaf people. To finally attain a position as a Deaf sport director was simply a bonus that led to new aspirations and further appreciation for the manner in which Deaf people worked to organize games and reach out to include an ever-expanding circle of Deaf persons.

In summary, community and cultural values are highly visible in Deaf sport. For newcomers to the Deaf community, sport allows a glimpse of a different lifestyle. There is no immediate threat of having to realign one's own beliefs and social behaviors with what initially might appear to be a foreign culture. This is the case because, like any other sporting event, the game itself can be the sole reason for a person's attendance. For those individuals who are already a part of the Deaf community, sporting events are likely to be a backdrop for socializing with others. For all individuals, Deaf sport inspires increased comprehension of their raison d'être, their place in life.

The Discovery of Self

> When [you are] talking with a hearing person, the conversation usually goes fine until another hearing person comes along and you are dropped cold. Then one of your deaf friends comes along so you talk with him. Then the hearing person feels left out. (Holcomb 1985, 52)

In the big picture, a fundamental interpretation of Deaf sport could be that it engenders a transposition of the "self." From within a hearing society, Deaf sport gives rise to an environment that reverses the role orientations of Deaf and hearing individuals. To be normal in Deaf sport, a person has to be deaf and know ASL. To achieve influence, a person must be proficient in the use of signs, recognize the values of the Deaf community, and be deaf. The status enjoyed by Deaf people in Deaf sport parallels that experienced by the hearing in society. But to fully realize the potential of the status endowed by Deaf sport, deaf individuals must first come to terms with the connotations of this status on their own behaviors and beliefs. In doing this, they must reexamine the question of who they are and what they wish to be.

Examination of one's place in society will invariably touch upon personal needs. The highest of all human needs (Maslow 1954) is thought to be self-actualization, which can be described as doing what one is capable of doing, realizing one's potential (Morgan, King, and Robinson 1979). The relationship of self-actualization and other personal needs is shown in the following descending hierarchy:

> Need for self-actualization
> Esteem needs, such as the needs for prestige, success, and self-respect
> Belongingness and love needs, such as needs for affection, affiliation, and identification
> Safety needs, such as needs for security, stability, and order
> Physiological needs, such as hunger, thirst, and sex.
> (Morgan, King, and Robinson 1979, 233)

The hierarchy is based on the notion that attaining each need is contingent upon already having attained the needs that precede it. Not everyone realizes his or her potential or achieves high self-esteem. How far a person is able to go in this hierarchy depends on personal attributes and social environment. For example, the hierarchy may be more applicable to males than to females, who may place more value on being sensitive to the feelings of others (Gilligan 1982; Knoppers 1988).

Society presents many challenges to the pursuance of high self-esteem, self-concept, and self-actualization. Even for Deaf persons who are strongly motivated, the achievement of goals may be frustrated by obstacles erected through stigma, communication differences, discrimination, lack of intimacy with fellow hearing workers and acquaintances, low expectations of significant others, failings of an ineffective education system, and many other factors. The situation is compounded by the presence of a rigid social conscience that makes social changes on a broad scale slow to occur. Thus Deaf people are left in a position of having to create their own social structures and to increase their opportunities for satisfaction of higher-order needs.

Deaf sport is one result of such social construction. It mentally and socially prepares Deaf persons to achieve higher-order needs. By presenting a wide range of opportunities, Deaf sport entices its participants, among other things, to seek out a sense of closeness with others, to attain self-respect and high self-esteem, and, whenever possible, to do things that fit their capabilities. In contrast to the larger society, which presents many restrictions, Deaf sport inspires a liberation of the ego to experience and react to whatever the environment has to offer. It gives Deaf persons the chance to be judged for what they are and not necessarily on terms defined by society.

The significance of a liberated ego is related to the way that people come to view themselves. The self has three parts: "our perception of how our behavior appears to others, our perception of their judgments of this behavior, and our feelings about their judgments" (Popenoe 1983, 128). It is difficult not to be affected by the way others see us. Thus, it is not surprising that deaf individuals who have not come to terms with their deafness tend to suffer from low self-esteem and self-deprecation, especially in their interactions in a hearing environment. Further, it is fair to hypothesize that deaf children living among hearing people tend to develop low self-esteem if others fail to acknowledge the implications of deafness and treat them as deaf individuals and not as faulty hearing individuals. In addition, deaf adults in their associations in a hearing environment are not immune to the constant reminders of society's negative expectations of them.

It has been stated that self-concept becomes stabilized during adolescent years (Wylie 1989). However, if the way people view themselves is contingent upon social experiences, then it is not unreasonable to expect that consistent interactions under a different set of sociocultural conditions may foster a change in self-concept. Changes should be facilitated especially where new conditions are not only in sharp contrast to former ones but are more desirable. This is the situation faced by deaf adults who have hearing parents and had attended local public schools while growing up. Their experience during their school years with Deaf culture would likely have been minimal. During this time their communication with their parents may have been limited. While growing up, they were likely exposed to few Deaf role models, and the only standards they truly understand are those established by and for hearing people. Later, when these individuals place themselves in an environment composed mainly of Deaf individuals, the more appropriate role models this environment provides can be more readily emulated. Deafness becomes the norm, and a readjustment in how these individuals see themselves is not unexpected and presumably is for the better.

In addition, on the basis of personal experiences and contacts within Deaf sport, I believe it is not unreasonable to suggest that improved self-concepts generated by new experiences in Deaf sport affect the way Deaf persons feel about themselves in the broader spectrum of a hearing society. The negative impacts of a hearing society are allowed to fade into the background as the advantages of participating in Deaf sport activities are realized. This is not to say that these impacts are forgotten. Nevertheless, Deaf individuals who have good self-concepts are better prepared to function in any community.

Deaf sport not only provides opportunities but it is also a source of motivation for individuals to satisfy their higher-order needs. For Deaf athletes, motivation can be found in newsletter accounts of sporting events, in the recognition of regional, national, and world records for Deaf athletes only, in the comfort of competing with other Deaf persons, and in the chance for a place in history. After all, Deaf athletes, unlike many of their hearing counterparts, are not insignificant competitors among millions of others. Rather, athletic achievements are noted throughout the Deaf community. For all deaf individuals, motivation is found in the accessibility of leadership roles, the enticement of politics between Deaf sport clubs, the increased friendship possibilities, the increased opportunities to socialize with other deaf persons, travel opportunities to sport tournaments for the Deaf, and other aspects of Deaf sport. All of these activities have implications for the psychological well-being of deaf individuals and encourage them to explore their own consciousness and to reformulate, when necessary, their roles and expectations in life.

Deaf Athletes and Deaf Coaches

Another way of looking at the psychological implications of Deaf sport is to examine Deaf athletes' and Deaf coaches' motives for being involved in sports. Motivation to participate in Deaf sport comes from many sources. Like any sport organizations, Deaf sport provides many tangible rewards for participation and performance. Medals, trophies, and certificates are bestowed on top competitors. Team and individual uniforms typically belong to the athletes. Jackets bearing the emblem of a Deaf sport organization offers the athletes visible prestige in the Deaf community. Photographs and program books augment memories of national and international competitions. Scholarships are available for promising deaf athletes. Records are noted and disseminated through newsletters and program books. Even the pins collected at various events and from national Deaf sport associations are among the extrinsic rewards reaped from Deaf sport. Extrinsic rewards can be a strong source of motivations for all athletes (Gill 1986). Although the effect of rewards on the performance of Deaf athletes has not been documented, extrinsic rewards likely account for some of their motivation to compete.

Another, and perhaps, stronger rationale underlying sport participation is intrinsic motivation. Intrinsic motivation encourages people to seek out and meet challenges (Gill 1986). Such behavior leads to confidence and self-determination in an individual (Deci 1975). Orlick (1980) pointed out that everyone likes to feel "competent and self-determining and this is one of the reasons they seek out challenges to overcome" (p. 12). However, various studies have shown that extrinsic rewards can undermine the effects of intrinsic motivation in sport activities (Gill 1986; Orlick and Mosher 1978; Ryan 1980; Ryan, Vallerand, and Deci 1984). Ryan (1980) noted that football players on scholarships reported that they were less intrinsically motivated than football players without scholarships. However, Ryan also found that wrestlers on scholarships were more intrinsically motivated than nonscholarship wrestlers. Ryan suggested that there may be other factors such as the availability of a scholarship that might also influence intrinsic motivation. More research in this area is needed before extending these findings to Deaf athletes.

On the surface it appears that Deaf athletes participate in Deaf sport for the same reasons any athletes compete, with the one exception that for them communication considerations are more critical. Even in this respect the Deaf community is not unique: other ethnic and linguistic minority groups form their own leagues and teams where they use their own language. Athletes participate for many reasons, among which the fun, fitness, and the feelings of togetherness that sport engenders are typical. Yet, when Deaf sport is probed in depth, it appears that these reasons may not adequately identify the dimensions of the motivations of Deaf athletes.

Participation in Deaf sport suggests a strong personal investment in the promotion of the infrastructure that gives rise to the playing of various sports among Deaf persons. It is proposed here that in addition to the physical and mental satisfaction gained from competing in Deaf sport, the athletes are motivated by their desire to assist in the survival and growth of the institution of Deaf sport. Deaf sport belongs to them. Without them, the Deaf community loses a primary vehicle for social events and a common meeting ground. The low incidence of deafness demands a high rate of participation of Deaf athletes if Deaf sport is to thrive and diversify.

The suggestion that Deaf athletes come under pressure to be involved in Deaf sport is reasonable. For instance, even in a relatively large Deaf community of 700 people, the availability of athletes for any one sport is affected by the diversity of interests in sports, the geographically dispersed nature of the community, the travel time involved in attending a sports event, the athletic skills of the population, work schedules, family commitments, and many other factors. A Deaf basketball team playing in a hearing league may be faced with league rules that prohibit a team from playing once their numbers have dropped below a certain level. Each player on this team is under pressure not to drop out for fear that the team might fold. Administrative skills are also at a premium, and many Deaf sport directors would admit that the reason they continue their involvement in Deaf sport is that there is no one else readily available or capable of taking over their positions. Thus, by participating in Deaf sport activities, athletes and other Deaf individuals become guardians of Deaf sport.

At the competitive level, playing with and against Deaf individuals is psychologically gratifying. This is not to say that competition against hearing athletes is undesirable. Playing against hearing teams and individuals may actually be preferred for its more intense competition, a situation not duplicated at the local level of Deaf sport because of the small number of available competitors (Stewart, McCarthy, and Robinson 1988; Stewart, Robinson, and McCarthy in press). Rather, the emotions and thoughts that arise from competing with Deaf athletes are unique. They appeal to an inner spirit of an individual in a way that goes beyond the elements of play and victory. Deaf people, in general, are concerned about one another's welfare. Therefore, although a Deaf athlete's determination to defeat a Deaf and hearing competitor may be equal, the bond between Deaf athletes includes a greater element of empathy. Possibly, for most Deaf players the prospect of competing against other Deaf persons is a strong motive because it promotes a sense of belonging among themselves.

At the athletic level Deaf sport is certainly not impervious to the presence of hearing individuals. Some Deaf teams have hearing coaches, and many teams that thrive on competition participate in hearing leagues. A chance to play against hearing competitors may also be a motive, however minor, for Deaf sport participation. Another motive comes from the prospect of parlaying athletic experience into coaching. For the Deaf athlete, the opportunities for becoming a coach and eventually a sport director are far superior in Deaf sport than in sports in the hearing community. Given a choice, Deaf athletes would prefer to have Deaf coaches. However, it is recognized that the expertise of hearing coaches is needed in many communities where qualified Deaf coaches are lacking. Indeed, the need is perceived to be so critical that the CDSA, in addition to sponsoring coaching workshops for Deaf coaches, has prepared materials for hearing coaches wishing to coach Deaf athletes (Robinson and Stewart 1987). Still, gaining control over coaching, especially at the national and international level (assuming that the vast majority of coaches at the local and regional levels are deaf), is another step toward self-determination.

One final psychological implication of Deaf sport for Deaf athletes and Deaf coaches is that it is an institutional haven for those who desire to leave their mark in history. It is difficult for people to "gain status in a social world to which they are denied admittance" (Schmitt and Leonard 1986, 1094). Deaf people rarely attain positions of prominence within the hearing community where they reside. In Deaf sport, accomplishments are disseminated through the Deaf network, which includes the national Hall of Fame for Deaf sport, newsletters, newspapers, forums, meetings, magazines, the grapevine, national television programs such as "Deaf Mosaic," local cable programming, and computer networks. Deaf athletes are able to transform themselves from an insignificant entity in a hearing world to a popular sport figure in the Deaf community. Where the accomplishments of even an elite Deaf athlete may be nothing more than a curious footnote to the general population, Deaf athletes are role models for many deaf youngsters. Motivation in this respect is further enhanced by the knowledge that accomplishments in sports will be remembered simply as memorable or record-breaking achievements. Their accomplishments will *not* be followed by an asterisk heralding them as examples of how deaf persons have once again demonstrated their capacity to "overcome their handicap" through sports. In Deaf sport, deafness is not a handicap.

Other Participants

Participation as an athlete or a coach is not a necessary condition for involvement in Deaf sport nor for enjoying its benefits. The implications discussed in the sections on adoption of community and cultural values and the discovery of self are applicable to all deaf individuals who come in contact with Deaf sport activities. In addition, there are a number of other psychological implications that apply specifically to nonathletic participants, a term that is used here to refer to all individuals other than athletes and coaches. Hence, game officials, sport directors, retired athletes, members of various athletic committees (for example, committees concerned with public relations, ticket selling, and technical rules), concession operators, newsletter reporters, and fans are among those classified as nonathletic participants.

The role of the fan is not entirely clear, even within the framework of sport in society at large (Leonard 1980). Edwards (1973), for example, suggested that sport provides fans with a sense of belonging and a socially acceptable outlet for hostile and aggressive feelings. But what function does Deaf sport have for its fans? Obviously, it encourages a sense of belonging and helps to create an identity that favors the role of Deaf individuals. It recognizes Deaf fans as being the norm, with little threat that hearing people will gain a social edge within the context of Deaf sport. A Deaf fan is not alone in a crowd where the demands of communication make socializing difficult. Indeed, it is proposed that the main reason why Deaf fans attend Deaf games is to socialize with other Deaf persons. For many fans at the local level, the games may be of secondary interest. Possibly, with each higher level of competition, more attention is paid to the games, with the peak of interest occurring at the international level. Nevertheless, just as there are some sport fanatics who attend Deaf games with the sole purpose of watching them, there are far more fans whose main motive is socialization. The need to be with others is also a motive for the actions of the other nonathletic participants.

For those participants who have a more direct connection with the organization of Deaf sport activities, the motive to participate may emanate from the need to feel wanted, to be recognized. In the workplace deaf people are typically underemployed and underpaid, in comparison with their hearing counterparts (Christiansen and Barnartt 1987). It is not uncommon for a deaf person to be shuffled aside while a less experienced hearing person gets promoted. Deaf people are bitter about their lack of control over the development of educational policies for deaf children and youngsters (Stewart 1982). Some may feel that the overall worth of a deaf person is relatively insignificant in a hearing society, which provides yet another motivation for participating in Deaf sport and other Deaf community activities.

Diane is a deaf teacher of deaf students who has managed hearing basketball teams at the secondary level. She became involved in Deaf sport during her mid-thirties. Her comments in the following passage illustrate the notion that a sense of self-worth motivates deaf individuals to participate in Deaf sport:

> It is not that hearing people purposefully ignore the contributions of deaf people in sport and anything else. Instead, I think they lack the understanding and ability of how to interact with a deaf person. In the classroom, hearing teachers are often uncertain of how much to expect of their deaf students. In sport, I have noticed that deaf athletes have to run faster and score more points than most others in order to get more than just passing recognition from their hearing teammates and coaches. An average deaf athlete is more likely to sit on the bench because of lack of rapport with the coach while other hearing athletes with the same or even lesser skill get more playing time. A deaf basketball player playing on a Deaf team will do or die by how well she plays. I think this is one of the reasons why so many deaf players like to play on Deaf teams and why deaf people like to go to Deaf games; they know their skills and enthusiasm will be recognized.

In this passage Diane raises the concern that uncertainty in the interactions between hearing teachers and coaches and their deaf students and athletes may adversely affect the performance of these deaf individuals. The basis for her observation was her tenure as a teacher of deaf students in a public school where all other staff members were hearing. It would appear that for deaf students in her school, participation in Deaf sport might have offered a welcome contrast to their day-to-day school activities.

Deaf individuals may also be unwittingly contributing to the low sense of self-worth they experience within a hearing society. We are all creatures of learned behaviors. If a society has low expectations of a particular group of people, then, perhaps, it is not surprising that some individuals in the group might adopt this level of expectation. Deaf youngsters who have had no exposure to older Deaf role models may be especially vulnerable to the expectations of their teachers and coaches. Edward, a hearing teacher of deaf students in a public school believed that deaf youngsters are caught in a treadmill of low self-esteem that they themselves perpetuate, along with those around them. He stated:

> I taught at a junior high school. I was coaching the grade 8 rugby team. I thought this would be a super chance for the deaf kids to have a coach who could sign. Two deaf students had quite a bit of potential. They could have been really good. I got them to come out for the team. I coached the team, which had about 20 players. I had the same expectations of all of them. I would sign the rules of the game. For my deaf players I would even talk about some of the rugby plays during language classes.
>
> I wanted them to succeed. They were happy to be on the team, but did not work very hard. I am really competitive and expect the students to try their hardest. I was able to inspire most of the players to put forth their best effort always. The two deaf players didn't try hard and that bothered me. I would go ahead and play them during a game. Once, they went out for ten minutes and then came up to me together and asked to be subbed off. In rugby, you are only allowed a limited number of substitutions. I told one boy to go back and try: "Look at the others, they kept at it." They both went back, but they simply walked about the field without giving any effort.
>
> Thinking back on that, I am still bothered. The deaf boys could have been good players. They were not used to being made to work. Everything was made easy for them. No one had expected much of them. Their parents had not pushed them, or instilled in them the

drive to do their best. When someone finally expected them to excel, they would have nothing to do with it. This lack of drive was still with them many years after they had graduated.

Edward felt that the lack of drive in his two deaf rugby players stemmed from a history of responding to low expectations. In rugby these two students passed up the chance to respond to the challenge presented by their coach. According to Edward, their lack of motivation on the field paralleled their equally unmotivated work in the classroom, where they did not value the work they did. Reflecting on his experience with these two players, Edward remarked that to remove themselves from the treadmill of low expectations that they were trapped in, they needed opportunities to succeed at levels they normally did not strive to reach.

Although the drive to succeed and test one's potential is a basic value of our society, it is also a learned behavior. Deaf children, like all children, need to be exposed to role models whose activities illustrate the rewards of determination and hard work. They also need to be given the chance to emulate this kind of behavior. The behavior of the two deaf rugby players suggests that all they had to do was show up for practice and games, and their work—their goals—were accomplished. In fairness to both of them, just being in a team uniform may well have been their only goal, and their lack of desire to try hard is an attitude shared by many of their hearing counterparts. On the other hand, their performance may also have resulted from years of having been denied opportunities to develop a healthy work ethic at home and in school. When carefully managed, sport can promote a desire to succeed in both athletes and nonathletes.

In Deaf sport the value of success for nonathletic participants is promoted through a range of organizational activities in which they can be involved. Because the success of these activities depends upon the contributions of deaf participants, the organizational work can become a reward itself. Diane explained her attraction to Deaf sport:

> What motivates me to work as a Deaf sport director is that it puts me in touch with other Deaf individuals and I can help improve the social, sport, and rec-

reational opportunities existing within the Deaf community. The harder I work the more opportunities that I can help create and the more involvement with other Deaf individuals that I receive.

Although Diane is a former high school athlete, her motivation to participate in organizational activities within the sphere of Deaf sport can be likened to that of many Deaf sport directors who have had little involvement in sport as athletes. Their activities and those of people like them help Deaf individuals feel good about themselves and the work they do for their community. Hence, Deaf sport promotes a sense of self-worth among nonathletic participants too.

Deaf individuals who feel better about themselves and perceive themselves to be valued contributors to the activities of Deaf sport enhance the overall character of the Deaf community. Their actions establish a positive example for others to follow. In this manner Deaf sport becomes a breeding ground for stronger leadership through the opportunities it provides individuals to satisfy their need for recognition and enjoyment.

Along with promoting a sense of belonging and self-worth, Deaf sport promotes a differentiation of roles among deaf individuals. From the athlete to the fan, roles are open to all deaf individuals. By comparison, the hearing community is a restrictive environment where roles for deaf individuals are often defined more by social conceptions of the limitations of deafness than by the ability to do the task at hand. In Deaf sport deafness is still critical, but judgment is based on other characteristics of the individual. Hence, individuals with little interest in sports are attracted to Deaf sport by the productive roles that they can assume to assure the continued growth of their own social institution.

Conclusion

Traditional beliefs of society have long held that the Deaf community is a subculture, a restrictive social environment, or a community of individuals who do not succeed in a hearing world. In contrast, Deaf sport clearly demonstrates that the actions and beliefs of the Deaf community create an oasis for Deaf persons. An investigation of the psychological implications of Deaf sport reveals how involvement in a range of sport-related activities affects the beliefs and behaviors of deaf individuals. Essentially, among the most important motivations to participate in Deaf sport are the sense of belonging, the convenience of communicating in signs, the lack of similar opportunities in hearing sport, and the need to see oneself as being a worthy contributor to a community.

Overall, the most striking implication is that Deaf sport empowers deaf persons to make self-determination a reality. It gives them access to the means to achieve higher-order needs. Self-actualization for many deaf individuals can more readily be realized via the activities of Deaf sport than in an environment that caters mainly to the needs of the hearing population.

In Deaf sport deaf persons have greater individual freedom in the choices they make in their capacities as athletes, coaches, sport directors, administrators, and fans. They are not bound by the negative expectations they face in society. Indeed, the hopes and opportunities for enhanced lifestyles lie in their control of their institutions. But having been raised in a hearing society and judged by hearing standards, they must first be acclimated to the empowering status endowed them by the culture and opportunities of the Deaf community. Deaf sport offers an ideal environment for this acclimatization.

CHAPTER 5

DEAF IN A HEARING WORLD
A Quest for Equity

In the common vernacular used in most literature on deafness, deaf persons are individuals "lacking the full complement of physical and mental capabilities" that are traits of those who possess hearing. The task is then to analyze the effects, which are invariably assumed to be detrimental, of not being a hearing person. This framework typically leads to the assumption that deafness is an abnormal and undesirable trait. Investigators therefore focus on how the lives of deaf people deviate from those of the majority of people.

Such a perspective hinders insights into the Deaf community and Deaf people that run contrary to popular societal notions. For example, although few hearing persons would argue that they would like to be deaf, many Deaf adults are proud of their deafness and do not wish to become hearing. The extent of this pride is evidenced in the fact that some Deaf couples would prefer to have deaf children—a wish that challenges the very notion of what is "normal." When Deaf and hearing groups are contrasted, care must be taken not to subordinate one group on the basis of perceived differences. Thus, it should not be said that deaf people use an inferior method for communication because many of them rely on signs and not speech. The standards derived from a hearing community provide a defective model for understanding the lifestyles and behaviors of deaf people.

Nevertheless, understanding how hearing people tend to view deafness is important because their viewpoint illustrates one aspect of the sociological dimension of being deaf. An alternative to such a perspective can be found by taking an ecological approach that assumes deafness as a normal characteristic. Having laid out both perspectives, one could then explore ways to promote social equity between deaf and hearing individuals.

Exploring Social Interactions

Today's society is a challenge for any inquisitive human mind that seeks to maintain autonomy in the face of strong social pressures. We are overly sensitive to the opinions of others (Popenoe 1983) and especially of those who we feel are in a position to "know." The advertising industry banks its success on projecting images of people who are "with it" and obviously know what is right in life. There may be little logic influencing the clothes we wear, the food we eat, the newspapers we read, and the way we vote other than a notion that our actions conform to the typical behavior of a particular social group to which we wish to belong. Hence, our desire to conform may be such that we allow our behaviors to be directed, to a certain extent, by what we believe others think is the right thing to do.

Our sensitivity to the opinions of others also reveals itself in the way we view sports and participate in them (Eitzen and Sage 1986). Eitzen and Sage proposed that sport "mirrors a society's basic structure and values" (p. 59). Hence, as in life, success in sport is critical, and the popularity of sport can be linked to its ability to draw people together who identify with a common goal—victory. Eitzen and Sage (1986) described the attraction and influence of sport in society as follows:

> Individuals living in an urban and bureaucratic society tend to feel alienated; in effect, they have feelings of isolation, powerlessness, self-estrangement, and mean-

inglessness. These persons need to identify with others in a cause that will give meaning to their existence and an escape from an otherwise humdrum world. Sports teams representing factories, schools, neighborhoods, cities, or nations—each pursuing victory—provide an important source of identification for individuals in American society. (p. 59)

Similarly, Deaf sport provides a means by which deaf people may identify with the culture and values of the Deaf community. But within the Deaf community, in addition to being sensitive to the opinions of others, Deaf individuals are sensitive to the experiences they share with others. The social experiences of 80,000 fans at a football game is not as important to each fan as is the experience of deafness for fans at a Deaf sport event.

That we are forever conscious of how others feel about us is at the heart of all social interactions. Popenoe (1983) defined social interactions as the "process in which people act toward or respond to others" (p. 104). By extension, social interaction is the essence of our place in society. We go about our daily events constantly evaluating the prevailing social contexts for clues to guide our behaviors. A hearing person meeting a deaf person for the first time might draw upon stereotypical conceptions of what deafness entails and proceed to converse in a rather loud and exaggerated manner. If the deaf person pulls out a pencil and paper and begins to communicate in print, the hearing person, wishing to appear sociable, is given little choice but to accommodate this change in communication strategy.

Sociologists have several theoretical frameworks from which social interactions can be viewed. It is not within the realm of this book to discuss these theories in detail. However, a brief description of symbolic interactionism will provide a basis for discussing Deaf people and social interactions. The following description is derived largely from the work of Popenoe (1983) and Blumer (1962).

Symbolic Interactionism

Symbolic interactionism attempts to understand human interactions through analyses of symbols and meaning. For instance, two persons shaking hands may indicate, among other things, a greeting, a business agreement, or a high bowling score, depending on the context of the interaction. Shaking hands is not a random act but conforms to a culturally accepted form of behavior appropriate for the social interaction at hand. In addition, the actions of each person depend on the meaning given to the situation, which is based on each person's past social interactions. As people interact, they continually interpret the situation in order to attach meaning to it and decide on further actions.

Embedded in the theory of symbolic interactionism is the requisite that we are able to understand the actions and intentions of other people. This raises the question about the extent to which Deaf and hearing people can come to understand each other and about the constraints working against an understanding. For example, members of society share common assumptions about various social symbols, the most obvious of which is language (Popenoe 1983). With respect to language, there is some evidence that the definitions of Deaf and hearing persons for the same words may be different. Whereas facial expressions are a part of ASL grammar (Baker-Shenk 1985), the linguistic role of the face in spoken language may not be so obvious. Therefore, certain facial expressions may convey different messages to hearing and Deaf individuals (cf. Padden 1980). Consequently, lack of shared definitions with respect to language may lead to confusion and misinterpretations in social interactions between Deaf and hearing individuals.

In Deaf sport, symbolic interactionism implies that there may be an added dimension to the personal characteristics and experiences of an individual that provides information about why that person participates in sport. Deaf individuals represent a linguistic minority that upholds a unique set of mores and beliefs. They also bring with them a different perspective of how they should behave either in the Deaf community or in the community at large. Finally, the symbols and interpretations that Deaf people attach to various social behaviors may contrast with those ascribed to these behaviors by most hearing persons. Thus, to fully understand the social forces involved in Deaf sport, one must analyze the characteristics of Deaf individuals.

Symbolic interactionism helps explain how Deaf athletes feel about themselves as athletes and illustrates some of the dynamics of being Deaf. Donald McCarthy, executive director of the CDSA, highlights the symbolic behavior of Deaf athletes in the following comparison of the way Deaf players interact in competition with hearing teams and among themselves:

> Deaf players playing against a hearing team in a sport like basketball, will be more open in their communication with one another and their coach and a lot less concerned about what the other team is thinking about them. They have nothing to hide because the hearing players won't understand their signing. . . . When a Deaf team plays another Deaf team the players become more secretive because they want to protect their game strategies and control the play. They don't want to give the other team any breaks. Deaf players look for communication leaks while they eavesdrop on the other team in an attempt to gain valuable information about game plans. Deaf players do not expect or even try to eavesdrop on hearing teams. Playing against a Deaf team inspires the players to play better. The play is more intense and there is far more enthusiasm when Deaf athletes play against other Deaf athletes.

> Deaf athletes will try hard to win against a hearing team. But a Deaf tournament or a Deaf league may inspire many of the players to play better. A good reason for this is the award system. In a Deaf tournament, each player has a chance to receive a team and an individual award, which inspires the players. In a hearing tournament or in a hearing league, a Deaf athlete has a harder time being recognized and selected for an individual award. In Deaf games, a Deaf athlete has more to look forward to during and after the games.

According to McCarthy's account, communication, inspiration, and recognition for performance influence the way Deaf athletes compete against hearing and Deaf teams. Thus, the very role of a Deaf athlete may undergo some change depending on whether two Deaf teams are playing against each other or one Deaf and one hearing team are playing.

On a more global level, some of the symbolic elements promoted by involvement in Deaf sport are power, security, and defiance. In a society that preaches the benefits of assimilating and mainstreaming deaf individuals with their hearing peers, Deaf athletes display an act of self-determination each time they participate in a Deaf sport event. For those athletes who have attended a school for deaf students, a desire to participate in Deaf sport during adulthood may reflect the ingraining of Deaf culture to a greater extent than the rejection of values associated with participating on hearing teams. There is a sense of security that comes from the continuation of social patterns that were embraced during the school years. For those athletes who have been educated in a public school, participation in Deaf sport could be interpreted as an act of defiance against the value of being fully integrated among hearing athletes.

This raises the question as to whether Deaf athletes see themselves as athletes first or as Deaf persons first. That is, does the sociocultural context of a competition influence whether a Deaf person views himself or herself first as a Deaf athlete, a Deaf person, or an athlete? In the previous chapter we saw how a Black Deaf person's sense of identity was influenced by the sociocultural environment in which he interacted. Briefly, among Blacks, Rohan considered himself Deaf first. However, in a largely white population or among white Deaf athletes, Rohan felt that his identity as a Black person was stronger than his Deaf identity or his identity as an athlete.

Similarly, Lawson, an avid bowler, described how environmental settings influenced the identities he embraced:

> I have been bowling competitively for the past 18 years with the exception of a five-year span when back pain sidelined me. There is no doubt that when I am all alone among hearing people that I feel my identity as a Deaf person stands out. I want to compete as hard as I always do, but the lack of communication and other Deaf people make me strongly aware that I am Deaf. When I bowl with a Deaf team in a league that has many hearing teams, then I am a Deaf bowler. I

am not just bowling for my score and team but also to impress hearing people about how good Deaf people are. In bowling tournaments for the Deaf where there are only Deaf people, I am strictly a bowler. In a Deaf tournament, I am out to get the highest score, have fun, and nothing else.

As shown in Lawson's comments, the ecology of a sport event will likely influence the self-identification of a competitor.

It would be of interest to investigate whether the degree of assimilation into Deaf culture influences the process of self-identification. Being Deaf in a hearing environment is a strong expression of one's cultural affinity. Exploring issues related to cultural affinity in greater depth should further our understanding of what the interactions of various sociocultural symbols are in Deaf sport.

Still, it is clear that Deaf sport has many roles depending on the sociocultural context in which it is placed. Some general statements can be made with respect to the identity of deaf people interacting in sport. For deaf individuals who have had no exposure to Deaf sport, the influence of the sphere of sport in general will provide the script for the sport roles they will assume. For Deaf individuals who attended a school for deaf students or those who are well aware of the sport activities of the Deaf community, then Deaf sport will likely provide the script. However, it is assumed that Deaf athletes who use signs as their primary means of communication have a stronger propensity than those who do not sign to participate in sport activities involving other Deaf persons. Finally, race, gender, and other biodemographic factors may also be influential. Further research is needed in this area.

The foregoing interpretation of social interaction in Deaf sport provides a framework for examining the interactions of deaf individuals within their social milieu. Symbolic interactionism suggests that during social interactions people are highly conscious of how others feel about them and the situation at hand. Conceivably, each instance of social interaction can lead to some alteration in our thoughts on how we should act. This process likely never ends, as we continue to evolve toward being a more socially acceptable being. This theory provides the basis for exploring social forces conducive to Deaf sport.

The Ecology
of Deafness

An ecological perspective of deafness uses "deaf people" as the central reference point for describing social behavior. Such a perspective represents a major departure from traditional portrayals of deafness. Levine (1981) noted that most publications on deafness focus on problems of being deaf with respect to behavior, rehabilitation and habilitation, research, communication, and other areas, with little or no concern given to the impact of the environment on the deaf individual. In contrast, someone working from an ecological perspective examines the interactions between deaf individuals and their social environment: What relationships with society are common to most deaf people? What social forces ensure the continuity of these relationships? How is the quality of a deaf person's life affected by these relationships? As with other ecosystems, does the ecology of deafness reveal any evolutionary trends?

Another rationale for adopting an ecological approach stems from the framework many researchers currently bring to the study of deafness: that is, deafness is presumed to be problematic to the deaf individual. This assumption creates a false sense of security in the field that relies heavily on many unchallenged principles. For example, deafness is viewed as a defect in the individual; it is presumed to be measurable in audiological and educational terms, and therefore it has an aura of tangibility to it; it is presumed to lead to predictable behaviors that can be systematically observed; causes and effects of deafness are thought to be easily delineated—the cause is related to the hearing impairment and the effect is documented as detrimental to the individual; and there are volumes of research on hearing individuals that can serve as a template for research on deafness. Within this framework, deafness and its implications become highly identifiable and understandable from a hearing person's point of view.

Likewise, the notion that deafness is problematic to the deaf individual leads to many seemingly logical and oftentimes simple-minded "solutions" to deafness. Deafness is seen as something that can be attacked and, if not cured (for example, with cochlear implants), then certainly hidden behind techno-logical wonders (for example, hearing aids) or educational mira-cles (for instance, speechreading and speech training). The cen-tral theme in all of these solutions is to make deaf persons more like hearing persons. Although the efforts made in these direc-tions are commendable, they obscure the reality of what it is like to be deaf and the accommodations that society can make to accept deaf persons for what they are and as they are. Study-ing the ecological niche that the deaf population possesses is a primary step toward recognizing the essence of deafness.

Allison (1987) suggests that play, sport, and leisure could logically be studied for insights into the way societies react against such developments as industrialization. Deaf sport is a social expression by Deaf persons who oppose complete accul-turation into a hearing society. Thus, an ecological perspective of Deaf sport is an examination of the way Deaf individuals have responded to sharing space in a predominantly hearing society.

A Hearing World's Perspective on Deafness

An overview of society's per-spective on deafness de-scribes how hearing people feel about deaf people, which one must understand in order to understand the challenges to the achievement of equity between deaf and hearing individuals. Such an overview reveals the social background against which deaf people have designed their lifestyles. Perspectives on deaf-ness will be examined in relation to disability and stigma, two issues associated with inequity.

Disability: Blinding Terminology

Society does not know how to deal with diversity. On the one hand, many people can accept that Deaf athletes represent a culturally distinct group and that Deaf games are needed to meet the social and communication needs of this group. However, under the rubric of sport organizations, Deaf sport is consistently categorized as a disabled sport group. Deaf athletes are not disabled in any way when competing in sport, and placement in the category of disabled sport merely reinforces the common social response to dealing with diversity. Rather than recognizing the distinctiveness within all groups of athletes, society finds it more convenient to separate those who conform to a societal norm from those who do not. Although it is true that Deaf sport shares some of the concerns of disabled sport organizations, the very qualities that distinguish Deaf sport cannot be compromised by the interests of people who have a range of disabilities and who are involved in sport. It is this threat of a compromise that urges Deaf sport teams to maintain a separation of their games from other sport groups. Thus, one of the strongest political battles being fought at the international level of Deaf sport is the resistance to interference from sport groups that meet the interests of a range of individuals with disabilities.

Jerald Jordan, president of the CISS, expressed this concern to the Inaugural General Assembly of the New Organization for Sports for the Disabled, in Dusseldorf, West Germany, September 21–22, 1989. He stated that Deaf people desire to cooperate with disabled sport groups in matters of mutual concern because of the similar problems encountered in dealing with the objectives of an able-bodied world that contrasts with "our hopes and aspirations." In other ways this partnership was not feasible because "our needs and concerns are so . . . different that it makes no sense, whatsoever, to put us together in one organization under one controlling body" (Jordan 1989, 7). The key word here is *control*. Deaf sport does not lack in Deaf leadership and has been organized at an international level since 1924, long before disabled sport established an international body. Whereas the CISS executive board consists entirely of elected Deaf sport directors, most disabled sport organizations are not administered by persons with disabilities. This is always a source of puzzlement for Deaf sport directors who attend disabled sport meetings (Robinson 1989), for Deaf people are committed to ensuring that they maintain control of their own sport institutions.

Thus, disabled sport is not defined by the type of sport played (for instance, kayaking, rhythmic gymnastic), age of athlete (for instance, senior sport events), or competitive nature of the sport (for instance, elite and recreational sports). Rather, it is a social construct that lumps together all athletes who are presumed not only to be "different" but also to be lacking in the full complement of skills needed to run a sport organization. In recent years umbrella sport groups representing the sport concerns of a diverse range of persons with disabilities are becoming common in many countries (for example, the Canadian Federation of Sport Organizations for the Disabled) and at the international level (for example, the International Paralympics Committee). Over the years governments have come to view these umbrella organizations as overseeing the interests of its members. This gives Deaf sport indirect access to funding, which is another concern for Deaf sport, as the strength of disabled sport groups such as Special Olympics and Wheelchair sport associations continue to grow and demand a larger piece of the pie.

The question that Deaf athletes often ask is why their games are thought to be just another type of disabled sport. Fine and Asch (1988) offered a reason for the way people are classified in the following description of why women with disabilities come to be placed in a similar category:

> Why should a limb-deficient girl, a teenager with mental retardation, or a blind girl have anything in common with each other, or with a woman with breast cancer or another woman who is recovering from a stroke? What they share is similar treatment by a sexist and disability-phobic society. (p. 6)

Thus, disability is commonly defined stripped of any social context that may alter the traditional charitable and compassionate attitude that the able-bodied person has toward the disabled. Disability is often defined "in terms of deviation from the norm," with the result that each of these "definitions finds the disability in the individual, not in the context of the environment" (Rogers 1987, 119). Disability is a form of deviancy that is based on impressions that society as a whole has formed about what constitutes normality and, by extension, abnormality. Individuals who do not conform to society's definition of normality are then presumed to be deviant.

In other words, the perceived worthiness of individuals will have a direct bearing on the labels attached to them. Thus, a stranger meeting an eight-year-old deaf girl might be overcome with compassion at the thought of this girl's going through life without experiencing the pleasures of music and the intimacy of hearing friends. The stranger might believe that the girl has an inherent incapacity to accomplish much in life and is therefore disabled, although the girl has yet to demonstrate any evidence of an inability to do something. Indeed, given the prevailing social context under which disability is placed, an individual with a disability must often contend with the belief that the disability "renders him less capable than an able-bodied person of similar age, sex, and social background" (Gliedman and Roth 1980, 28).

George Herbert Mead, in his theory of symbolic interactionism, views the judgment of others as an ongoing process that continually shapes the way we respond to others (Popenoe 1983.) Unfortunately for people with disabilities, judgments are not entirely influenced by the primary actors in an interaction. Individuals tend to adopt current social definitions to guide them in their interpersonal interactions. Moreover, these social definitions are rarely defined by mutual agreement of all members of society. Only those who occupy the dominant positions within a social structure are able to define for themselves and others the "skills, abilities, and the characteristics needed to be 'normal'" (Higgins 1980, 173). In other words, the able-bodied persons are often the key players in defining the people with disabilities.

Extrapolating the theory of symbolic interactionism to persons with disabilities raises the question of how much influence societal notions have on the way persons with disabilities view their own self-worth. That is, are they inclined to internalize negative stereotypes of themselves because this is the message society is relaying to them in the schools, the workplace, the mass media, and even the home environment? Perhaps more significant, can widespread positive descriptions of persons with disabilities be used as a means of improving the way the general population perceives them as well as how they view themselves? To some extent, the mass media are making an effort in this direction. More positive images of persons with disabilities are beginning to appear on television and in newspapers. And messages that are pro-Deaf are being conveyed. For example, Sara in *Children of a Lesser God* sent a message to the public that she and not hearing people will define the terms for being Deaf.

Sara's message needs to be repeated over and over again, as hearing people are still responsible for society's prevailing conceptions of deafness. Without any prior contact with deaf persons and without any knowledge about deafness, many people have preconceived negative notions about a deaf person's capabilities. One possible reason for this is that to many people the term *deaf*, like the term *disabled*, indiscriminately declares that there is something wrong with an individual. These two terms along with others become signals that announce without qualification that an individual does not have a full set of physical and mental capacities. Thus, deaf individuals are seen not only as people who cannot hear and therefore cannot enjoy some of the everyday activities taken for granted by others, but also as individuals who cannot hold their own in a community (Gliedman and Roth 1980)—they are disabled, a burden on society.

A major problem with society's lay method of evaluating deaf persons is that deaf individuals are not given fair opportunities to demonstrate their abilities. They are not allowed to show that deafness is not necessarily a disability when the context is taken into consideration. More generally, persons with disabilities are not allowed to prove their skills and knowledge, and the social assumptions about their lack of abilities is so great that there exists severe doubt as to the benefits of such demonstrations. A case in point is illustrated by questions often asked by both lay people and professionals working in the field of deafness that center on the type of work that deaf people *can* do or *will* eventually end up doing. These questions indicate blatant negative expectations of the mental and physical capacities of deaf individuals to hold a decent job in the community. A more positive outlook on deafness would result if the question asked was, "What *can't* a deaf person do?" This outlook is not necessarily naive. Obviously, deafness does impose some limitations on career opportunities, especially where the use of hearing is essential to the type of work at hand. Nevertheless, given the multitude of careers available, asking what deaf persons can do betrays a skepticism as to whether they are able to do many of the things others take for granted.

In sum, biased assessment in society results in a false accentuation of the disability of deaf individuals. Although it is undeniably true that deaf persons may be communication disabled with respect to functioning in a speech-oriented environment, the label *disabled* used out of context does injustice to their true capabilities. In today's business-oriented society, the term *disability* leaves the impression that a person has more liabilities than assets. Despite the fact that sign language is a viable alternative for interpersonal communication, society pinpoints the inability to hear normally and therefore communicate effectively through speech as a failing of a deaf person. Indeed, it can be argued that the label *disabled* perhaps does injustice to all those who meet its social definition. As Gliedman and Roth (1980) observed:

> If one thing is clear from the autobiographies of the handicapped, it is that the first hazard many face is the demoralization that can result from having one's competence as an individual constantly challenged while one is growing up—not because one actually is incompetent but because the able-bodied think one is. (p. 71)

Deaf sport offers Deaf persons a forum from which they can disassociate themselves from the social handicap of being disabled. In addition, although hearing persons may see Deaf sport as a "disabled sport," Deaf individuals are empowered by their games to demonstrate in a physical way that they are fully capable and competent to run their own show.

Stigma: The Penalty for Being Different

In a society that is becoming increasingly media oriented, it is imperative that individuals are aware of the impact of symbols in their lives. Indeed, in every facet of our lives there are reasons to question the control that symbols exert. Are our taste buds so alike that Coke is it? Is Christmas the only time of the year during which we feel compassionate enough to donate food to the needy? The answer is that commercial products (and sporting events) are symbolic of the values that many Americans uphold. These symbols appeal to various images that do not necessarily relate to the product or events being sold.

Stigma is also related to the manipulation of symbols in society. The Webster's *New Universal Unabridged Dictionary* defines stigma as "something that detracts from the character or reputation" of a person or a group. Goffman (1963) used stigma to refer to an attribute that is deeply discrediting. Higgins (1980) likened stigma to mean a failing, a handicap, or a shortcoming. In all of these definitions, the attribute of an individual that leads to stigmatization does so on the basis of its symbolic representation of an inferior status. A stigmatized person is portrayed as being in some way inferior to most others with respect to personal characteristics and behaviors.

The stigma itself is either immediately obvious or known, in which case an individual is said to be discredited, or it is hidden, and the individual is then said to be discreditable (Goffman 1963). Discreditable individuals can become discredited by revealing characters that society associates with inferiority. Two deaf people sitting in a bus might show no signs of being deaf, but they are discreditable. If they were to begin signing to one another, they would then be discredited. Signing symbolizes deafness. Deaf persons have traditionally been perceived to be inferior to hearing persons. Therefore, signing is a social stigma.

In general, as long as people think of deafness as an indication of the inferiority of a person, then any characteristic that reveals a person to be deaf could be a stigma. Obvious examples of such characteristics are attendance at a school for deaf people or other similar educational programs, signing, speech that is unlike what is commonly heard among hearing persons, and hearing aids. Not so obvious stigmatizing traits would include the tendency to have the television volume on loud, the possession of a telecaption device, shyness among hearing persons, and an appearance of obliviousness to surrounding noises.

A deaf individual is placed in a socially disadvantaged position because of society's unfounded assumptions about the implications of deafness. Guiding these assumptions are symbols that society associates with what is right and what is wrong, normal and abnormal, and disabled and able-bodied. Thus, the indiscriminate beliefs of a hearing and speaking community have succeeded in promoting deafness as a stigma. Little if any consideration is given to the environmental conditions from which a stigma is derived. Indeed, it may well be that when an understanding of deafness is not present, egocentric perceptions by hearing people will always ensure societal maintenance of the stigma of deafness.

For some people Deaf sport might also be seen as an undesirable social system. Parents might not want their deaf children to participate in Deaf sport because of their own stigmatization of deafness. Deaf individuals who harbor strong awareness of the social stigma of deafness may resist becoming involved in various sports with other deaf people. For these individuals Deaf sport deviates from the normal activities associated with the general world of sport in the nature of its participants and in its acceptance of deafness as the status quo. On the other hand, for those who choose to participate in Deaf sport, it is a means of expressing their own preference for a Deaf identity.

Equity: Is Society Ready for the Challenge?

Equity implies a justness between humans. Equity could also be thought of as a willingness to formulate opinions of others on the basis of personal experiences and devoid of biased information gleaned from the existing social consciousness. A stigma is a sign of inequity. Parents' learning to sign so that they may communicate with their Deaf child is a sign of equity. Equity can also lead to a greater intimacy between people. Goffman (1963) would refer to people who have established an intimacy with the stigmatized as "sympathetic others," whom he described as persons

> whose special situation has made them intimately privy to the secret life of the stigmatized individual and sympathetic with it, and who find themselves ac-

corded a measure of acceptance, a measure of courtesy membership in the clan. (p. 20)

Similarly, Higgins (1980) used the term "courtesy members" to refer to hearing people who have achieved some degree of intimacy with deaf people and where membership is in reference to the Deaf community. However, given the low incidence of deafness in the population, the number of people who have achieved intimacy with deaf individuals is likely very small. Thus, as most of the hearing population continues to lack opportunities to achieve intimacy with deaf persons, the question still remains as to what can be done that will make society a more equitable environment for the deaf population.

The political system offers one means of establishing equity. This implies a strategy that is not only geared toward deaf people but could include other minority groups such as those with various physical or mental disabilities. Gliedman and Roth (1980) suggested that "to do justice to the complexity of disability—and to dismantle the structures that have excluded the disabled from the mainstream,"

> a political perspective is essential because only a civil rights movement, supported by a massive federal commitment to the integration, can end the exclusion of handicapped people from the mainstream. . . . An ethnographic perspective . . . also draws upon the minority-group lessons of the past decades: we must discard the intellectual straitjacket of the social deviance analysis and devote as much effort to understanding the handicapped person in terms of his own norms and social situation as to seeking to reduce or cure his specifically biological limitations. (p. 50)

An example of a political strategy for combating social inequity with respect to the deaf population is found in a Council on Education of the Deaf report that contains fifty-two recommendations to the federal government related to the improvement of educational standards for the deaf students (Commission on the Education of the Deaf 1988). Although all of the recommendations require government intervention in order to be implemented, recommendation number 26, in particular, exemplifies the political support needed to promote equity. This recommendation states:

> The Congress should amend the Education of the Deaf
> Act to require that a majority of the members of the
> governing and advisory bodies of Gallaudet University,
> the National Technical Institute for the Deaf, and the
> Regional Postsecondary Education Programs for the
> Deaf be persons who are deaf.

Implicit in recommendation 26 is the recognition that the cultural, linguistic, and educational experiences of deaf individuals cannot be preempted by the experiences of hearing individuals. It recognizes the necessity of designing a safeguard against situations in which deaf persons have little or no control over their social destinies as manifested in the education system. However, although political action is desirable because of its potential to promote equity, politicians are not always obliging to the needs of deaf people. It is questionable whether the deaf population by numbers alone carries any significant political weight.

The mass media can also be used as an effective tool for facilitating equity. By increasing public awareness, mass media can help destroy misconceptions about hearing loss, deaf persons, the Deaf community, sign languages, schools for deaf students, and other aspects relating to deafness. In recent years the mass media have demonstrated a move in this direction; there has been a noticeable increase in exposure to deaf people in motion pictures and on television, as well as to the technology (for instance, hearing aids) and behaviors (for example, signing) associated with deafness. Following are examples of how the mass media have focused on deaf and hard-of-hearing people and on the various issues related to deafness.

The hearing loss of former President Ronald Reagan led to numerous comments about the fact that he wore hearing aids, which may have helped reduce the stigma associated with wearing hearing aids in public. However, it would be of interest to know if a real reduction of the stigma did in fact occur, or if it occurred only for elderly users of hearing aids. Since hearing loss is a common occurrence in the elderly and Reagan, as president, was an elderly citizen, perhaps the generalization that hearing aids are acceptable in public did not extend to the younger generations. Another recurrently popular news item, especially in newspapers and magazines, concerns the cochlear implant, a surgical technique that implants an electronic device in the inner ear, which is then capable of responding to certain sound frequencies, making it analogous to the nerve cells it seeks to imitate. Stories about cochlear implants are usually accompanied by interviews with successful implant patients. However, the mass media focus on hearing aids and cochlear implants does not necessarily imply a positive impact on the public. It is possible that only the reinforcement of negative stereotypes will occur if the public sees technology as a possible cure for deafness—a quick fix that will make deaf individuals more like hearing people.

Signing has also gained mass media exposure through episodes in television series such as "Magnum P.I." and "McGyver," in made-for-television movies such as *And Your Name Is Jonah* and *Love Is Never Silent,* and in motion pictures, including the Oscar-winning *Children of a Lesser God.* Marlee Matlin, the deaf actress in *Children of a Lesser God,* signed her acceptance speech as she picked up her Oscar for best actress in 1987 and then again used signs when she took a part in announcing the Academy Awards in 1988. (She stopped signing and used her voice while presenting the award. Her decision to do this caused quite a stir in the Deaf community from individuals who viewed her actions as a betrayal to the goals of total communication; Wilson 1988.) The first deaf president of Gallaudet University was interviewed on "60 Minutes." On "Sesame Street," Linda Bove, a Deaf actress, uses only signs in her interactions with others. Hearing individuals have also used signs on various occasions on television and in motion-picture roles. Amy Irving portrayed a deaf woman who relied on signs in *Voices.* Louise Fletcher, who has Deaf parents, used signs when she accepted an Oscar for best actress in 1972. Finally, there are many instances of the sign for "I love you" being flashed across the television screen. Various politicians, news reporters, deaf individuals, and fans watching sports events have waved the "I love you" sign at television cameras. Thus, mass media presentations of signs, whether planned or unplanned, has meant that an increasing proportion of the population is becoming accustomed to the use of signs.

The media can make a greater contribution to creating equity by monitoring the context of its presentations. Lessening the social stigma of deafness will be facilitated if references to deaf individuals, signing, hearing aids, and other characteristics are portrayed in a positive manner. An excellent example of the way this can happen is shown in a news segment delivered by Peter Jennings, anchor for the "ABC Evening News." Reporting on the bugging of the U.S. embassy in Moscow in the spring of 1987, Jennings quoted a government employee who stated that perhaps diplomats should learn ASL so that they can talk behind closed doors without having their conversations bugged. Associating ASL with diplomats, even if in a tongue-in-cheek remark, says a lot about the favorable status ASL is gaining in our society.

But not all mass media attention is necessarily beneficial. In an analysis of the ways persons with disabilities are portrayed in television and motion pictures, Longmore (1987) revealed the perpetuation of several distinctly negative images. Remarking on the types of characters traditionally played by persons with disabilities, Longmore noted that

> giving disabilities to villainous characters reflects and reinforces, albeit in exaggerated fashion, three common prejudices against handicapped people: disability is a punishment for evil; disabled people are embittered by their "fate"; disabled people resent the nondisabled and would, if they could, destroy them. (p. 67)

More recently, television appears to be portraying persons with disabilities in a more positive manner, as demonstrated by such shows as "Wolf" and "Life Goes On." However, it still might be the case that mass media tend to create an image that associates disability as an individual rather than a social problem. Disability is often shown as a psychological problem, and social prejudice is rarely implicated. Able-bodied characters are shown to understand better than those with a disability the nature of the problem associated with the disability. Furthermore, it is often an able-bodied person who eventually offers a solution, which is typically one of self-adjustment by the person with a disability.

Longmore (1987) also observed that commercials offer the most positive images of disabled people. One example is a McDonald's commercial about two deaf students taking time out from their studies to enjoy a meal. Both students signed their parts, which were interpreted in subtitles so that viewers could understand what was being signed. This commercial indirectly emphasized not that it is all right to be deaf and to use signs but rather that there are deaf people in this society who do use signs and no judgment was called for on the part of the viewer.

Biklen (1987), analyzing the treatment of disability issues in print journalism, concluded that the media have standard ways of presenting disability issues. For example, disability "is typically cast in terms of tragedy, of charity and its attendant emotion, pity, or of struggle and accomplishment" (p. 81). Biklen's findings concurred with those of Longmore (1987), and together they indicate that mass media are, for the most part, stereotypical in their representation of disability and tend to uphold society's negative conceptions of the disabled and of disability issues.

Beyond the domains of the political system and mass media, society has a moral obligation to extend equity to all individuals. This raises the question of whether the social conscience and empathy of the general public is at a level that is supportive of equity-related initiatives. Are hearing people ready and willing to acknowledge the values of the Deaf community? Can hearing people accept that other people may choose not to be an integral part of the social infrastructure of the hearing community? Can they accept that the biological, social, and environmental conditions that led deaf individuals to create their own language and cultural activities are the same conditions that will assure their continuation?

The importance of values cannot be overlooked. Although a vast majority of deaf persons have hearing parents, the values they uphold as adults may in many respects differ from those of their parents, and hence the hearing community. Eitzen and Sage (1982) defined values as the "culturally prescribed criteria by which individuals evaluate persons, behaviors, objects, and ideas as to their relative morality, desirability, merit, or correctness" (p. 57). They identified the most dominant American values as being success; competition; the valued means to succeed through hard work, continual striving, and deferred gratification; progress; materialism; and cooperation and conformity with respect to laws and customs.

Obviously, not all Americans subscribe to these values. Pepper (1976) identified several differences in value orientations, for example, between the dominant culture in America and that of Native Americans. Native Americans value good relationships and mutual respect above success, progress, materialism, and rugged individualism; and where in the dominant culture people are judged by their credentials, Native Americans tend to judge others on the basis of what they do. The cultural characteristics of Hispanics also differ from those of the dominant culture in that among Hispanics there is a preference for cooperative rather than competitive activities, attention is given to present rather than future tasks, and close family relations and loyalties are vital (Condon, Peters, and Sueiro-Ross 1979; Rodriguez et al. 1979).

For Deaf persons there are not only cultural characteristics that distinguish them from their hearing counterparts but also those that accentuate differences between various deaf ethnic groups (Delgado 1984; Hairston and Smith 1983; Moores and Oden 1978; Stewart and Benson 1988). Only limited information is available on the cultural differences of deaf individuals from various ethnic-minority backgrounds (Moores 1987), although it is known that in education the academic achievements of non-Caucasian deaf students typically lags behind that of deaf students from the dominant culture (Wolk and Allen 1984). In short, in a society that caters to the needs of the dominant culture, deaf ethnic-minority students may be handicapped because of their ethnic backgrounds as well as their deafness (Moores 1987).

On the other hand, cultural differences are more obvious between the Deaf and the hearing communities. The Deaf community is characterized by a distinct language, ASL (Stokoe 1960); commonality of experiences; a tendency toward endogamous marriages; Deaf sport; Deaf cultural activities; and activities or associations that typically exclude hearing individuals from directly participating. The exclusion of hearing individuals from certain Deaf community events is not by itself a rationale for cultural distinctiveness. Nevertheless, it deserves to be mentioned because the Deaf community is one of the few minority groups where this form of reverse discrimination is not only common but acceptable to the dominant society. Hearing people do not argue that they should be allowed to compete in the World Games for the Deaf. The exclusion of hearing people from direct participation in many Deaf community activities helps Deaf persons maintain tight control over their own cultural activities. Hence, the means by which Deaf persons are able to design their own culture and maintain control over their destinies are unique aspects of the Deaf community.

Stewart (in press) conducted a preliminary investigation of the value orientations of Deaf adults within the context of sports. His study was based on research on the game orientations of youngsters in the general population (Blair 1985; Knoppers, Schuiteman, and Love 1986; Maloney and Petrie 1972; Webb 1969) and adults (Loy, Birrell, and Rose 1976; Snyder and Spreitzer 1978). These studies showed a tendency in younger children to display a play orientation in which one of the characteristics is that fair play is valued ahead of winning. Older youngsters, on the other hand, tended to favor winning over fair play (that is to say, a professional orientation).

The subjects in Stewart's study were Deaf adults involved in the planning and directing of various sporting events in the Deaf community. These Deaf sport directors ($n = 21$) were asked to rank the values fitness, skill, success, socialization, and equity with respect to their importance in sport among Deaf persons and sport among hearing persons. There was no evidence of a professional orientation found in either sociocultural context. Analysis of these rankings showed that socialization was ranked significantly higher and equity received a significantly lower ranking when the context was Deaf sport. The results of this study confirmed the thesis that socialization was a critical aspect of Deaf sport (Stewart 1987). The high ranking given to equity in the hearing community may indicate Deaf individuals' desire for fair treatment by their hearing peers. Stewart (in press) suggested that

> societal stigmatization of deafness, generally poorer scholastic performances of deaf children when compared with their hearing counterparts, low self-esteem, and poor outlooks for career possibilities may all contribute to different experiential frameworks upon which value orientations are developed within deaf adults.

Thus, the context of Deaf sport provides some evidence that the value orientations of Deaf individuals may differ from that of hearing persons.

Still, the existence of the Deaf community does not mean that all deaf individuals must adopt its norms and beliefs. Deaf individuals are a part of both Deaf and hearing communities, and their value systems may be more complex than those of their hearing counterparts. The achievements of Jeff Float, an American swimmer, illustrate the influence of a dual value system. In 1977 at the World Summer Games for the Deaf in Bucharest, Romania, he won ten gold medals in swimming events. His performance showed his desire to compete, succeed, discipline himself to achieve success, and conform to the goal of many Deaf athletes to compete in the World Games for the Deaf. At the 1984 Summer Olympics in Los Angeles, Float won a gold medal as part of a U.S. swimming relay team. His performance demonstrated his desire to progress and compete with the best in the world. Not only had Float enjoyed the status of being the best deaf swimmer in the world, he had also gained recognition as one of the world's best swimmers, deaf or hearing.

In summary, the road to equity may be facilitated by means of politics and the mass media; and through acceptance of the value orientations characteristic of Deaf individuals. Whether a significant proportion of society is ready to proceed in this direction and acknowledge the rights of those who have chosen a set of beliefs and norms that differs from that of the dominant culture still remains to be seen.

A Challenge for All

The only certain truth about deafness is that the hearing is impaired. Beyond that, a majority of society is unqualified to make judgments about the deaf population. Less reliance on negative social symbols would make society more equitable for all populations, which would likely give Deaf people the benefit of being perceived as individuals with a unique identity within a culturally diverse community. Although there are certainly some common characteristics that can be attributed to a large number of deaf people, deafness is not a static entity. It is a dynamic force in the interactions between deaf individuals and their environments. Society needs to increase its awareness of the social behavior of the deaf population from an ecological perspective and actively encourage a social conscience that will ensure that equity between deaf and hearing populations will one day be a reality.

A change in society that brings about more equity between deaf and hearing individuals will likely have a positive impact on the popularity of Deaf sport. Legal recognition of ASL as a language, greater accessibility in telecommunications (for example, widespread use of telecommunication devices for deaf people and a nationwide message-relay service), complete captioning of all television programs and home videos, and promotion of cultural pluralism in schools will facilitate equity. They will also help the activities of the Deaf community become recognized by society as desirable cultural activities. Greater equity will make promoting and marketing Deaf sport events easier as the general public's awareness of these events increases. Hearing parents will be more likely to view Deaf sport as a viable cultural alternative for their deaf children. Deaf sport and all other Deaf cultural activities will likely flourish in a more equitable society.

Conclusion

A motto for our society could well be "You are what others think you are." In all forms of social interactions we act according to what we think is appropriate social behavior, which is determined by a social consciousness of what is right and normal. Fifty years ago signing was not the right way to behave. Deaf people were humiliated for using their hands to communicate and congregating among themselves to nurture a social life that could not be found elsewhere. Signing was a symbol of intellectual inferiority, and signers were less than human. The Deaf community was ostracized for embracing values that differed from those of the dominant culture.

Today, ASL has come of age and is recognized as a foreign language (ironically, in its own native land.) Mass media have increased their exposure of signs, and through a proliferation of ASL courses in adult education programs, more hearing than deaf people have some knowledge of signs. For the deaf population, "what others think you are" is beginning to take on a different meaning. The universe as they see it is slowly becoming more accessible. Although equity between the deaf and hearing populations has not yet been achieved, there is a light at the end of the tunnel. The next chapter discusses how Deaf sport is propelling the Deaf community toward this light.

CHAPTER 6

SOCIALIZATION
in Deaf Sport

An examination of the social processes that socialize individuals into Deaf or hearing sport reveals the popularity that sport holds for Deaf people. Sport, in general, offers a unique circumstance for the investigation of social processes and relationships (Coakley 1982), and it provides a context for looking at the social behavior of Deaf individuals and their value orientations. In such a paradigm Deaf sport can be perceived as a microcosm of the Deaf community.

The Structure of Deaf Sport

Clearly, there are strong incentives encouraging Deaf people to create their own sport network. Deaf sport organizations are not established because Deaf athletes are restricted from participating in sport clubs commonly found in communities. They are formed because social processes found in Deaf sport are designed specifically to satisfy the physical, psychological, and social needs of deaf individuals. These social processes or values include using ASL, a natural inclination toward solidarity among Deaf individuals, the advantages of self-determination that is demonstrated through the control that Deaf individuals maintain of Deaf sport activities, and a sense of concern among Deaf individuals for the physical and mental welfare of all deaf people.

The first three social processes mentioned above have received extensive coverage throughout this book. However, a Deaf person's concern for the well-being of other members of the deaf population is seldom, if ever, mentioned as a reason for why Deaf organizations exist. Donald illustrates this sense of commitment in the following, in which he describes his motivation for organizing Deaf sport events:

> I like to think that there are lots of things for Deaf people to do at night other than sitting at home. But, I know that unless we do the work there would be no Deaf community activities available for them. Deaf people need the exposure to Deaf culture and socializing is the best way to do this. In sport activities it doesn't matter who wins or loses as long as people get out to meet each other and enjoy themselves.

A commitment on the part of the Deaf community to enhance the social lives of deaf people also in part shapes the type of sports offered in each community. Volleyball, basketball, and bowling are common in many North American cities because the necessary equipment is minimal and many individuals have at least an elementary grasp of how to play these sports. Slo-pitch is another sport that is rapidly catching on in many communities. It started as a community sport in the 1970s, and by 1982 the CDSA sponsored its First Annual Canadian Deaf Men Slo-Pitch Tournament. The First Annual Canadian Deaf Women Slo-Pitch Tournament was sponsored in 1987.

The rapid progress made by slo-pitch in Canada illustrates the close links between organizations from the grassroots through international levels of Deaf sport. Elite competitions such as national tournaments are largely defined by their appeal to individuals who enjoy sport as athletes or fans, at the local level. This contrasts with professional sports, where the popularity of a sport is more likely to be defined by grassroots support of fans in the stands and in front of the television set.

But the social and athletic concerns of local Deaf communities are not the only forces that encourage the formation of

Deaf sport organizations. The CDSA was founded so that Canadian athletes could compete in the World Games for the Deaf. The move was necessary because the CISS recognizes only those athletes who represent a national Deaf sport organization.

Some organizations are founded to foster both recreational and competitive sports. The United States Deaf Skiers Association (USDSA) is a case in point. Along with its social and athletic functions, the USDSA organizes annual ski tournaments that help recruit and prepare skiers for the World Winter Games for the Deaf.

Other organizations focus mainly on the competitive aspect of a sport. The Canadian Hearing Impaired Hockey Association (CHIHA) and the American Hearing Impaired Hockey Association (AHIHA) sponsor camps to develop youngster's skills. The Canadian Deaf Ice Hockey Federation (CDIHF) and the AHIHA prepare elite hockey players for international competitions. Interestingly, all three organizations are not viewed by some people as Deaf sport organizations because they allow hearing people to occupy executive administrative positions and do not actively strive to uphold the values of the Deaf community. Still, the work of these organizations is accepted by the CDSA and AAAD because high ice rental fee, equipment costs, and the scarcity of hockey players are disincentives to many capable Deaf sport directors, who would prefer to invest their time in organizing sports that have a wider appeal in the Deaf community.

At the local level Deaf sport organizations typically provide opportunities for three levels of participation. At the recreational level, leagues are established that place a premium on the pleasure and social benefits of sports. Volleyball, badminton, tennis, slo-pitch, and, in Canada, curling are examples of some popular recreational sports enjoyed in many Deaf communities. Mixed leagues for men and women are also found at this level. At the next level, competition is emphasized, and players tend to be more serious than when they are playing in a recreational league. Leagues usually consist entirely of Deaf players, although in some sports such as bowling and curling, Deaf teams may participate in hearing leagues if there are not enough Deaf teams to form a league. On the other hand, if there are many players and teams interested in participating, organizations will attempt to accommodate the demand by expanding teams and forming leagues. Tournaments are popular at this level, and they are usually followed by banquets that bring together large numbers of Deaf individuals. At the third level, competition and athletic skills are stressed, and many players at this level aspire to compete in regional, national, and international competitions. At this level, coaching and practice become important, and tryouts for teams are not uncommon.

Outside of the Deaf community, some Deaf athletes participate in hearing leagues and teams. The work of Stewart, McCarthy, and Robinson (1988) and Stewart, Robinson, and McCarthy (in press) showed that Deaf players felt that playing on hearing teams or against hearing individuals provided a more competitive environment that facilitates the development of athletic skills. In addition, Deaf communities usually do not have the numbers nor the demand to provide clubs for sports such as swimming, shooting, and track. Therefore, keen athletes may join hearing clubs in order to pursue the sport that most interests them.

The Greater Vancouver Association of the Deaf (GVAD) is representative of Deaf sport at the local level. The GVAD is a typical community-based association that promotes a range of activities including sport, social clubs, banquets, fund raising, and advocacy. Over the years the GVAD has sponsored recreational leagues in volleyball, basketball, badminton, slo-pitch, and tennis. It has also fielded teams in hearing leagues such as the slo-pitch team that in 1989 won the Vancouver Division D city championship. All GVAD sport activities are the responsibility of a sports director who reports to the GVAD board of directors. The sports director selects coordinators and committees to look after each of the various sports that the GVAD sponsors.

To ensure that its players and teams have access to a higher level of Deaf sport competitions, the GVAD is affiliated with the British Columbia Deaf Sports Federation (BCDSF). Among its activities at the provincial level the BCDSF sanctions tournaments, provides guidance to local clubs on the development of sport programs, promotes the development of youth sport programs, pursues fund-raising ventures, and provides financial assistance to help athletes train and attend national and international games.

Along with nine other provincial Deaf sport associations, the BCDSF is affiliated with the CDSA. Each of these provincial associations consists of a number of local clubs. Through this network of Deaf sport organizations, the CDSA promotes the general welfare of Deaf sport in Canada, which it accomplishes largely through its selection of athletes and teams to compete in international competitions, its sponsorship of the Canada Deaf Summer Games, its coordination of national tournaments in curling, slo-pitch, bowling, and darts, and its ongoing recruitment and development of young athletes and coaches, as well as fund raising and public relations. It is run by an elected board of directors and by provincial delegates at its Annual Congress Meeting. There are no hearing sport directors in the CDSA or in any of the provincial and local Deaf sport organizations in Canada.

At the pinnacle of Deaf sport organizations is the CISS, which regulates competition between countries and sanctions the World Summer Games for the Deaf (WSGD) and the World Winter Games for the Deaf (WWGD). To remain in good standing with the CISS, national Deaf sport governing bodies are required to seek approval from the CISS when they travel to another country to compete. There are eight elected members on CISS's Executive Committee; each is from a different country. The executives meet at least once each year. National Deaf sport organizations send two representatives to CISS Congress meetings at each WSGD and WWGD. The constitution of the CISS stipulates that all executives and representatives must be deaf.

In the United States a large population and a large number of states present the AAAD with logistical problems as it reaches out to grassroots communities. Currently, the AAAD relies on regional affiliates and national affiliates to encourage the development of state and local Deaf sport organizations. The regional affiliates are responsible for conducting annual tournaments in slo-pitch, volleyball, and basketball. Regional winners then compete in a national tournament. The national affiliates are responsible for promoting participation and competition in their respective sports—skiing, hockey, tennis, volleyball, aquatics, and racquetball.

Both the AAAD and the CDSA are concerned with recruiting deaf youngsters and adult members of Deaf clubs into Deaf sport. In Profile 2, Martin Belsky, president of the AAAD, discusses this concern. To counter declining sport programs in schools for deaf students, he favors a national sports festival for

Profile 2
Martin Belsky
President
American Athletic
Association of the Deaf

Martin Belsky has been living in a Deaf mainstream environment for most if not all of his life. His parents were deaf, and he now lives with his deaf wife and their two deaf children. He attended the New York School for the Deaf (NYSD) and graduated from Gallaudet University. His first job after graduation was a teaching position at Michigan School for the Deaf (MSD), where he has been employed ever since and is presently the principal of the high school department. He was a stellar basketball player at NYSD and continued to play at Gallaudet and in a city league in Flint. It is noteworthy that Belsky got his job at MSD because he was willing to coach basketball and football. After many years of involvement in local Deaf sport organizations, the Central Athletic Association of the Deaf, and in the AAAD as an officer, Belsky is now its president.

Belsky's goals as president illustrate his sensitivity to the future prosperity of Deaf sport:

"With declining enrollment at residential schools for the Deaf and the increasing number of deaf students attending mainstreamed programs in public school environments, there is an urgent need to establish regional and national sport festivals for all deaf high school-age students. It used to be that nearly all elite Deaf athletes attended residential schools where sports programs included regional or sectional tournaments. Today, declining enrollment and a smaller pool of high-caliber athletes has forced many of these schools to cancel various sport programs. Football programs are being dropped in favor of soccer, and basketball programs have eliminated the junior varsity teams to concentrate only on varsity teams.

"One way of countering this deterioration in the number of sports programs would be to offer a national sports festival for school-age deaf students. This would provide a valuable source of motivation, competition to enhance athletic skills, and an opportunity for deaf students both in schools for the Deaf and mainstreamed programs to learn more about each other. Such a festival would provide high exposure to Deaf adults involved in state, regional, and national athletic organizations. Workshops conducted by Deaf adults and related to various aspects of Deaf sport could be made available that would increase deaf youngsters' exposure to excellent Deaf role models.

"Oftentimes, the World Games for the Deaf Team Committee discovers outstanding deaf athletes after the Games are completed. A national Deaf sport festival held on a regular basis should help improve the caliber of athletes competing in international games. At the festival, Deaf coaches would work closely with young athletes to prepare them for tryouts for the World Games for the Deaf.

"Another area that needs much attention and improvement is in bridging the communication gap between local clubs of the Deaf and the AAAD. During regional and national basketball and softball tournaments this gap is usually narrow because the AAAD holds its board meetings at these tournaments. This allows AAAD officials and tournament participants to interact and learn about each other. However, many clubs do not sponsor athletic teams and therefore may not receive any benefits from the AAAD. Given the size and number of Deaf clubs across the United States, the task of bridging the communication gap will not be an easy one to accomplish. Yet, the AAAD has already begun efforts in this direction. Our hope for the future lies in nourishing the products of our educational system and the members of our Deaf communities."

school-age students, which would also be used to expose deaf youngsters to Deaf role models. He admits the AAAD faces a tough challenge in getting local adult clubs to sponsor various sports. In this respect, the problems faced by the AAAD are representative of those of the Deaf community in general. Nearly all Deaf associations must grapple with how to stir enough interest in a small population dispersed over a wide area to make the sponsorship of various sport and social activities possible (Fleischer 1990).

Beyond the local level, provincial, national, and international games in Canada and regional tournaments in the United States provide further competitions for deaf athletes. Table 1 shows the number of athletes and countries participating in the 1981, 1985, and 1989 WSGD and in the 1976, 1979, 1983, and 1987 WWGD. The first WSGD was in Paris, France, in 1924, and the first WWGD was held in Seefeld, Austria, in 1949. The location of each world competition is determined by delegates at the CISS Congress six years prior to the games. Countries bid for the chance to host the games, and lobbying can be intense as these countries try to win support prior to voting.

The WSGD in Christchurch, New Zealand, marked the first time that the games were held in the southern hemisphere. The cost of sending a team to a remote country like New Zealand is high. More countries and athletes are likely to participate if the games are held in Europe, where transportation is more affordable. However, the CISS recognizes the value of reaching out to Deaf communities around the world and of enhancing Deaf awareness in the hearing communities of the hosting nation.

Social Processes in Sport

Sport provides a fertile turf for the processes that promote social interaction. Through a common interest in sport, athletes and nonathletes are exposed to a variety of social elements that serve as a blueprint for guiding their behaviors

TABLE 1.

Countries and Athletes Participating in Selected World Winter Games for the Deaf and World Summer Games for the Deaf

	Countries	Athletes
World Summer Games for the Deaf		
1981 Cologne, West Germany	32	1,663
1985 Los Angeles, United States	29	1,423
1989 Christchurch, New Zealand	27	959
World Winter Games for the Deaf		
1976 Lake Placid, United States	15	268
1979 Méribel, France	14	180
1983 Madonna di Campiglio, Italy	16	191
1987 Oslo, Norway	15	225

within a society. These elements include the transmission of cultural values, attitudes, and norms (Leonard 1980) that help guide individuals through their interpersonal interactions. Further, the manner in which these elements are transmitted may depend on the type of sport played and the traits of those individuals participating in it. The overall message conveyed through social interactions reflects the values and beliefs upheld by a society and is not typically unique to a particular group of sport enthusiasts. Thus, sport serves to socialize individuals in a manner that is commensurate with the ideals of a particular society.

In addition, participants are socialized into sports. That is, through a variety of experiences an individual gets drawn into a sport and learns the social behaviors associated with a specific sport role. Given the variety of sports and sport roles available for athletes and nonathletes, it is obvious that there are numerous influential forces that promote the specific types of involvement. Indeed, there are several models that attempt to explain how members of the general population become involved in sport. In particular, the works of Kenyon and McPherson (1973), Leonard (1980), and Snyder and Spreitzer (1978) illustrate how elements of the family, peer groups, school, community, and mass media become agents for the socialization of individuals into sports. Implicit in each of these models is the assumption that a mode of communication and a common language exist between the agents of socialization and the individuals being socialized. Alternatively, in Deaf sport a model is needed that incorporates the impact of communication and other aspects of deafness on the socialization of Deaf individuals into sport.

The Socialization of Deaf Individuals into Sport

The existence of Deaf sport organizations increases the deaf individual's opportunities for involvement in various sports. Given the availability of sport activities in the hearing community, it would appear that deaf persons have greater access to sport than do hearing individuals. This is true even after accounting for the opportunities for involvement that Deaf sport provides to hearing individuals. Nevertheless, the existence of a greater number of opportunities does not necessarily lead to greater involvement on the part of deaf individuals. Likewise, personal attributes such as athletic inclinations and athletic skills are not necessarily key factors determining the type of sport deaf persons participate in or the level of competition they choose. Instead, participation results from a combination of internal and external forces that guide individuals toward optimum social, physical, and mental gratification. To fully understand socialization processes, one must not only examine the influence that significant others, socializing agents, and personal attributes have on these processes, but also understand the intricate nature of these influences (Allison 1982).

Of the many forces that impact sport participation, the idiosyncratic forces of the individual and the external forces emanating from Deaf and hearing communities are most notable. These forces consist of those personal attributes that, taken together, determine the appropriateness of a particular sport or sport-related activity for an individual. Examples of some key attributes are (1) athletic abilities, (2) athletic inclinations or the preference for participation in certain kinds of sports, (3) past experiences with sport in either an athletic or nonathletic capacity, and (4) anticipated rewards stemming from one's involvement. Thus, a fourteen-year-old deaf male who is a fast runner, enjoys rough sports, and has some experience in organized football may decide to play rugby on a predominantly hearing team because of the team's highly successful play-off record. On the other hand, past experiences on a hearing team, if negative, may lead this person to avoid rugby and try out, for example, for the track team, a sport that is oriented to the individual and may not demand much communication effort. Hence, experiences, skills, and desires all influence the type of sport an individual will select.

External forces that affect individuals' participation in sport include the influence of family, peers, school, community, and mass media. In Stewart's (1987) model, the value orientations of Deaf and hearing communities influence the extent to which a deaf individual will participate in Deaf or hearing sport. This can be shown by exploring the influence of the hearing community as perceived within the sociocultural contexts of the community, family, peer groups, and school, and comparing it with the influence of the Deaf community within these same contexts.

The Influence of the Hearing Community

Socialization into sport in the hearing community refers to the processes that induce a deaf person to participate in sport among hearing individuals, typically in environments in which there are no other deaf individuals present. At a young age this is most common for the deaf children of hearing parents. Many of these parents are unaware of opportunities for involving their children with other deaf children in sport. Further, because of the low incidence of deafness, there are many communities in which deaf individuals have not formed their own sport groups, where only a narrow range of sport activities (for instance, bowling, volleyball) is provided, or where no sport activities for youngsters are offered. Thus, for many deaf children the prevailing local restrictions on participation in Deaf sport tend to make the hearing community a more likely source of sport activities.

As adults, deaf persons are in a position to determine for themselves the community in which they will interact. Deaf adults may experience an isolation within hearing environments that results from their different communication and social status. For such persons, an assessment of the value of participating alone in sport among hearing persons against the cost of their isolation within the group may tip the decision toward the Deaf community.

Another factor affecting deaf persons' involvement in hearing sport is the prevailing attitude within the hearing community that deafness is negative. Although this attitude reflects the orientation to sound that our society possesses, it is a value that greatly affects the behavior of deaf individuals. One example of this affect, mentioned earlier, is the amount of literature devoted to defending ASL as a language. The inclination of authors to defend ASL underscores the inequity that exists in society.

Indeed, it may be difficult for some hearing persons to view deaf persons from an untainted perspective—always, the disconcerting question arises of whether a deaf person is able to lead a normal life. Chapter 3 provided an example of this kind of published perspective in an article in the June 2, 1988 *New York Review of Books*, where it was suggested that deaf people often see themselves as incompetent, a comment that, intentional or not, is insensitive to the historical and educational experiences of many generations of deaf people. Comments like this only reinforce society's suspicion that deaf people do not lead a so-called normal life. I have never met a deaf person who "supposes" himself or herself to be childlike or incompetent. I have met many who understand the challenges they face in a society that is oriented to sounds. I have also met many whose response to these challenges is to seek social gratification within the Deaf community and a comfortable relationship with the hearing community.

Thus, deaf individuals participating in sport with hearing persons may face the prospect of being judged not only for their athletic skills and sportsmanship but also for their social status and communication skills. These will determine the effectiveness of their interactions with teammates and other hearing individuals. Although it would appear that hearing players and coaches might be more concerned about the ability of deaf players to play a game well and to benefit the team than they are about communication skills, how they judge a deaf player might still be influenced by societal and personal notions about deafness.

Society appears to be more obsessed with overt indicators of deafness than with the personal attributes of deaf individuals. Examples of this obsession can be found in many articles written about deaf athletes. *Sports Illustrated* in 1987 profiled Jim Kyte, a defenseman for the Winnipeg Jets of the National Hockey League. The article is accompanied by a picture of Kyte using a blow dryer to dry his hearing aid, which gets wet from Kyte's sweating during games and practices. The article is almost entirely devoted to discussions about Kyte's hearing impairment and includes only brief comments about Kyte the hockey player. The article begins with the following statement: "Veteran defenseman Jim Kyte of Winnipeg is such a scrappy player that not even a hereditary hearing impairment can bring him down" (Newman 1987, 109). Down in what way? Reporters too often assume that deafness is a tragedy and that only with much effort can a person learn to live with it. Reporters may inadvertently shape the attitudes of other hearing people who have yet to meet a Deaf individual.

A *Los Angeles Times* article on Jeff Float, a gold medal swimmer at the Los Angeles Summer Olympics, stated that "broadcasting is for people who speak fluidly. Float slurs his words. But he has an excuse. He has impaired hearing. Float wears hearing-aids and is also proficient at lip-reading. The combination allows him to carry on a conversation with little difficulty" (L. Stewart 1985, 3). Comments such as these reinforce society's fixation on "deviating" characteristics of the deaf population.

One reason for this fixation may be that as reporters interview and observe Deaf athletes, they are overwhelmed by the experience and find themselves confronting basic assumptions about communication and social interactions. Perhaps because their time among Deaf athletes is usually short, they do not have time to fully recognize and appreciate the diversity to which they have been introduced. Hence, their stories may reflect their own attempt to understand the unique culture of the Deaf community. This reflection is shown in the following quote taken from a *USA Today* story about Gallaudet University's football team: "The hearing impairment of Gallaudet players varies. Some are totally deaf, relying on sign language. Some have only partial loss. Some, like Woods, talk and hear almost normally" (Moores 1989). Statements such as these do little to enlighten the reader about the athletic skills and character of Deaf athletes.

Sign language also grabs a lot of the media attention. Signing is different. There is something mystical about it that entrances those who do not know it. In a *Los Angeles Times* article (Newman 1985) about the "Quiet Olympics," communication was highlighted through a comparison of the 1984 Los Angeles Summer Olympics and the 1985 World Games for the Deaf, which were also held in Los Angeles:

> At the 1984 Olympics, the thundering roar could be heard from the crowd of 92,655 even before the first nation, Greece, entered the Los Angeles Coliseum. When Greece entered there was a roar.
>
> At UCLA's Drake Stadium Wednesday, there was no noise, just the sound of whispering. In the crowd of 7,000 there were arms waving; the crowd was cheering in sign language. When France, the host nation of the first Games for the Deaf in 1924, finally entered, arms were thrust into the air. In sign language, the applause was thunderous.

A thunderous applause in sign language? Articles written about Deaf sport and deaf people in general are seldom short on cute phrases. Such phrases tell the reader little about the athletes and Deaf Games themselves. Yet, a major attraction in reporting about Deaf athletes appears to be the public's fascination with those characteristics of the Deaf community that set them apart from the rest of the population. Little if anything is reported about the controversies that exist in Deaf sport, the politics played by Deaf sport organizations around the world, the lifestyles of Deaf athletes, or a multitude of other topics one would expect to read about during international sport events.

Coverage of issues other than those associated with hearing impairment would enhance public awareness about the various social dimensions of being Deaf. In politics, for example, media could cover the maneuvers of Deaf sport organizations to remain autonomous and not fall under the control of disabled sport governing bodies, strategies that are used to ensure that sport directorships and other administrative positions are occupied by Deaf persons, the ways regional disparities in economics and populations influence sport activities and the ambitions of Deaf athletes, the power struggle between those who desire to maintain long-term control over organizations and those who advocate the empowerment of new blood to help strengthen the overall leadership in the Deaf community, and attempts to deal with inequity issues involving gender and ethnic minorities. Other important issues are related to the ability of athletes to reach their athletic potential and include quality of coaches, corporate sponsorships, access to affordable training facilities, and fund raising.

In addition to issues related to politics and athletics, the living experiences of athletes and sport directors might affect the value of sports to them. In Stewart's (1987) model of sport participation it is suggested that the unique life experiences of Deaf persons lead them to perceive the value of sport in a way that differs from the perceptions of hearing persons. Essentially, many experiences of Deaf individuals bear little or no resemblance to those undergone by hearing individuals. Examples are attendance at a school for deaf persons, the use of sign language as the primary means of communication, difficulty in communicating with significant others through the speech modality, less exposure to the influence of radio and television, and social stigmatization. Like other minority groups, Deaf people also face a different set of choices in their social activities. The ways in which these unique experiences affect the perceptions of a Deaf person have yet to be completely understood, and further research on the perceived value of sport may make a significant contribution to our understanding of deafness within the total context of society.

Thus, given that hearing and Deaf persons have different experiences and subscribe to different beliefs, it seems reasonable that their value orientations will also show differences. However, value orientation has received relatively little attention in the literature, and research findings on hearing individuals cannot simply be generalized to the Deaf population. Indeed, care must be taken not to indiscriminately impose mainstream logic on any minority population. The identity of any such group as the Deaf population must not be lost as a result of efforts to fit our knowledge about deafness onto existing templates that are often derived from research on individuals without disabilities.

Still, research evidence suggests that the value orientations of a hearing community create an atmosphere that is ill-suited to the social and communication needs of Deaf people (Padden and Humphries 1988; Stewart 1987, in press). Hence, participation in hearing sport does not necessarily offer the same benefits to Deaf individuals that it does to other individuals in society. Deaf athletes playing on hearing teams may perceive little social gratification stemming from their involvement. Indeed, investigation of the value orientations of Deaf sport directors has shown that socialization ranked behind equity, fitness, skill, and success as a value associated with participation in hearing sport (Stewart in press).

Moreover, there may be fewer opportunities for a deaf person in hearing sport to participate in an administrative capacity. Those deaf persons who aspire to contribute to the administration and direction of hearing sport organizations are faced with a communication challenge. However, participation does occur, especially when a Deaf person is representing a Deaf sport organization. For example, the AAAD-United States World Games for the Deaf Team Committee has a representative on the U.S. Olympic Committee's Committee on Sports for the Disabled. If Deaf individuals do not participate in the administrative structure of a hearing sport association, it may be because there are few benefits associated with the experience. I was once a director at a community ice rink but left because of my desire to concentrate on playing hockey on a Deaf team and to become involved with the infrastructure of Deaf sport. It became readily apparent that in Deaf sport, Deaf individuals have a better chance to realize their leadership potential.

Nevertheless, competing on hearing teams does offer Deaf athletes some advantages. Two studies of Deaf sport directors and Deaf athletes found that both groups felt that hearing sport offered a more competitive and intense atmosphere conducive to the development of athletic skills (Stewart, McCarthy, and Robinson 1988; Stewart, Robinson, and McCarthy in press). It was also felt that training sessions on hearing teams were more intense and that the overall challenge of competing was greater than on a Deaf team.

Another factor favoring participation on a hearing team is the low incidence of deafness; it is estimated that one person in a thousand has a severe to profound degree of hearing loss (Clarke et al. 1977). In addition, the already relatively small pool from which deaf athletes might come is further reduced by factors that are specific to an individual (for example, propensity to participate in a particular sport, physical fitness) or extrinsic to the individual. Examples of factors in the latter group include work schedule (for example, afternoon shifts), financial status (for example, the ability to pay bowling fees), family responsibilities, and community responsibilities (for example, involvement in a Deaf cultural society). Hence, participation in the sport opportunities provided by the Deaf community may be severely limited by the size of that community.

It is not uncommon for Deaf individuals to participate in hearing leagues as a means of expanding their participation in sport. Bowling provides a prime example of how people in the Deaf community use hearing community sport to their own advantage. For example, in a bowling league in Michigan, there are twenty teams, two of which consist entirely of Deaf bowlers. The benefit of this arrangement is that, from a competitive perspective, the bowlers on any team are exposed to different levels of competition among the nineteen other teams, which helps improve bowling skills. At the same time, being on a team that has all Deaf players means that communication is facilitated among all the players. For the players, the competition with hearing players is seen as good preparation for competition at higher levels, where more than one hundred Deaf teams may compete for top prize money. Obviously, in larger cities a league with twenty Deaf bowling teams would offer the same advantages.

Thus, some variables that may positively influence a deaf athlete's participation in sport operating within the framework of a hearing community are lack of similar opportunities for involvement in Deaf sport, age restrictions for participating in Deaf sport, lack of awareness of opportunities for involvement in Deaf sport, and a desire for intense training and competition. The major adverse influences on hearing sport participation are negative attitudes toward deafness among hearing persons and the existence of a less than optimal environment for socialization due in large part to barriers to communication.

The Influence of the Deaf Community

Deaf sport exemplifies the value orientations of the Deaf community. For some deaf individuals, especially those who are about to become involved in Deaf sport for the first time, the values associated with communication, socialization, and shared experiences are incentives for this involvement.

In a survey of Deaf sport directors Stewart, McCarthy, and Robinson (1988) asked each to indicate the type of community he or she preferred to interact in and his or her preference for participation in Deaf or hearing sport. Descriptive data on the directors revealed that, in general, they all had a severe to profound hearing loss, with a majority becoming deaf at birth or prior to the acquisition of a spoken language; ASL was preferred by all as the primary language of communication; most had learned to sign by the time they had reached school age; and most never use hearing aids.

With respect to community preference, all 21 directors stated that they preferred to interact socially only within the Deaf community. Thus, even among those who used hearing aids all of the time ($n = 3$ directors) and those who preferred English as their language of communication ($n = 3$) or had equal preference to English and ASL ($n = 5$), the Deaf community offered the most attractive environment for social interaction. The following comment by one of the subjects who was a hearing-aid user and gave equal preference to the use of ASL and English illustrates the underlying rationale for Deaf community participation:

> The deaf community offers a less stressful situation. Even with my hearing aids, talking and listening to hearing people is a difficult task that I would rather not have to face day in and day out. In the deaf community we understand the lifestyles of each other and do not have to spend a lot of time explaining about deafness to others. Also, I feel that deaf people must

become strong advocates of the things they enjoy, such
as Deaf sport, and therefore should stick together.
(Stewart, McCarthy, and Robinson 1988, 239)

Hence, the common themes of communication and likeness of
life experiences are major forces propelling Deaf persons
toward a community of their own.

So that their preference for participating in Deaf or hearing sport could be explored fully, subjects were asked to quan-
tify their responses using the categories *always, most of the time,
some of the time,* and *never.* Overall, Deaf sport directors preferred
to participate in Deaf sport to a greater extent than hearing
sport. However, only two directors stated that they wished never
to participate in hearing sport. Comments made by the directors indicated that competition in Deaf sport was favored for
its "social benefits, opportunities for physical fitness, high degree of enjoyment, communication compatibility among players, equity among players (i.e., deafness is the norm and players
perceive each other as social equals), and positive experiences
involving deafness" (Stewart, McCarthy, and Robinson 1988,
240).

The Deaf community offers its participants a different set
of conditions under which they may comfortably interact with
others while simultaneously reaping the rewards that their participation as athletes or nonathletes entails.

Stewart, Robinson, and McCarthy (in press) replicated the
foregoing study with 21 Deaf athletes who had participated in
the 1989 World Games for the Deaf in Christchurch, New Zealand. There were some marked differences in the biodemographic characteristics of these athletes and of the sport directors examined in the previous study. In contrast to the sport
directors, who indicated a strong preference for using ASL,
only 6 (28.5 percent) athletes preferred to use ASL over English
and another 5 (23.8 percent) athletes had an equal preference
for ASL and English. All 5 French Canadian athletes preferred
French over LSQ. With respect to community preference, 12
(57.2 percent) athletes preferred to interact in a Deaf community, 5 (23.8 percent) preferred to be a part of a hearing community, and the 4 others (19.0 percent) had an equal preference
for both communities.

The community preferences of the athletes contrasted with
those of the sport directors. Stewart, Robinson, and McCarthy

suggested that the differences noted in communication and community preferences between athletes and sport directors may be attributed to factors such as degree of hearing loss (9 of the athletes had a moderate or moderate to severe hearing loss, whereas all sport directors had a severe or profound hearing loss), educational background (9 of the athletes attended public schools where a spoken language was the language of communication), and the fact that nearly all of the athletes who had attended public schools had been exposed to ASL only during Deaf sport competitions. Because most of the athletes were still of school age, the authors are planning a follow-up study to see if the athletes from public schools will become more involved in the Deaf community during their adult years.

The athletes were also asked about their preferences for training and competing with a Deaf or a hearing team. As did the Deaf sport directors, the athletes found hearing teams to be more athletically challenging. However, for some of the athletes belonging to a hearing team or club was the only option available. The athletes did show a stronger preference for competing with hearing teams than for training with them, and the opportunity to socialize before and after practice with Deaf team members was the main reason for this preference. Thus, Deaf athletes are faced with accommodating their need to socialize and their desire to excel when deciding their options in sports.

In addition to the complex issues related to competitiveness and the training of athletes, Deaf communities often face logistical problems in organizing sport for a small population. An example of how a Deaf community does this is found in hockey. Because hockey requires skills that are not commonly taught in physical education programs, the number of Deaf hockey players in any given community might be too small to make fielding a full team possible. Alternatively, five or six Deaf players may join a hearing team and try to play together as a line. As in bowling, the Deaf players will likely use the team they play on as a way of preparing themselves for competition in a tournament for Deaf hockey teams. In Canada and the United States there are also the options of attending a national hockey camp sponsored by the CHIHA or the AHIHA at the end of the hockey season (see Schappell 1986) or trying out for the national team. These options rely on the possibility of drawing players from many different provinces and states.

Another strategy that combines Deaf hockey players with hearing players is illustrated by an experience I had while playing for a Deaf hockey team. At that time, although there were just enough players to field a team, the team was plagued by player absenteeism stemming from shift work, travel, and other conflicts. The solution to this was to incorporate a reverse form of integration whereby a few hearing players were allowed to play on the Deaf team. However, although hearing players may be welcome to participate on a Deaf team playing in a hearing league, they are not allowed to compete on a Deaf team during a Deaf tournament.

In addition to devising strategies to compensate for the limitations that a small Deaf population could impose on opportunities for sport participation, some Deaf communities attempt to diversify the interests of its members in sport. This can be accomplished through the establishment of leagues that allow many novice players to participate, which helps to expand the range of sports offered by a Deaf community. Furthermore, astute Deaf sport directors will schedule leagues so that a minimum of overlap occurs, which allows players to participate in a variety of sports throughout the year. Such a set-up is found in British Columbia, where the GVAD has at one time or another offered its members soccer, slo-pitch, curling, basketball, volleyball, badminton, tennis, table tennis, skiing, and hockey (Stewart 1987) despite the fact that its own membership is usually only approximately two hundred.

Conclusion:
The Influence
of the Community

In a sense, current evidence suggests that Deaf sport caters to the social instincts of Deaf individuals and hearing sport to their physical capabilities—social versus physical gratification. The sociocultural context and the perceived athletic advantages of the Deaf and hearing communities appear to be critical in determining the propensity of Deaf individuals to participate in them. For those who are keen on developing their skills in a certain sport, playing on a hearing team is perceived as having a distinct advantage over playing with a Deaf team. Likewise, the more recreationally oriented a Deaf athlete is, the less appealing hearing sport might appear.

Therefore, in addition to social and communication considerations, deaf persons draw from their own athletic attributes and inclinations for reasons that may influence their choice of participating in sport with Deaf or with hearing individuals. Relevant issues would include such future athletic aspirations as making a regional or a national Deaf team, desire for a competitive atmosphere, desire for social interactions with others, and intensity of desired physical activities. It appears then, that the ideal situation for Deaf athletes is one in which there are opportunities for positive involvement in both Deaf sport and in sports available to all members of society.

The Influence of Hearing Families

The impact of the family unit on sport socialization is well documented (Greendorfer and Lewko 1978; Kenyon and McPherson 1973; Loy, McPherson, and Kenyon 1978, 1981; Sage 1980; Sofranko and Nolan 1972). Sofranko and Nolan (1972) found that adults who were favorably socialized into certain leisure or sport activities at a young age tend to introduce their own children to these activities. Also, interest in a sport at an early age is likely to be present at later stages in life. In general, the impact of the family on sport participation can be summarized by looking at the role of the family as one that

> serves as socializing agent for the learning of sport (especially mothers for their daughters); it provides a structure from which ascribed and achieved attributes impinge on an individual in a sport system, and it uses sport as an expressive microcosm of the larger society in its attempt to socialize children. (Loy, McPherson, and Kenyon 1978, 226)

In addition to encouraging sport participation, parents in particular promote their children's success in athletic activities (Eitzen and Sage 1982). In a review of the research on the impact of the family on socialization in sport, Greendorfer (1987) criticized research methodologies for being incomplete, unidirectional, and gender biased, among other faults. Still, the literature provides some indication of a strong relationship between the social institutions family and sport.

The processes by which families socialize children into sport is also important. In most cases a common language and communication system facilitates socialization in a variety of settings. Casual conversations while watching a baseball game at a park or on television can reinforce values that parents attach to the rituals of baseball within the domains of the athlete and spectator. Parents who favor fair play in sport signal to their children a precise value that is generalizable to other aspects of life. Subscription to sports magazines or faithful reading of the sports section in newspapers can lead to many dinner table discussions on various issues in sport. Parents who actively partake in the activities surrounding their children's community sport involvement become sources of information related to the coaches, teammates, and other families associated with the team. In many instances, sport contributes to a special kind of intimacy between child and parents, and even between siblings. Although communication per se is not a sole condition for development of this intimacy, it undoubtedly affects the degree to which this intimacy develops.

In contrast, deaf children in hearing families are socialized under a different set of conditions. More than 90 percent of deaf children have hearing parents, a large number of whom will never learn to sign. Thus, the influence of verbal communication as a facilitator of socialization processes in the family is likely reduced. Discussions on issues related to sport would be, for the most part, nonexistent or only superficial.

A family that is unable to communicate effectively with a deaf child has already imparted a significant value to that child—the value of speech as a tool for social interactions. If deaf children are unable to eventually acquire functional speech skills, then speech may have negative connotations. When deaf children become older, they become acutely aware of the role speech plays in social relations. They resent that their families have refused to learn to sign although they themselves have spent ten or more years trying to learn to speak. If resentment results from the lack of communication within the family, deaf individuals may shun competition in hearing sport.

Although the notion of a deaf child's playing sports with hearing peers is entirely appropriate, parents who do not accept their child's deafness may unwittingly pressure their child to behave in a manner for which he or she is inadequately prepared. This occurs, for example, when a parent continually encourages a deaf youngster to interact socially with other teammates, to chat it up, to be like the others. If the deaf child, when attempting to do this, experiences too many failures, the encouragement may backfire and lead the deaf child to lose interest in playing on a hearing team.

Hearing parents may even deny their deaf child any opportunities for participating in Deaf sport. If parents believe that their child should be completely integrated into the hearing community and should conform to a hearing model of normality, then they will prefer sports involving hearing peers. Even when these parents are aware of opportunities in Deaf sport, they may choose not to have their child participate in them. A friend related a story about parents who preferred to have their deaf son participate in sports for athletes with a disability rather than in Deaf sport. Perhaps these parents feared the influence that Deaf adults might have on their child. However, by placing their son, who did not have a physical disability, in sports for athletes with a disability, these parents may have established a harmful precedent in shaping their son's understanding of who he is and what deafness is all about. Thus, in some families access to the Deaf community is either limited because of lack of information or denied because involvement with other deaf individuals is not desired.

It is also true that not all deaf youngsters desire to associate with their deaf peers. A teacher of deaf students in a public school related her experience with some of the students she had over a ten-year period:

> My students are integrated for all of their courses and only come to my room for assistance with their coursework. At first some students feel uncomfortable coming to my classroom because they don't want to be different from their hearing friends. This is very true for those students who use speech and not signs for communicating. However, if they come to me, they soon appreciate the help I can give them. While in my classroom they may get to know other deaf students.

> They see signing and begin to learn it themselves. Even
> then, for some students it may take one or two years
> before they feel comfortable around other deaf stu-
> dents. And some deaf kids leave school wanting only
> to associate with hearing people.

Hence, there are some deaf students who perceive speech to be
their primary means of communication and hearing persons as
their preferred social group. It may be that they have had little
exposure to Deaf individuals or are acutely aware of the social
stigma attached to deafness. Parents may also persuade their
deaf children to not associate with other deaf individuals. Thus,
socialization into sports for many deaf children of hearing parents will occur within an environment that does not include
Deaf sport.

Whatever factors influence a person's social group, it is
clear that mainstreaming deaf students into public schools has
impacted their socialization behaviors. Mainstreaming reflects
the value orientation of parents who must decide in which sociocultural environment (that is, deaf or hearing programs) they
desire their children to be educated and which method of communication will become the primary tool for instruction. How
mainstreaming has affected deaf children's opportunities to
participate in Deaf sport is discussed in the next chapter.

Without information on the long-term benefits of participation in Deaf sport or sport for hearing persons, one cannot
possibly clearly identify the effects of being involved in one or
the other. Although preliminary investigations of deaf youngsters and adults showed that they felt there were benefits to be
gained from participation in both kinds of sport (Stewart, Robinson, and McCarthy in press), parents are likely to depend
upon their own experiences and beliefs as they socialize their
children into sport. For some hearing parents this could mean
focusing only on sports for the hearing, whereas others might
view a combination of sports for hearing persons and for Deaf
persons as ideal.

Further information about the impact of a hearing family
is seen in the following account, which I have related to groups
of parents. My own mother was never supportive of my playing
sports because she wanted me to attain a good education first.
My dad, however, was always signing me up for various sports

because he felt that I needed as many skills under my belt as possible in order to be competitive with my peers.

My first encounter with organized sports was when I was seven years old and my dad signed me up for lacrosse. For the two years I played it, I was a goalie. Now that I look back on that experience, I think the choice of making me goalie was intuitively wise of my dad. Goalies don't have to communicate with their teammates—at least, I never did. I just stood in front of the goal and blocked shots. Fortunately, I played for a good team that had a winning reputation. We would win 35–0, 17–1, and that had nothing to do with my goal-tending skills. As a matter of fact, I hated being a goalie. I wanted to run and score. But always being a winning goalie, I was the one who received the pats on the back at the end of the game, and that was the closest I ever got to talking to anyone at games other than my dad.

When I was nine years old, I switched to hockey, where I wasn't the goalie. In hockey I was always the fastest and good enough to play on any team for my age. This meant four to five games a week plus practice, which dad would drive me to. I found myself talking more than during lacrosse, partly because my own communication skills had improved over the past two years and partly because the talk was complimentary and predictable—"Great game!" "I got two goals and three assists." "Who do we play next?" As a young player, this was fine, but as I got older and the things that were said got more complicated, I used to try to head out of the dressing room after a game as soon as possible. I just didn't like having to ask someone to repeat what they had said and then often not understand anyway. I quit hockey when I was sixteen years old and concentrated on high school sports like rugby and track. But I continued to faithfully watch hockey on television with dad twice a week and spent hours reading about it in the newspaper.

I don't regret my lacrosse and hockey experiences and do wish I had not quit either of them. I just saw a dead end. When you're a teenager, interacting with other people on a social basis overtakes the importance of sports. On one hand, I enjoyed the recognition others would give me because I was a good athlete. But handling questions about the victories and having to fumble through a conversation was tiresome and difficult since I wasn't skilled at handling my deafness in public. Until I became an adult and got involved in Deaf sport, I never saw the long-term benefits of sports. I never saw myself being involved competitively as an adult, although I did enjoy watching sports with some close friends as well as playing pick-up basketball, baseball, and football with them. The stress of talking to others was too much to handle. I don't blame my parents for not introducing me to Deaf sport because until I told them about it they had never heard of it. For that matter, until I became an adult, I had never really met a Deaf person. Today, my parents are proud of my involvement in Deaf sport.

Several issues are apparent in my experience. First, socialization into sport meant participating on hearing teams because that was the only avenue known to my parents and because I went to a hearing school. This is interesting, because there was a school for deaf students in the city where I lived. Yet I cannot recall any competitions involving my school and that school, although both did compete against other hearing schools in the city.

Second, although I excelled as an athlete, I withdrew from the socialization activities associated with my teams except for walking home with a friend after a game or practice. When I was a child, my dad would do most of the talking when parents or other kids asked questions because I could not understand them and they had difficulty understanding me. Thus, outside of active participation in sports, my dad, some close friends, and some high school coaches were my main connections with sport-related social activities. This does not mean that there were no other processes involved in socializing me into sport. Passive forces may also have played a role, as I did watch a lot of sports on television and was an avid reader of the sports section in newspapers and novels about sport.

The third issue arising from my experience is that it suggests that sport at a younger age is oriented to the thrill of playing, and only later does the participant confront the realities of socialization. This concurs with my proposition (Stewart 1987) that adolescent years might alter the values that deaf individuals attach to sport, especially in the domain of social interactions. When I was younger, I did not know how to interface my enjoyment for playing sports with my restricted ability to communicate in the speech mode. Assistance in this regard not only might have prolonged my involvement in lacrosse and hockey but also might have changed my outlook on the value of sports in my adult years.

In summary, hearing parents tend to socialize their deaf children into sports for the hearing because they are usually unaware of the opportunities in Deaf sport or might see this type of involvement as being the best means of normalizing the life experiences of deaf children. Obviously, there are some hearing parents who allow their deaf children to participate in both types of sports. Parents who use this type of socialization strategy might be influenced by their children's attendance at a school for deaf students or other deaf educational programs, by their desire to expand opportunities for competition, by their own association with Deaf adults, and other factors. Further research in this area could prove useful in the development of guidelines for parents who desire a range of sport options for their deaf children.

The Influence of Deaf Families

In this section the term *Deaf family* will refer to those families in which at least one of the parents is a member of the Deaf community. Deaf siblings are not a necessary component in the current criteria of a Deaf family. Nor is a family considered a Deaf family when all of the siblings are deaf but the parents are not, although a strong case could be made for the influences that deaf siblings have on each other with respect to value orientation. Deaf siblings often share common experiences, attend similar educational institutions, and, in the absence of parents with adequate communication skills, rely upon each other for moral support and guidance. In a sense, an older deaf sibling could, in time, assume some of the roles characteristic of Deaf parents, introducing the values of the Deaf community to a younger deaf brother or sister. Hence, deaf siblings may have a significant impact on each other. Nevertheless, the decision not to discuss their role here stems from the lack of research on deaf siblings and the number of varying conditions (for example, deaf twins; older deaf sister and younger deaf brother; three deaf sisters) that may complicate generalizations.

There are no data to tell us the number of deaf children who come from a Deaf family when the above definition for Deaf family is used. If we consider that there are also some deaf parents who do not see themselves as being a part of the Deaf community, then a reasonable estimate might be that 4 to 6 percent of all deaf children come from Deaf families.

Not all Deaf parents have deaf children, but those who do tend to more readily accept their child's deafness. Deaf children in Deaf families are exposed to signing at an early age and learn ASL as their native language. Having a firm language base at a young age puts them in a better position to more readily absorb the values held by their parents than are deaf children of hearing parents, who often do not acquire a firm grasp of language until after they have begun school. Thus, for many Deaf children of Deaf parents, initiation into the Deaf community begins at an early age.

Deaf families introduce their Deaf children to various cultural, social, and sport events associated with the Deaf community and fully expect them to become active members in this community. With these types of experiences and expectations, along with high acceptance of deafness and sharing of a common sign language, the ecological perspective of a deaf child growing up in a Deaf family is inarguably different from that of a deaf child growing up in a hearing family.

In sport, a Deaf family will expose children to sports played in the Deaf community and their accompanying social activities. Although the size and location of a Deaf community affects the type of sports played, it is the experience of participating and watching Deaf individuals participate that provides the primary rewards. Thus, on one hand, all children have opportunities to watch professional and amateur sports live or on television, and all families, hearing or Deaf, are able to do this together. However, a deaf child watching Deaf adults play these same sports is treated to dynamic portraits of life in a Deaf world. Deaf families are more likely than hearing families to introduce their children at a younger age to situations that generate these portraits.

Another insight that Deaf families bring to their children is found in the planning and staging of Deaf sport events. Where Deaf parents are involved in the organizational aspect of Deaf sport, their Deaf children will be cognizant of similar opportunities that will be available to them during their adult years. The exposure to Deaf adults with positions on boards of directors, organizational committees, executive boards, and in other influential roles is a crucial ingredient in the cultivation of healthy and meaningful aspirations in all deaf children. It is a goal that has all too often been neglected in our educational system and in the home.

Exposure to Deaf people in administrative roles is significant because there is evidence that parts of society still adhere to the notion that deaf persons are to be helped by others rather than do the helping. The comments of a hearing chairperson of a university board of trustees is a prime example of how deaf people are stigmatized by this notion. While defending the choice of a hearing person (with no experience in deafness) as president of Gallaudet University, she stated that "deaf people are not ready to function in a hearing world" (Williams 1988, A20).

Deaf sport, as opposed to deaf education, is a haven of administrative opportunities for Deaf adults. Deaf children who are exposed to this aspect of Deaf sport are given a unique standard for assessing their place in society.

Conclusion:
The Influence of the Family

With more than 90 percent of deaf children having hearing parents, there are distinct advantages to be gained from increasing these parents' awareness of Deaf sport. To this end, much can be learned from the role Deaf parents take in inducting their children into various elements of the Deaf community. In addition, because it is not expected that hearing parents duplicate the roles of their Deaf counterparts, the characteristics of hearing parents who have fostered a successful relationship with their deaf children should be examined. Deaf children deserve exposure to the activities of Deaf sport because it is one option that they have as citizens in our society. Likewise, they should also be allowed to determine what sports in the general population has to offer them—Deaf parents along with hearing parents are obligated to provide learning experiences within this domain.

The Influence of Hearing Peers

Association with peer groups can impact an individual's participation in sport. Research in this area suggests that lack of association with a sport-oriented peer group tends to reduce individuals' participation in sport (Loy, McPherson, and Kenyon 1978). Early sport participation also provides opportunities for individuals to compare their athletic abilities with others, which might then influence their perception of the value sport has for them (Snyder and Spreitzer 1978). With deaf individuals, the influence of peer groups is likely to take on other dimensions. The communication of a deaf person is likely to influence interactions with hearing peers in sport.

This relationship may, however, be affected by age. My own experience was that there came a time when there was more to sport than just playing the game, and during this time I keenly felt the need to socialize. During early childhood the rewards for playing with hearing peers may override the frustrations of interpersonal interaction, and deaf children may be receptive to involvement in formal or informal sport activities with their hearing peers. During adolescent years the increasing importance of social interaction may change deaf youngsters' perception of the benefits derived from continuing involvement with hearing peers. Finally, for youngsters and adults striving to develop talent in a particular sport, there is again an inclination to participate in sports with hearing individuals, as the socialization aspect of hearing sport is now less important than access to a competitive environment.

My personal experience suggests that a deaf person's involvement with hearing peers during the adult years may be less stressful than during adolescent years. As an adult, my perceptions of the realities of deafness and my personal niche in a predominantly hearing and speaking world were honed. Gaining access to the adult Deaf community provided me with an alternative viewpoint of my place in society. My rationale for participating in hearing sport also changed decisively. As an adolescent who had no exposure to Deaf sport, I had no options other than to play with hearing peers and on hearing teams. Therefore, I strove to achieve excellence in all competition and had no choice but to accept the frustrations of communicating with my hearing peers. When I reached adulthood, competition with hearing persons became a matter of choice, and it was no longer a goal by itself. Contrary to popular notions about the competitiveness of Deaf athletes, I do not compete to demonstrate that deafness can be conquered. Nor do I compete to show that I am just like any other hearing person—because I am not. My participation in sport is in the spirit of fitness, competition, and pleasure. Although, I still experience breakdowns in my communication with hearing individuals, the fault is mutual and, in the speech modality, inevitable. I have come to accept my deafness and all that it entails as reality, and my lifestyle as something to be shaped and treasured in its own unique mold rather than distorted to fit a defective social conscience of what it could be. Deaf sport provided the context through which my philosophical outlook on life was developed.

However, there are instances when hearing players may be actively recruited to participate on a Deaf team. This typically occurs when there is an insufficient number of Deaf players to support a Deaf team. Donald explains how he handles this situation at a local level:

> We play in local hearing leagues because that is how we prepare for Deaf tournaments and a Deaf player on the bench may feel that he is losing valuable game time and experience. Because of this I try to keep the same hearing players all of the time so that the players can get used to them and play them only when the Deaf players are tired or if their skills are badly needed. For example, we have a small team, so I often use a tall hearing person as center. Also, sometimes a good hearing player will model the type of skills I want my Deaf players to have, and if the Deaf player is competitive he will try to beat out the hearing player. So there are some benefits for having hearing players on the team. Whenever I can, I will recruit a hearing player who is related to a deaf person or is a teacher

of the deaf. This way, it is easier for all of us to accept him. It is also a game of numbers. If there are enough Deaf basketball players available, I won't use hearing players at all. When hearing players are selected, they must fit in with the short- and long-term goals for the development of the Deaf team.

When asked about communication needs and how a hearing person fits into the total team picture, Donald stated that the hearing players on his team come to play the game and never socialize to any great extent. In other words, a hearing person playing for a Deaf team faces a situation that is similar to that facing a Deaf person playing for a hearing team. In both instances, socialization does not appear to be a significant motivational factor for playing.

The Influence of Deaf Peers

ASL is an identifying characteristic of the Deaf community. In the United States and Canada, where only a fraction of the population is deaf, it is little wonder that ASL seduces Deaf people into congregating at every opportunity. Obviously, Deaf peers are in a better position than hearing peers are to perceive one another's values.

Deaf sport provides a setting that encourages deaf individuals of all ages to socialize with one another. Within this context they are able to react to each other's ideas and behaviors unhindered by (although very much aware of) the presence of deafness. Through a network of Deaf friends, one can learn much about the meaning of the Deaf community and the activities surrounding it. Deaf friends may come under the same peer pressure as their hearing counterparts do when it comes to sport participation. Indeed, the mutual influence among Deaf peers may be greater than among hearing peers because of their unique social position in society (Meadow 1972; Padden and Humphries 1988; Padden and Markowicz 1976).

Another dimension of Deaf peer relationships is found in the interaction of Deaf sport and hearing sport. One's view of the rewards of participating in either is likely to be influenced by the prevailing opinions of one's peers, and participation in individual sports can be used as an example of the way Deaf individuals influence their friends to participate in sports for the hearing. The Deaf community is often too small to sponsor particular individual sports, and Deaf individuals interested in these sports typically train and compete on clubs composed mainly of hearing individuals. Through their membership in these clubs they help develop a club's reputation for being accessible to deaf athletes. There can be many benefits that accrue to the Deaf community when other Deaf individuals join these clubs. To use swimming as an example: participation by more Deaf athletes can mean a higher awareness of deafness and its implications among swim coaches, swimmers, and parents; an adjustment to the communication needs of the Deaf swimmer by the coaches and others; the incorporation of visual aids to signal starts during races; more familiarity and less curiosity among competing clubs about what it is like to swim against deaf swimmers. Often, one result is increased financial support for swimmers' competitions in Deaf games. In sum, Deaf athletes may indirectly be responsible for promoting the integration of other deaf athletes with their hearing peers.

With respect to team sports, being a part of an optimal social environment is one well-defined factor encouraging Deaf athletes to play on Deaf teams. In addition, the cohesiveness and strength of the group may be facilitated when the team is a Deaf team. Support for this concept comes from a study by Eitzen (1973) on 288 high school basketball teams. Eitzen examined the background characteristics of (hearing) players and found that homogeneity of background with respect to religion, socioeconomic status, and neighborhood background were positively related to team success. On Deaf teams it is likely that deafness and linguistic compatibility promote greater cohesiveness among the players, which positively contributes to the team's performance. The following comments by Donald help illustrate possible reasons for this cohesiveness:

> Team spirit is very much the most important aspect of basketball, volleyball, and soccer. When we play against hearing teams we are out to win, but if we don't win we are not devastated because our pool of potential players is so small. We recognize our limitations. We want to win and in trying to do so we want all players to give their best. That's why having an all-Deaf

team is so important. Although my team will occasionally use a hearing player to help fill out the team, there is some resentment among the players that we are unable to do it ourselves. There's a feeling that once again, a hearing person must come to the rescue. The Deaf player who is benched because of a hearing player might not perform as well when playing because he is too caught up in his emotions about the hearing player.

According to Donald, being deaf is what binds the players as a team.

From Donald's comments it is difficult to discern whether having a hearing player on the team had an effect on the Deaf team's performance. For some Deaf players, it may be that the presence of a hearing player is detrimental to their playing efforts, yet for others it may stimulate them to try harder. Clearly, there is a need for research investigating the effects of Deaf and hearing teammates on individual and team performance levels.

Conclusion:
The Influence of Peers

Research has shown that peer groups may exert an influence on an individual's participation in sport. However, the effect of hearing peers on the sport participation of deaf individuals appears to be complicated by communication factors as well as societal and individual perspectives on deafness. Deaf peers, on the other hand, experience life in much the same way, and their interactions with one another reflect a common language and set of values that are related to their Deaf experiences. Hence, the impact of Deaf and hearing peers on a deaf individual will likely be different. Moreover, gender might also be a factor, although no research could be found that attempted to determine if peer (Deaf or hearing) influence affects deaf females and Deaf males differently. More research in the area of peer influence should help delineate differences between hearing and deaf peers, and the importance of gender, race, age, and other factors.

Researchers interested in this area should also consider investigating the effects of Deaf individuals on the lives of hearing persons. The lack of research that examines the reciprocal effects of interacting Deaf and hearing individuals is possibly a result of the ethnocentric perspectives of researchers who seek to examine the characteristics of Deaf people but who overlook the fact that they themselves may not be impervious to the influences of these populations. Some interesting questions that could be asked are: What processes lead hearing persons to work with Deaf people? Are these processes a result of social (for example, they had known a Deaf person while growing up), financial (for example, the pay is good), psychological (for example, they need to feel that they are helping others), or some combination of these and other factors? How does the presence of Deaf athletes affect the performance and attitudes of hearing athletes on the same or the opposing team?

The Influence of Hearing Schools

Schools are in a prime position to influence the participation of individuals in sport. Physical education classes and intramural and extramural competitions all function to socialize children and youths into sport roles (Loy, McPherson, and Kenyon 1978). Through their sport programs schools promote the dominant values of a community along with particular lifestyles, but they leave little room for individuals to question the values they advocate (Schafer 1971, cited in Loy, McPherson, and Kenyon 1978). That is, school sport programs are typically tailored to the needs and ideals of a community rather than to the physical, psychological, and social needs of an individual.

School is the major means by which society attempts to integrate deaf students into the hearing mainstream of life. With the passage in the United States of the Education for All Handicapped Children Act (PL 94-142) in 1975, the number of deaf students receiving an education alongside their hearing peers increased dramatically, while there was a decrease in the number of students enrolled in schools for deaf students. Consequently, public schools are more than ever in a position to socialize a large percentage of deaf students into sport.

In hearing schools deaf students are often associated with programs that cater to the educational needs of more than one deaf student. Deaf students from the same program are able to communicate with one another, which encourages friendships to develop between them, often without regard to age differences. Thus, in these programs there will always be someone with whom students can interact comfortably. Indeed, there is a tendency for deaf students to form their own social groups that meet during noninstructional time (for example, before school begins, during lunch or recess) throughout the school day. This tendency is also shared by members of other ethnic and racial minorities.

However, it is not clear what the impact of socializing in a deaf group has on the amount of time deaf students spend with hearing peers. For example, does the presence of a Deaf group mean that deaf students will be exposed to fewer opportunities to communicate with their hearing peers? Or does the presence of a deaf group create a situation whereby information gleaned from communications with hearing persons are shared within these social groups, which could lead to greater input for all of the deaf students involved?

Another consideration is the larger number of students interacting and competing in physical education classes and sport groups. Many deaf students obtain part or most of their education in self-contained classes that have on average four to six students. The social skills they learn in these classes along with those they acquire through their interactions in deaf groups may be different from those used among hearing individuals. Also, large groups of hearing persons may force a deaf student to adopt the prevailing set of social skills. Thus, if there is a discrepancy between the social skills learned in the deaf and hearing groups, a deaf athlete from a self-contained class may need time to learn the social characteristics of hearing teammates. On the other hand, sport also makes allowances for those who have exceptional athletic abilities and whose value to the team is greatly appreciated. In these instances, the social behavior of the deaf athlete may not affect his or her performance on the team, and he or she may be free to behave according to familiar social standards.

Participation in school sport is also affected by prevailing attitudes toward deafness. In general, negative attitudes breed negative interactions. Teammates might falsely assume that deaf athletes are also in some way athletes with a disability, and therefore they may be reluctant to be partners with them or include them as an integral part of a team's playing strategies. Hearing teammates in physical education classes during team games such as basketball and soccer might hesitate to pass the ball to a deaf person on the assumption a deaf player would be ineffective in carrying out a play. Team sports often incorporate interactive communication during play that may work against the inclusion of a deaf teammate.

For deaf athletes, hearing coaches might also be one of the negative aspects of attending a hearing school. The coaches might inaccurately attribute lesser athletic ability to deaf athletes without fully assessing their potential. This can easily happen to coaches who develop strong rapport with their hearing players but not with their deaf players. These coaches could then fall into the trap of favoring those players with whom they have rapport. In this respect, it might be said that coaches in individual sports such as swimming, track and field, tennis, and wrestling are less susceptible to underestimating the talents of deaf athletes than are coaches of team sports, because performance standards are either preset (for instance, height jumped; time for the 100-meter backstroke) or are based on individual won-lost records.

On a more positive note, hearing schools can take measures to prepare classes for the integration of deaf students (Stewart 1984a). Deaf adults with experience in social interaction with hearing persons can be brought in to speak to a class and help dispel misconceptions about deafness as well as explain techniques that can be used to facilitate social interactions. Having a successful Deaf adult as the guest speaker is an excellent method of demonstrating to hearing students and teachers what expectations are realistic for deaf youngsters (Stewart, Benson, and Lindsey 1987). If possible, a Deaf athlete should be recruited to talk about his or her sport experiences as a youngster. Another option is to have a deaf youngster from the school recount personal experiences in physical education classes and on sport teams.

Finally, deaf students in hearing schools may have less contact with the Deaf community. One reason is that there are few Deaf teachers teaching outside of schools for deaf students (Stewart and Donald 1984). Deaf teachers are valuable resources for information pertaining to Deaf community events. Social events, talent shows, and sport events are activities available in Deaf communities, but information about them is seldom relayed to students not attending a school for deaf students. The small size of many deaf education programs may also work against students' having contact with the Deaf community. Still, there may be some deaf students who have Deaf parents or personal contact with the Deaf community and are well aware of Deaf cultural, artistic, and sport events occurring in the community. However, the small size of many programs reduces the possibility that such students are enrolled in them.

The Influence of Schools for Deaf Students

Schools for deaf students are in a good position to capture the essence of Deaf sport and the value orientations of the Deaf community. By their very nature they encourage participation in Deaf sport. Physical education classes and intramural and extramural sport teams are composed entirely of deaf individuals, which replicates the conditions found in most sports for Deaf adults. Within deaf educational programs only a relatively small percentage of teachers are Deaf; however, more of the physical education teachers and coaches in schools for deaf students are Deaf. Deaf adults bring to the sport they coach or to the physical education classes they teach firsthand knowledge of Deaf sport outside of the schools. They thus serve as one of the primary means by which deaf children are initiated into Deaf sport. Indeed, a large percentage of Deaf sport directors are themselves products of a school for deaf students (Stewart, McCarthy, and Robinson 1988).

Schools for deaf students promote Deaf sport by other means as well: (1) They have a higher percentage of Deaf teachers and Deaf teacher aides than do other educational programs, people who serve as role models of Deaf community values. (2) Their coaches and physical education teachers tend to emphasize the sports that are popular in the Deaf community or are recognized at the World Games for the Deaf. (3) They allow Deaf sport clubs to use their gymnasium and field facilities as a home base. (4) They indirectly act as a clearinghouse of information on Deaf community events, including local, national, and international games for the Deaf. (5) Their student bodies may be given free membership in local or regional sports associations (for example, all senior students at Jericho Hill School for the Deaf, in British Columbia, are offered free membership in the British Columbia Deaf Sports Federation). (6) Students who attend such a school are more likely than others to associate in the adult Deaf community. In sum, schools for deaf students are ideally suited to socialize deaf youngsters into Deaf sport.

Conclusion: The Influence of Schools

Students attending a school for deaf students tend to have greater access to Deaf sport activities than do those attending schools catering primarily to the educational needs of hearing students. However, the passage of the Education for All Handicapped Children Act of 1975 has led to the greater enrollment of deaf students in general education schools. Stewart, Robinson, and McCarthy (in press) found that there is an increasing number of athletes from public schools on national Deaf teams. As deaf children increasingly become recognized as individuals who have bilingual and multicultural needs, schools will need to assume more responsibility for providing information related to the activities of the Deaf community. In their effort to integrate deaf students into the hearing mainstream of education, educators cannot forsake the unique cultural and linguistic heritage of Deaf individuals. All schools should have a curriculum designed to account for this.

The Social Implications of Deaf Sport

Deaf sport is a culturally distinctive set of activities that offers its Deaf participants a viable, and to many, a preferable alternative to sports for the hearing. Its promise of carefree communication and interactions with others in shared experiences is a strong enticement to Deaf individuals who use signs. Deaf sport also attracts deaf individuals unaware of the Deaf community but who are intrigued by the possibility of interacting with others who have firsthand experience with deafness. Because of its accessibility Deaf sport is, to many Deaf individuals, the mainstream of the sporting world.

In this chapter I have examined the ways in which value orientations affect the socialization of deaf individuals into sports. When we consider those components of the community, the family, peer groups, and school that relate mainly to hearing individuals, we are not surprised to learn that negative value orientations with respect to the acceptance of deafness and the use of speech as the primary means of communication are the major incentives for Deaf persons to explore alternative options for involvement in sport. Within the Deaf communities, Deaf families, Deaf peer groups, and schools for deaf students, values are influenced by deaf persons themselves and are positively oriented to their cultural and linguistic needs. Therefore, Deaf sport offers all deaf individuals a unique opportunity to find the physical and social gratification they desire from sport.

There are several implications of the observations made in this chapter:

1. *The socialization processes that introduce deaf individuals to Deaf sport sidestep conventional societal wisdom and seek to congregate deaf individuals in their own groups.* It may well be that the social environment created by the hearing members of society creates in deaf persons a propensity to associate with each other. Deaf sport may be the catalyst that brings many of them into the Deaf community. Deaf children of hearing parents who grow up unaware of the existence of the Deaf community may be introduced to the community through their interest in sport. Once

involved in Deaf sport, they learn about Deaf culture, acquire ASL skills, meet others who have similar experiences, and eventually come to adopt the community's values.

2. *Deaf children and youngsters should be made aware of their options for involvement in sports.* Deaf sport need not be the preserve of deaf individuals who are from Deaf families and schools for deaf students, or who were introduced to it during their adult years. As with all children, deaf children must be given the tools and knowledge that will make them productive and participating members of society. The Deaf community is one component of our society that is ideally suited to meet the social needs of many deaf individuals. Schools, in particular, should expose deaf students to various aspects of the Deaf community, including Deaf sport. Community and school coaches should be familiar with opportunities for deaf athletes to compete in regional, national, and international Deaf sport competitions. This is especially important for those athletes who excel in individual sports such as swimming, track and field, tennis, skiing, speed skating, and cycling. These athletes can use a hearing club as a home base for training and competing and the Deaf sport tournaments as one source of competition. Even for those who are not athletically inclined, Deaf sport offers an environment that is socially accessible.

3. *Society needs to commit itself to the promotion and preservation of Deaf cultural activities, including Deaf sport.* Since the turn of the century the Deaf community has been ostracized for segregating its members and using signs to communicate. One of the strongest opponents of the Deaf community was Alexander Graham Bell, who advocated genetic counseling for the deaf, outlawing intermarriages between deaf persons, the suppression of sign language, the elimination of residential schools for deaf students, and the prohibition of deaf teachers of deaf students. Fortunately current philosophy is not as radical as Bell's, and there are many oralists who recognize the value of the Deaf community. From a Deaf person's perspective, deaf people have always been an oppressed minority group, and it is only within the sanctuary of the Deaf community that they have been able to establish a normal social relationship with others. As the twentieth century comes to a close, it is time to recognize that we live in a culturally diverse society and that the assimilation

of all people into a common "norm" is not only an unattainable but also an undesirable goal.

The promotion and preservation of Deaf sport can occur through mass media coverage of the World Games for the Deaf, national tournaments (for instance, the AAAD National Basketball Tournament), and regional games (for instance, the Western Canada Summer Games for the Deaf). The results of these games should be broadcast on local radio and television news programs, as well as reported in the newspapers. Athletes and game organizers can be interviewed, and information of upcoming games announced. This type of publicity would help reach deaf individuals, parents, and coaches who are unaware of the opportunities available in Deaf sport. In addition, the general public will benefit from increasing awareness of the cultural distinctiveness of the Deaf community.

Conclusion

The social significance of Deaf sport is best analyzed in terms of its contribution to the socialization processes that affect the participation of deaf individuals in various sociocultural activities. Deaf sport is attractive to deaf individuals because it provides an environment that is protected against society's stigmatization, and its predominant form of communication is compatible with the needs of its participants. Deaf sport allows for the full involvement of all deaf individuals, unlike sports with hearing persons, where deaf athletes may find it difficult to advance to the level of their athletic ability because of sociocultural differences.

Essentially, the social satisfaction gained through interpersonal interactions assures the survival of Deaf sport. As a cultural entity, Deaf sport enables Deaf individuals to influence their own social activities. Society's acceptance of the notion that Deaf individuals will continue to determine their own place in society as well as their own set of values would represent a major step toward creating a more equitable society.

Moreover, affiliation with Deaf sport does not negate participation in sports for the hearing. Sports for the hearing offer a more competitive atmosphere for the development of athletic skills. Deaf athletes are therefore in a position of being able to optimize the social and physical rewards they receive through sports by managing the sociocultural contexts of the sports they play.

CHAPTER **7**

THE EDUCATIONAL IMPLICATIONS
of Deaf Sport

There are sharp contrasts between the spheres of influence of Deaf sport and deaf education. In Deaf sport the experts are Deaf; in deaf education most of the experts are hearing. In Deaf sport Deaf people administer; in deaf education there are few Deaf people involved in decision-making processes. The success of Deaf sport depends on the input of Deaf athletes and Deaf sport directors; many of those regarded as experts in deaf education are from outside the field of education. In Deaf sport ASL is the language of Deaf persons; in deaf education ASL receives little recognition. Although it is clear that deaf children bring to school a diversity of personal and sociocultural characteristics, educators and administrators have not found a way to meet this diversity. Deaf sport is ideally suited to meet the diversity among the deaf population.

Where It All Begins

By the time most deaf students graduate from high school at the age of eighteen they have spent up to sixteen years in educational programs for deaf people. Much of their time in residential or public schools is devoted to instructions in core subjects. Beyond academics, the education of deaf students becomes a mosaic of policies, practices, and promises. Educators and administrators constantly juggle their options as they attempt to fit each student with special instructional programs in speech and auditory training, language development, and literacy; develop strategies for eliciting parental support; and arrange schedules that will allow integration with hearing peers. Some programs might also tangle with curricular options that allow for learning about causes and types of deafness, Deaf culture, ASL, Deaf sport, and Deaf heritage. Although programs may be diverse in their educational approach, the field as a whole has much to learn about promoting academic success among deaf students.

Deaf people are acutely aware of their position in society and the contribution of the education system to this role. This awareness is translated by many deaf adults into bitterness, which is compounded by their lack of influence in education decision-making processes. Nonetheless, the cumulative effect of educational practices is the silent promotion of the social activities of the Deaf community. A sense of discontent slowly ferments in the minds of deaf students as they endure years of educational neglect of their Deaf identities. Many of them have been told that being deaf in a hearing world carries with it a host of disadvantages, that in order to succeed, they must conform to the standards and values of a hearing world.

But for many deaf students the capacity to conform is prevented by communication and language barriers, and later by inadequate education. As they work to hold their own in society, they are struck by the contrast in expectations for themselves and their teachers. They are expected to conform to the value orientations of society, which often breed negative stereotypic images of deaf persons. Teachers are not required to be conversant with the values of the Deaf community. Deaf students must spend many years learning to speak and to use hearing aids so that they may interact in a hearing and speaking environment. This effort is not reciprocated; not enough teachers learn to be effective signers. Some teachers are indifferent when years of learning to speak results in few benefits to a deaf individual. Students' opinions of their teachers' communication behavior are not relevant and therefore do not contribute to the formulation of educational practices.

Through all of this, integration with hearing peers is stressed. However, integration is seen strictly as a one-way street; hearing teachers seldom seek out the company of Deaf adults in an effort to learn more about Deaf persons. These and other issues play a major role in deaf students' search for a social identity.

Conversely, preparation for the Deaf mainstream of life is not deemed to be a necessary aspect of our schools' role. Yet, by pooling deaf students together in special educational programs, schools speed their students' initiation into the Deaf community. Indeed, the net social impact of schools is to increase the appeal of interacting in a Deaf environment. Deaf students learn much through their interactions with Deaf peers. Their encounter with efficient communication conditions them to crave more of it. Signing becomes their ticket to an expanding circle of meaningful relationships, both in and out of school.

One dimension of education worth examining for its implications for Deaf sport is the effect physical education has in shaping the deaf individual's interest in sport. But before discussing these two dimensions, I will present a brief overview of the educational practices commonly used with deaf students.

Educational Practices: Communication Methodologies and Placement

Total communication and oral education are the two most common educational practices used with deaf students. Total communication can be broadly defined to mean the use of any form of communication that will facilitate understanding in the classroom. In practice, total communication teachers tend to rely mostly on signs and speech for instructional purposes. Oralism, on the other hand, is the practice of using a deaf child's residual hearing, speech, speechreading, and/or vibrotactile skills as the major modes of communication, and signing is strictly prohibited. Whereas some total communication programs may be receptive to the concerns of the Deaf community and may endorse the use of ASL for instructional purposes, the implications of Deaf culture typically hold no place in the educational agenda of an oral program.

Regardless of methodological orientation, all educational programs have the potential to influence participation in Deaf sport. Some programs, for example, schools for deaf students and total communication programs located in general education schools, are more direct in their influence than others because of their endorsement of signing as an instructional medium, which implies an acknowledgment of the value of sign language to deaf people. Oral programs usually emphasize the integration of their students with hearing peers and at first glance may not seem directly supportive of Deaf sport activities. However, their historical opposition to signing, strong pursuance of mainstreaming, and the conspicuous lack of deaf adults in their professional ranks may indirectly establish a mindset in oral deaf students that prompts them as adults to seek out participation in Deaf sport and other Deaf cultural activities.

Deaf sport often plays an important role in the initiation of oral deaf students into the Deaf community. It is not unusual for oral deaf students to transfer to a total communication program during their secondary school years. After such a transfer, these students may experience some problems while they learn enough signs to be socially conversant. Normally, students in total communication programs are supportive of their oral deaf cousins who are making the transition to signing. For oral deaf athletes who transfer to a school for deaf students, extramural and intramural sports can act as a buffer during the initial transition period. Mindful of their inability fully to take advantage of social interactions, they are able to develop intimacy with their peers on the playing courts and fields.

Another implication of the consequences of an oral education is that the values of a hearing society cannot be imposed on the deaf population. Oralism plays out the consequences of what happens when a hearing society maintains a stranglehold on the deaf population. Unless they excel in their speech and speechreading abilities, deaf adults do little to confirm the oralist's mission. They cannot act as role models exemplifying all that oralism stands for; therefore, their other talents and skills cannot be displayed. In other words, Deaf adults and the things they uphold are at cross purposes with the oralists and their aims. Deaf individuals sense in oralism the inequity they experience in society. Oralism and society at large are alike in their treatment of deaf individuals: neither fully recognizes the precedence established by the values and standards of the Deaf community. They do not accord signing and socializing among Deaf adults as logical outcomes of deafness. Nor do they provide a social option for those who do not adhere to a set of hearing norms. Yet the activities of Deaf sport clearly demonstrate the prosperity and fullness of the lives members of the Deaf community lead, many of whom are graduates of oral education programs.

Thus, when oral education does not provide its students with the necessary tools to function adequately in a hearing and speaking environment, Deaf sport serves as a beacon, directing students toward a more viable means of communicating and, with it, a new social status. By focusing on athletics and associated activities such as those of the spectator, Deaf sport offers a variety of avenues for sampling a Deaf way of living.

Total communication programs make a significant contribution to Deaf sport in that they bring many deaf children and youth together for their first sampling of life in a Deaf community. Although most total communication programs do not directly encourage the use of ASL, their emphasis on signing has created an environment favorable to the widespread use of ASL among students and Deaf teachers and, to a much lesser extent, hearing teachers. To handle the logistics of educating relatively few deaf students, school districts often resort to a central school model, which groups deaf students in total communication programs that are located in a single school. By pooling deaf students, they create more opportunities for increasing students' awareness of Deaf cultural values and activities of the Deaf community.

Total communication programs bring together geographically scattered deaf individuals with their varying experiences into a coalition with similar perspectives and goals. Essentially, by increasing the exposure of deaf peers to each other, these programs serve to prepare deaf students for Deaf sport and other activities of the Deaf community.

Transportation can affect the opportunities that deaf students have to pursue athletic activities in either oral or total communication programs. Because some education programs have deaf students brought to a central school, many students spend long hours being transported to and from their schools. Unless alternative methods of transportation are found (for instance, parents who can transport their sons and daughters), participation in sports might not be feasible for some students.

In sum, total communication and oral programs both lay the groundwork for initiating deaf students into the Deaf community. This occurs despite the fact that educators tend to see mainstreaming deaf students with hearing peers as a major goal.

Educational Practices: Schools for Deaf Students

Historically, schools for deaf students have been the primary source of sport activities for deaf children and youth. Gannon (1981) has documented some achievements and contributions of Deaf athletes in the world of sport and made extensive reference to the accomplishments of athletes at schools for deaf persons. The following sampling of Gannon's (1981) listings illustrates the strengths, influence, and diversity of Deaf sport:

> 1918—J. Frederick Meagher won the 108-pound Amateur Athletic Union (AAU) wrestling championship and repeated in 1919.
>
> 1929—The Arkansas School for the Deaf wrestling team coached by Nathan Zimble won the first of 13 consecutive state wrestling championships spanning a period from 1929 to 1941.
>
> 1946—The Michigan School for the Deaf track team, coached by Earl Roberts, won the Class D State title. The school repeated the feat in 1947, 1950, and won three straight titles from 1961 to 1963.
>
> 1950s—The Gallaudet College wrestlers won a string of 36 consecutive Mason-Dixon Conference matches.

1960—The North Carolina School for the Deaf Negroes won its first of three straight National Schools
for the Deaf Negroes basketball championships.

1976—Marvin Tuttle, one of Iowa School for the
Deaf's outstanding basketball players, was inducted
into the Iowa High School Athletic Association's Basketball Hall of Fame. (pp. 273–274)

Further influence of Deaf sport and Deaf athletes were noted
by Strassler (1976) and Gannon (1981). Included in their reports
were the historical accounts crediting Gallaudet University's
football team with having invented the huddle and of the influence of a professional deaf baseball player, Dummy Hoy, in the
creation of umpire signals for ball and strike.

For many Deaf athletes, their involvement in sport began
with their participation at a school for deaf students. In fact,
until the 1970s most deaf students were educated at residential
schools. Thus, a major contribution of these schools to Deaf
sport, and therefore the Deaf community, was that they brought
deaf students in contact with a large number of deaf peers. Students were transplanted from the hearing environments they
encountered at home and in society to one in which deafness
characterized the total student body.

Within a school for deaf persons, students evolve a deaf
consciousness peculiar to the environment of a residential
school but compatible with that of the Deaf community. In the
past students usually did not go home other than for major holi-
days and summer vacations. Except for the usual supervision,
they were left to themselves during the evenings and weekends,
and dormitories became the headquarters for the evolution of a
Deaf identity. In this situation Deaf supervisors were the crown
jewels, as they shared with students stories of their own experiences at residential schools, anecdotes of interactions with hearing people, the values of the Deaf community, and in general
provided moral and educational support to assist students as
they learned to live away from home and assimilate a wealth of
Deaf cultural experiences.

Deaf sport was a part of this identification process.
Whereas oral communication was the favored approach in
many schools for most of the twentieth century, oralism was not
normally enforced during after-school sport activities among

athletes and spectators. Homecoming events and Deaf alumni games brought in an infusion of Deaf ASL role models. Thus, in its entirety, the residential school was and still is an educational oasis for deaf students.

Today, the Deaf spirit of residential schools has been challenged by key changes in the educational placement of deaf students. Since the beginning of the 1970s most schools for deaf students have been faced with drastically declining enrollments (Moores 1987; Schein 1987) because of the impact of the Education for All Handicapped Children Act of 1975. Consequently, many deaf students are now educated in total communication programs located in public schools and commute to school on a daily basis. A transformation in schools for deaf students also occurred; they are now either residential-day schools that provide housing for those students requiring it, or day schools where all students commute daily. Most schools for deaf students also now require their students to go home on weekends. Total communication is the recognized practice in many of these schools, and ASL remains the primary language in use among students, with English as the instructional language of the classroom.

The decrease in institutional enrollment has not gone unnoticed by adult Deaf sport groups. Sport programs at schools for deaf students feed athletes into Deaf sport at the adult level. But a reduction in enrollment has led to the scaling down of the number of extracurricular activities. High-caliber teams capable of bringing home city and state championships have become more rare, as coaches consolidate the skills of fewer athletes into fewer sports. Speaking at the First National Deaf Sport Conference in Ottawa, Ron Stern noted that coaching has also suffered as (1) the presence of fewer students has diminished the overall enthusiasm of staff members to become involved in coaching, and (2) potential Deaf teachers are lured away by an increasingly diverse job market that affords more opportunities for higher salaries (Stern 1989). In addition, day students must arrange for transportation before they can make any decision to compete. Still, in those schools with enough students, sport continues to play a prominent role in shaping after-school activities.

Deaf adults have taken some steps to counteract the impact of declining enrollments in schools for deaf students. For example, the CDSA recently created the position of Youth/Recreation Director. Among a number of responsibilities, the director is charged with (1) ensuring that students at schools for deaf students are aware of their opportunities for involvement in sports and recreation with Deaf adults, and (2) disseminating information about the CDSA and its ten provincial affiliates to students attending educational programs outside of a school for deaf students.

Sport in schools for deaf students is a part of the overall structure of Deaf sport. The basic characteristics of sports in these schools resemble those of adult Deaf sport. School teams are composed entirely of deaf players and typically compete in a local league against hearing schools and/or in an interstate league composed only of teams from schools for deaf students. Intramurals are popular in those schools having a large enough student body. Deaf alumni events promote greater cohesion between sport in the school and the community. At many of these events spectators are present, and the social aspects of sport are prominent.

It would be interesting to compare the social motives of spectators at school games with those at adult sport events. Deaf student spectators may have less of an urge to socialize. This would be the case if their social needs are being satisfied through their interactions with deaf peers throughout the school day and, for those students who live in school residences, in the evening as well. In contrast, many Deaf adults crave social interaction because their day-to-day work usually does not involve contact with other Deaf adults. Attendance at Deaf sport events gives them the chance to meet social needs which, more often than not, overpower their interest in the game.

For certain sports there are annual tournaments involving schools from several states that clearly illustrate the type of sport activities students can come to expect as Deaf adults. For example, the Western States Basketball Classic (WSBC) is an annual tournament for both boys' and girls' teams from schools for deaf students (Strassler 1988). Schools also send cheerleading squads to the tournaments, which are held at a different school every year. In 1988 the tournament was held in Phoenix, and teams came from Washington, Oregon, California (two), New Mexico, Arizona (two), and Idaho. These tournaments have a strong impact on Deaf identity. There is the thrill of competing against other deaf athletes. Students learn that there is comfort in numbers, that they are not alone in a hearing world, and many of their experiences are similar, regardless of geographical location. There is much socializing, as students swap stories about sport, school, home, friends, the hearing world, and Deaf culture. Deaf adults from local communities flock to these events, inspired by similar social opportunities and a chance to meet Deaf friends who are coaching or chaperoning for the visiting schools.

Deaf graduates from schools for deaf students are appreciative of the social opportunities, lasting friendships, and memories gained through their "Deaf school." It is within the walls of these institutions that many deaf children learn about being Deaf. Because being Deaf is a favorable condition from the perspective of the Deaf community, it is perhaps more appropriate to refer to these institutions as being integrated rather than segregated schools. The adoption of such an attitude would be another step toward creating equality between Deaf and hearing individuals and institutions in society.

The Implications of Physical Education for Deaf Sport

In all of Canada and in many parts of the United States, physical education is a required course for all children and youngsters throughout most of their schooling. However, it is not dealt with in any of the leading texts written on the education of deaf people and is scarcely mentioned in research literature on deafness. One possible explanation for this omission is that deafness does not overtly appear to affect motor abilities. It might be that educators assume that after communication considerations have been handled, there are no other accommodations necessary in physical education. Nevertheless, the physical education needs of deaf students do raise some unique considerations and implications for Deaf sport.

Before discussing these unique considerations, I want to briefly examine some goals and effects of physical education for youngsters. Thomas and Thomas (1986) summarized their overall importance as follows: "Physical education and sport each make valuable and unique contributions to the development, health, knowledge, and skill of children, youth and adults. The need to justify either one beyond their unique contributions is unnecessary and usually without cause" (p. 450). More specifically, Vogel (1986) reviewed studies on the effects of participation in physical education programs with respect to various outcomes. Positive effects were found for academic performance, and increased time in physical education classes was not found to have an adverse effect in academic performance. However, academic benefits in general are secondary goals in physical education classes. Physical education classes were found to positively influence students' feelings about physical activity and health or fitness, and students in these classes also tend to be more knowledgeable about healthy lifestyles. Evidence indicated that physical education positively affects motor performance and muscular endurance, power, and strength. All of these findings suggest that physical education has desirable effects for any student. Certainly, physical education classes seem to be ideally suited for physically and mentally preparing deaf students for direct participation in sports during their adult years. Thus, if participation in physical activities as an adult is desirable, then one implication of physical education classes is that they can help to condition the mind and the body to meet the challenge of Deaf sport.

For deaf students, self-esteem is an important issue, especially in view of their social status and their comparatively low educational attainments. Deaf students with average physical abilities can participate in games and sport with their hearing peers without any discernible academic weaknesses or major communication concerns. This may also be true for hearing students who are average or below average academically. If they have an interest in athletics, then they may have a chance to interact on a more equitable basis during athletic activities—in this way their self-esteem may be raised. Thus for some segments of the population, sport may be a great equalizer in society.

There has been little or no research examining how deaf students feel about their own ability to perform various physical activities (that is, perceived competence). The effects of physical education in schools for deaf students on the development of self-esteem would also be of interest, because even in these schools students face constant reminders that they lag behind their hearing peers in academic achievement. If physical education leads to improved perceived competence and self-esteem in deaf students then this dimension of physical activity would add to the appeal and the importance of Deaf sport.

With regard to deaf students, there has been little research in the area of physical education, and a majority of research efforts that were done investigated motor proficiency skills. The following overview of the research in this area was derived mainly from a review of the literature by Dummer, Stewart, and Haubenstricker (1988). Much of the research in this area has focused on the balancing skills of deaf children. This interest may stem from the fact that the vestibular system is close to the auditory system, and both share a common origin on the phylogenetic scale (Kileny 1985). In any case, the vestibule is believed to have a prominent role in maintaining a person's balance, and certain etiologies of deafness (for example, meningitis, nonhereditary prenatal and perinatal conditions) are also related to poorer balance performance (Boyd 1967; Brunt and Broadhead 1982; Butterfield 1987; Butterfield and Ersing 1986; Effgen 1981; Lindsey and O'Neal 1976; Morsh 1936; Myklebust 1946; Potter and Silverman 1984; Wiegersma and Van der Velde 1983).

Studies on the motor skills of deaf children and youth revealed mixed results, with some showing inferior performance when deaf children are compared with hearing counterparts (Boyd 1967; Wiegersma and Van der Velde 1983) and others finding no differences (Brunt and Broadhead 1982; Cratty, Cratty, and Cornell 1986). Dummer, Stewart, and Haubenstricker (1988) noted that where differences were found, they usually reflected the results of the deaf children's performing less well on balance tasks. Stewart, Dummer, and Haubenstricker (1990) questioned the validity of many of these studies because test administration procedures often neglected the complex communication behaviors and needs of deaf students.

Only two studies have reported on the personal-social effects of physical education on deaf students. In these studies 21 Deaf sport directors (Stewart, McCarthy, and Robinson 1988) and 21 Deaf athletes (Stewart, Robinson, and McCarthy in press) were asked to identify the personal or material sources that introduced them to Deaf sport. (Note: in both of these surveys, participation in Deaf sport did not include attending physical education classes.) The athletes surveyed were younger (average age = 22.9 years; range 12–34 years) than the directors (average age = 36.3 years; range 22–57 years). This age difference is significant because the push to mainstream deaf students in public schools did not become popular until the mid–1970s. Thus, as students, the athletes faced a greater range of school settings in which they could be educated than did the directors. Whereas, 18 (85.7 percent) of the directors had attended a school for deaf students, only 9 (42.9 percent) of the athletes went to such a school. For the directors, Deaf physical education teachers ($n = 4$; 19.0 percent) and hearing physical education teachers ($n = 2$; 9.5 percent) accounted for 28.5 percent of all initial introductions to Deaf sport. For Deaf athletes, only 1 (4.8 percent) Deaf physical education teacher and no hearing physical education teacher was involved in introducing them to Deaf sport. These findings appear to confirm Stern's (1989) observation that declining enrollments in schools for deaf students and a lack of awareness of Deaf sport activities among public school teachers will make recruiting athletes for Deaf sport a more difficult proposition.

In conjunction with what is known about the effects of physical education on the general population, there appears to be enough evidence to justify further exploration of the roles and effects of physical education on deaf students. Physical education teachers are in an ideal position to influence the participation of deaf students in sport. By including knowledge about Deaf sport in the training of physical education teachers, public schools would be in a position to assist younger deaf children in learning about Deaf sport.

Physical Education in Schools for Deaf Students

Preceding discussions have alluded to the potential influences of physical education programs in schools for deaf students. Typically, these programs have a higher percentage of Deaf teachers than is found in the field in general. Deaf teachers tend to be more active in promoting various Deaf sport activities. They are also more aware of sports commonly played by Deaf adults and are likely to emphasize certain athletic and sport skills that are congruent with the interests of the local Deaf community. It makes sense, for example, that intramural sport programs would focus on volleyball, basketball, and slo-pitch when these are the sports commonly played in adult communities.

Often adult Deaf sport programs use the facilities of a school for deaf students as their home base. At these schools students benefit from watching Deaf adults perform as athletes, sport directors, and spectators. In some adult leagues deaf students sixteen years and older are allowed to participate as athletes. Some of the more organized Deaf sport associations have a student representative from a school for deaf students who sits on their board of directors.

There are two ways by which physical education teachers in schools for deaf students can encourage the participation of students in Deaf sport. First, because sport in such schools is a component of the total array of activities falling under the institution of Deaf sport, any physical education program that promotes the appreciation of sport and physical fitness will indirectly promote Deaf sport.

Second, many teachers can intentionally attempt to educate deaf students about Deaf sport. An exemplary physical education program would contain instructional materials relating to the options and advantages that Deaf sport offers to all deaf individuals. This should include information on lifelong physical fitness; opportunities and strategies for involvement in Deaf sport; the names and functions of various levels of Deaf sport associations; a historical overview of the CISS and the

World Games for the Deaf; and the relationship of Deaf sport to the overall function of the Deaf community. A concerted effort to educate deaf students about Deaf sport also benefits those who are not inclined to participate in sports. These students may be inspired by knowing that during their adult years there will be chances for involvement in sport administration, volunteer work during games, and various avenues for socializing with others.

In educating deaf students about Deaf sport, Deaf physical education teachers will obviously have a distinct advantage over hearing teachers, especially if they are involved in it themselves. However, like any other teaching position in the field, physical education is not only for Deaf teachers. Hearing physical education teachers can and do exert a positive influence on the participation of their students in Deaf sport inside and outside of their schools. At the start of their teaching career they may be at a substantial disadvantage. Until recently, the import of Deaf sport has always been taken for granted by Deaf individuals, and awareness of it has been largely confined to the Deaf community. Consequently, teacher-preparation programs have not responded to the need to address the contributions of Deaf sport. In fairness to these programs, it should be noted that the incorporation of curricular materials dealing with any aspect of the Deaf community, including ASL, has only recently been adopted by a handful of programs. Still, hearing physical education teachers, like other hearing teachers in the field of deaf education, must compensate for their disadvantage by actively seeking more knowledge about the culture, language, sport, and social activities of the Deaf community.

Alternatively, a school for deaf students may already have as part of its curriculum courses on Deaf Studies. Here is another mechanism for presenting materials on Deaf sport. To some educators, this type of course would alleviate the need for physical education teachers and others to incorporate information relating to the Deaf community into their own courses. However, given the extent to which many Deaf adults become involved in activities of the Deaf community, astute educators will constantly explore their own lessons for occasions that lend themselves to incidental instruction about deafness and Deaf people.

Physical Education in Public Schools

From the vantage point of deaf students, there are several factors that may affect the outcome of their physical education classes in public schools, including the size of their classes, students' characteristics, the school level, and teacher qualifications. Size is an important consideration, as many physical education classes for deaf students at the elementary level are selfcontained and small (that is, an average range of four to eight students). Students in small classes may benefit from the increased intimacy that they develop with their teacher, who is then able to structure activities precisely suited to the motor skills and interests of the students. There might also be some disadvantages in that students may have fewer opportunities to meet objectives in areas such as social competencies, communication, being a part of a team, sportsmanship, and competitiveness.

Some students' characteristics that can affect physical education outcomes are hearing status, gender, and age. Physical education classes may be composed entirely of deaf students or a mixture of deaf and hearing, male and female students. Studies have shown that hearing females tend to dislike physical education and that their fitness levels drop as they progress through the grades (Knoppers 1988). Knoppers also noted that physical education programs are geared toward the needs and interests of males.

The last and perhaps most significant characteristic is age. The age range in self-contained classes for deaf students is highly variable. Granted that most programs attempt to minimize the age range in a single class, they nevertheless have little flexibility. This is especially true in those elementary programs that have only a few deaf students (four to six) and must function under further limitations brought on by hiring practices that are based on numbers and not educational requirements. Under these circumstances a self-contained physical education class may end up with students who are as much as four years apart in age. Alternatively, programming arrangements could group these students with their hearing peers, which would likely lead to a closer match of physical abilities.

In physical education, diverse student characteristics demand that teachers have greater instructional flexibility when designing lessons. In other classes for deaf students, the individualization of lessons, one-to-one assistance, and a heavy reliance on seatwork are techniques useful in accommodating varying levels of skills in one classroom. However, in physical education classes these techniques have limited application, and the spirit of team play and competition is not easily accomplished in classes with few students. At the secondary level the logistics of handling diversity in physical education is to some degree taken care of by the integration of students into larger hearing classes.

At all school levels physical education teachers must attempt to carry through their educational agenda with their deaf students. This is an important point, because teachers might bypass instructing students in certain areas because of communication difficulties. Or they might assume that deaf students are assimilating their instructions without attempting to verify the extent of a deaf student's understanding of principles and values being taught. A Deaf sport director with the CDSA, Wayne Goulet, had this to say about his experiences as a student at a school for deaf students, where he had physical education teachers who used speech to communicate:

> I found my physical education teachers to be reluctant to teach the values of gamesmanship and leadership in sport. Neither did they take the time to develop a winning instinct in us. The drive to win requires a certain discipline that many of us have to learn. When a physical education teacher used only speech while teaching deaf children, it is hard to learn about or understand what a "winning formula" is. This affected how we played our games, which was often a struggle because we lacked critical mental training in sport.

Physical education teachers should make an effort to ensure that their deaf students do not miss out on important information.

The qualifications of any teacher who assumes responsibility for teaching physical education to deaf students is a third major challenge for schools. Preparation programs for teachers of deaf students do not normally include discussions of the implications of physical education for deaf students. Few graduates of these programs ever have to teach physical education to their students, and those who do are invariably in schools for deaf students. As a consequence, in public schools physical education for deaf students is the responsibility of general physical education teachers or of those who have an endorsement in adapted physical education.

Physical education teachers, like other teachers in general education, have little if any knowledge about deafness. What they do know is often negative and reflects the education system's orientation to the weaknesses of deaf students in relation to their hearing peers. General education teachers faced with having a deaf student as part of a larger hearing physical education class or with teaching a self-contained class of deaf students should have the assistance of a teacher of deaf students or other resource personnel in the education of deaf students.

Teachers in adapted physical education are much better prepared to work with deaf students. Adapted physical education has been defined in various ways. In general, it implies the "modification of traditional physical activities to enable the handicapped to participate safely, successfully, and with satisfaction" (Auxter and Pyfer 1985, 7) and the provision of a "comprehensive service delivery system designed to identify and ameliorate problems within the psychomotor domain" (Sherrill 1981, 10). Teachers with endorsement in this area have an advantage over others in that their training includes an overview of selected characteristics of deaf individuals and adaptations teachers can make to suit the special needs of their students. Examination of several adapted physical education textbooks and journal articles shows that the most emphasized adaptation is in manner and type of communication (Auxter and Pyfer 1985; Berges 1969; Butterfield 1988; Cratty 1980; Eichstaedt and Seiler 1978; Masters, Mori, and Lange 1983; Schmidt and Dunn 1980; Sherrill 1981; Stewart 1984a; Wiseman 1982). Surprisingly, given that deaf children tend to experience more difficulty in balance tasks than their hearing peers, balance techniques received relatively little attention (for example, Butterfield 1988; Schmidt 1985; Wiseman 1982). Only a few texts and articles suggested that teachers be aware of opportunities in Deaf sport (Auxter and Pyfer 1985; Seaman and DePauw 1989; Sherrill 1981; Stewart 1984a).

If textbooks are used as a benchmark, even adapted physical education teachers are treated to stereotypic and negative images of deaf persons. They learn that deaf students have language and communication "problems," that socialization is another "problem" of deaf persons interacting among hearing persons. What is rarely pointed out, and this is true of most literature on deafness, is the importance of sociocultural settings as a contributor to these so-called problems. Conversely, it should be clear that these "problems" are mutual between deaf and hearing individuals. The responsibility of communication is a two-way street, and it takes two to socialize.

Deaf students do not bring communication and socialization problems to the classroom; rather, it is the sociocultural orientation of the classroom that creates these problems, with a detrimental effect on everyone involved. To counteract this, it is helpful if hearing persons learn to sign in order to interact with deaf people who rely on signing as their primary communication mode. However, hearing persons learning a few signs simply indicates a commendable starting point, which does not guarantee efficient communication. Extra effort to use whatever communication skills one has is required by all parties involved before meaningful social dialogue becomes possible.

Sign language interpreters provide a viable option. In addition to respecting the normal responsibilities of educational interpreters (Caccamise et al. 1980; Solow 1981), deaf students and their hearing classmates and teachers should be encouraged to use interpreters for social conversations. Hearing persons need to be aware that an interpreter is present to interpret all of the dialogue that one would normally expect to transpire between two individuals who are able to communicate freely with each other. However, the better use of interpreters does not negate the need to learn to sign. Signing enhances the overall intimacy felt between deaf and hearing persons, whereas the use of interpreters reduces the impact of nonverbal communication, including the importance of eye contact between speakers.

Another implication of physical education in public schools is that its goals for deaf students should be modified to include information about Deaf sport. It is not enough for adapted physical education texts merely to mention that the Deaf community has its own sport institutions. Teachers should know the function of various Deaf sport associations such as the AAAD (Ammons 1984) and the historical significance of the World Games for the Deaf (Ammons 1986, 1990; Panella 1974). They should know of opportunities for their secondary-school deaf students to participate in Deaf sport. Deaf athletes and Deaf sport directors should be invited to speak to students and teachers. Teachers should be aware of the technical modifications to various sports (for instance, Robinson and Stewart 1987) and whenever possible incorporate them into the sports played at school. These modifications are not extensive and do not in any way change the way a sport is played. They often simply involve the use of visual cues in place of commonly used auditory ones. In swimming, for example, special lights or flags may be used to start races. In wrestling the referee taps the wrestlers with both hands, and "stop of play is signaled by scorekeepers throwing in a towel or sponge" (Robinson and Stewart 1987, 25).

Conclusion

Deaf children of hearing parents are born into the fringes of a social system until school brings them into contact with other deaf children or until efficient communication has been established between them and their parents. Although many deaf children and youngsters achieve fluency in ASL, few parents learn to sign well enough to carry on conversations at a sophisticated level with their deaf children. Schools for deaf students and public schools provide students with two different sociocultural perspectives. Schools for deaf students are in a better situation than public schools to expose students to various aspects of the Deaf community. However, *all* schools must assume the responsibility of providing students with the kind of knowledge and experiences that will help them determine their relationship to Deaf and hearing communities. Thus, it is imperative that schools focus as much on Deaf orientations to living as on hearing values.

Physical education teachers must be knowledgeable about the benefits of Deaf sport and the ways they can help introduce deaf students to various aspects of Deaf sport. Responding to the advantages of Deaf sport must not be interpreted as a failing of the education system. Society must respect the unique linguistic and cultural heritage of deaf students. To this end, the incorporation into physical education programs of goals related to Deaf sport would demonstrate that cultural pluralism is more than just a buzzword in the schools.

CHAPTER 8

DEAF SPORT
as a Vehicle for Deaf Integration

At first, the notion of Deaf sport as providing a setting for the integration of deaf individuals with one another appears to contradict prevailing concepts of integration. After all, the schooling of other students within their own ethnic groups is better known as segregation. However, segregation from hearing individuals is not the central issue in Deaf integration. The systematic placement of deaf students in environments that foster the assimilation of Deaf values such as ASL, togetherness, the preservation of mechanisms that ensure the self-determination of Deaf individuals, and international friendship among Deaf people transcends ethnic and political divisiveness experienced by hearing members of society. Thus, the assimilation of Deaf values becomes an underlying rationale for integration.

Integration: A Two-Way Street

The integration of deaf and hearing students is a goal that many educators and parents share. It typically refers to the participation of handicapped students in social and instructional activities with their nonhandicapped peers (Kaufman et al. 1975; Schultz and Turnbull 1983). Rightly or wrongly, *integration* is often taken to be synonymous with the term *mainstreaming*, which has been defined as the "inclusion of special students in the general educational process" (Lewis and Doorlag 1987, 4). In the education of deaf students, the key notion embedded in either term is that modification of the educational status quo of deaf students is required—they are to be removed from their self-contained classes or a school for deaf students and placed with their hearing peers. Hence, deaf students are integrated into the hearing mainstream of education.

An important impetus for integration was Public Law 94–142 (the Education for All Handicapped Children Act) in the United States, which stipulated that all handicapped children have a right to a free and appropriate education, to be educated in the least restrictive environment, and to be evaluated in a nondiscriminatory manner. For many mainstreaming proponents, PL 94–142 translated to mean the right of handicapped children to an education in neighborhood schools with their nonhandicapped peers. The degree of restrictiveness is commonly thought of in terms of the degree of isolation from non-handicapped peers. Within this framework, schools for deaf students are seen by many as being a highly restrictive environment. Consequently, PL 94–142 has led to a significant decrease in their enrollments.

Today, the process of integration is being increasingly questioned. After more than ten years of aiming to place as many deaf students as possible in general education classes, schools have not experienced the success they had anticipated (Commission on the Education of the Deaf 1988). Wholesale reallocations of teaching personnel and classmates are not sufficient to meet the educational and social needs of deaf students. Indeed, schools have not been responsive to the special needs of deaf students. Riding the tail of oralism inspired by the Milan resolution in 1880, educators took approximately ninety years before they again accepted the value of signing and endorsed total communication programs. It took Gallaudet University 124 years before it hired its first Deaf president. It is only in recent years that Deaf Studies has been integrated into the curricula of a few programs. Whereas hearing students are allowed to take ASL for foreign-language credits in a handful of states, a vast majority of education programs for deaf students have yet to utilize the instructional value of ASL. Integration is still a unilateral proposition for entry into a hearing environment.

The foregoing discussion is not meant to imply that integration is an unworthy objective. The proliferation of other materials on the integration of deaf individuals into the hearing mainstream is justification for not repeating the argument here. Rather, it is suggested that integration needs to be reconceptualized from the perspective of deaf individualism. It is especially critical that social dimensions of integration (Gresham 1982; Sabornie 1985; Strain, Odom, and McConnell 1984) and psychological ones (Saur et al. 1986) are accounted for before educational placement decisions are made. Further, in conjunction with all that has been expounded in this text, integration into the mainstream of the *Deaf* community must become a viable option for all deaf students (Stewart 1984b).

Although there has been much written on issues related to the educational integration and mainstreaming of deaf students, I could find no study that explored the long-term social effects of integration. Yet, the full impact of integration during the school years must be examined in relation to the long-term social behavior of deaf adults inside and outside the Deaf community. In the absence of such research, it must not be assumed that Deaf adults participating in Deaf sport or socializing within the Deaf community have failed to meet the goals of integration during their school years. The Deaf community is not a stain in the social fabric of society. It is a thriving host to a number of social activities that give Deaf people unparalleled opportunities to fulfill their physical, social, and emotional needs. It is in this spirit that schools should consider the benefits of Deaf integration.

Defining
Deaf Integration

Deaf integration is the transition from interacting in a predominantly hearing environment to one in which the social dynamics of being Deaf are in force. With this definition of integration, it is not unreasonable to expect all facets of our educational system to provide some exposure to the values and activities of this community. In this respect, Deaf sport provides some direction. For example, deaf athletes who attend an oral program and do not know signs are not barred from competing in Deaf sport. It is not unusual for those with exceptional athletic abilities in a certain sport to try out for the World Games for the Deaf. Jeff Float, a winner of ten gold medals at the XIIIth World Summer Games for the Deaf in Bucharest, Romania (1977) and one gold medal at the XXIIIrd Summer Olympiad in Los Angeles (1984) is a product of the oral education system.

Although it is rare, not all Deaf sport teams are composed mostly of Deaf players who use signs. As a member of the British Columbia Deaf Hockey team, I played in a series against the Chicago-based American Hearing Impaired Hockey Association in Vancouver in 1981. On the British Columbia team only one player was considered a weak signer, and all of the others were members of the Deaf community. The composition of this team was typical of a Deaf sport team. At the opposite end of the rink stood the American team, which was decidedly not typical of a Deaf sport team. The team had nineteen players who had minimal if any knowledge of signs, and one, whom we will call Doug, who was a fluent ASL signer. All of the team officials and coaches were hearing, whereas on the British Columbia team only the coach was hearing. At the banquet following the series, Doug spent his whole time interacting with the players from British Columbia. During this tournament he met a Deaf woman from Vancouver whom he eventually married.

The enlightening aspect of this episode is that the American team was composed mostly of school-aged players. These oral deaf players through their affiliation with Doug and their four-game series in Vancouver gained insight into the Deaf community that they might never have had before. This insight may eventually influence the directions the players pursue in their adult social lives.

The one player who was just learning to sign on the British Columbia team offers another example of Deaf integration. This player, whom we will call Terry, came from a small town about five hundred miles from Vancouver, where the Deaf hockey team played. His father worked on the railway and was able to arrange for his transportation to weekly practices. Terry had attended public schools all his life and was a senior in high school when he found out about the Deaf team. Within just one short year his involvement in Deaf sport had a lasting impact on his education and social life. His interactions with Deaf teammates convinced him to attend Gallaudet University. At Gallaudet he rapidly improved in his signing skills, and his association with other Deaf individuals came to define new standards for him in his social interactions. Terry now has the option of interacting in either a Deaf mainstream or a hearing mainstream.

Terry's participation in Deaf sport as a school-aged adolescent illustrates another aspect of Deaf integration. The decision to play on a Deaf hockey team was one that Terry had made for himself. At the beginning he was well aware that he was an outsider. He could not communicate effectively with most of his teammates, and if he wanted to stay on, it was obvious that it would be to his advantage if he learned to sign. However, at no time did anyone tell him that he had to learn to sign and assimilate other cultural values of the Deaf community if he was to be welcomed to play. On and off the ice, his Deaf teammates did their best to ease his social predicament. This was often accomplished by using another Deaf player as an interpreter. The decision to remain on the team was strictly Terry's. Integration into the Deaf mainstream was not forced on him. Integration into the Deaf mainstream had been presented as an option, not a requirement for social acceptance. Indeed, integration into a Deaf mainstream does not preclude involvement in a mainstream of hearing individuals.

Schools could learn much from Deaf sport. A goal for all deaf educational programs could be to inform their students of various social options and provide experiences that allow them to determine their own social destinies. Likely, Deaf individuals will choose those aspects of both worlds that best suit their individual needs. The task of schools is to ensure that the decisions deaf students make are not unduly influenced by bitter educational experiences. This is especially true for those experiences that reflect educational measures that do not lead to academic successes. All schools must arrange educational activities that allow students to sample the conventional wisdom of *both* the Deaf and hearing worlds. In this way integration would reflect a more realistic representation of society.

Deaf integration, like Deaf sport, should not be viewed as a threat. If implemented, even to a minimal extent, it will undoubtedly promote cultural pluralism in our increasingly multicultural society.

Deaf Integration: The Example of Deaf Sport

Two fundamental principles should underlie all types of integration for deaf individuals: (1) integration is most effective if it puts deaf persons on a par socially with those with whom they interact, and (2) the purpose of integration is defeated if integration serves to emphasize weaknesses or differences that are viewed negatively by one group of people or party in the interaction. In short, mutual respect for one another is absolutely essential for effective integration. Deaf sport provides a vehicle for showing how these two principles can be applied to Deaf integration.

The participants of Deaf sport reflect the cultural mosaic of the Deaf community. The diversity of these participants is shown in a number of factors, including educational background, hearing status of the nuclear and extended family, racial configurations, number and type of social activities (for example, sport banquets, tournaments, fund-raising activities), sophistication of a local Deaf association as evidenced by its affiliations (for example, the Toronto Association of the Deaf—Ontario Deaf Sports Association—Canadian Deaf Sports Association—North American Deaf Sports Association—Comité International des Sports des Sourds), and type of sports offered (for example, bowling, darts, basketball, skiing). In Canada, and to the best of my knowledge in the United States, Deaf sport associations do not discriminate against deaf people who wish to participate in their activities. Hence, one objective of Deaf integration is to ensure access for all deaf people.

The diversity of participants in Deaf sport make it a valuable source of Deaf role models. Deaf people have not enjoyed a substantial amount of success in the labor force (Christiansen and Barnartt 1987). Part of the negative stereotype of deaf people questions their ability to hold professional types of employment. Moreover, deaf students are not unaffected by this misconception, which is why they need Deaf role models. Because educational programs outside of schools for deaf students rarely have Deaf teachers, they must actively search the community for Deaf individuals. Thus, establishing contact with Deaf sport associations is one way the schools may access a pool of Deaf role models.

In Profile 3 Art Kruger, one of the founding fathers of the AAAD, highlights the value of exposing deaf youngsters to the experiences of international Deaf sport competitions. He views these experiences as a means of strengthening the character and leadership in local Deaf communities. This is a message that should be heeded by all educational institutions. Within their own facilities and staff, schools are limited in the number of Deaf role models and Deaf experiences that they can provide. We need conscientious effort by the schools to impart information about Deaf sport and other Deaf cultural activities to all deaf students. Access to this information demands that schools tap the Deaf resources of their community.

Association with individuals involved in Deaf sport would help teachers in all educational settings understand the implications of deafness and of the social and educational options available to deaf persons. Deaf sport provides vivid proof that Deaf people are a cultural entity who constantly create and design their own set of social behaviors that meet their unique social, communication, and personal needs.

Thus, irrespective of educational setting, contact with the Deaf community is necessary if the educational needs of deaf students are to be recognized and met. It might be said that any program that brings deaf students together encourages Deaf integration. Nonetheless, the curriculum is a vital part of a total

Profile 3
Art Kruger, Ped.D.
Chairman Emeritus
United States
World Games for the Deaf
Team Committee

Art Kruger is one of the grandfathers of the American Athletic Association of the Deaf (AAAD). Deafened at the age of three years, Kruger completed grammar school in an oral setting, attended the Pennsylvania School for the Deaf, and then went to Gallaudet University, where he graduated in 1933. In 1982 Hofstra University granted him a Doctor of Pedagogy degree. Kruger used the popularity of basketball among Deaf people to take the bold step of organizing Deaf sport on a national level. Acting as chairperson of the First National Deaf Basketball tournament in 1945, Kruger got together with a few other sport enthusiasts and founded the AAAD in Akron, Ohio. He was the first president of the AAAD and since that time has served a number of years as its secretary-treasurer. He later assumed the positions of team director and chairperson of the United States World Games for the Deaf Team Committee. In these latter two positions he has raised an estimated $2 million for U.S. athletes. Such an effort illustrates the strong commitment he has devoted to enhancing the athletic endeavors of many deaf individuals. In the following comments he offers an insight into a major driving force behind his many contributions to Deaf sport:

"The World Games for the Deaf or the 'Deaf Olympics' is an inspiration to our younger deaf children. Watching older students attain success through sport helps them realize the many accomplishments that they can strive for. Success in sport also gives deaf children greater pride in their school. But competition is not the only value of the World Games. They provide a rare opportunity for participants to learn about the nature of competition, about themselves, and about places and people from around the world.

"For myself and other Deaf adults, it is an enlightening experience to watch the growth of young deaf athletes during the World Games. Their independence and knowledge expands in a manner that is hard to match in any other environment. The medals may be the initial justification for young deaf athletes seeking to compete internationally. But the typical six weeks of competition and socializing associated with the World Games reaps far greater rewards in the areas of friendship and understanding. These come from the common experiences that Deaf individuals from all over the world share with each other. Another important factor is the confidence that youngsters gain during the World Games that contributes to the development of their leadership skills. In this way, the benefits of the Games can flow right back to the local level where Deaf sport all begins.

"Communication behavior associated with the World Games for the Deaf is also an eye opener for our young deaf athletes. Athletes from all over the world come together in a social experience that knows no language barrier. Although each country enjoys its own unique kind of sign language, Deaf persons use their signing skills and the visual field to strike up meaningful communication with one another.

"These are just a few of the advantages of international competition for young deaf athletes. International experiences lead to an overall improvement in the quality of life of a Deaf individual. Ultimately, the greater self-esteem that comes with these experiences will result in later pay-offs as deaf youngsters become a part of the adult Deaf community. By promoting the participation of deaf youngsters in international sports, Deaf adults can strengthen the leadership in their own communities. In this way, I feel that my involvement in World Games is one way in which I can contribute to the grassroots organizations of Deaf sport."

educational package for deaf children, and it must provide a means for educating students about Deaf sport and other aspects of the Deaf community. This could be accomplished in a number of ways. A Deaf education program could be established that parallels certain parts of the regular curriculum used with deaf children. This parallel program could incorporate a module on Deaf Studies that would include ASL studies and events related to Deaf sport and other activities of the Deaf community. For example, to increase Deaf awareness, one could arrange for a community-based Deaf basketball team to play the staff at a school for deaf students or at a public school.

Alternatively, or in conjunction with a parallel Deaf studies program, information about Deaf people and their culture could be infused into the curriculum. For example, reading materials about Deaf people such as *Great Deaf Americans* (Panara and Panara 1983), *Angels and Outcasts: An Anthology of Deaf Characters in Literature* (Batson and Bergman 1985), *Deaf Heritage: A Narrative History of Deaf America* (Gannon 1981), *Deaf in America: Voices from a Culture* (Padden and Humphries 1988) could be used as part of a language arts curriculum. More generally, stories and factual information about deaf people could be extracted from numerous Deaf publications such as newspapers and magazines (for instance, *Canadian Deaf Advocate, NAD Broadcaster, The Deaf American, Silent News, Deaf Life*). Doubtless, there are many other ways in which the curriculum could be used to prepare deaf students for their social and cultural options.

In physical education, curricular adaptations should include visits by Deaf athletes, schedules of Deaf sport events in the community, information on how to join a Deaf sport club and participate in various Deaf sport tournaments, and readings of articles written about Deaf athletes. Examples of such readings would be the "The Deaf in Sports," a regular column in the *NAD Broadcaster.* Highlights of the U.S. national Deaf team appear in *Spotlight,* a newsletter put out by the United States World Games for the Deaf Team Committee. The official sport newsletter of the CDSA, *The Competitor,* has stories about Canadian Deaf athletes.

All of these curricular suggestions can be implemented in programs from any educational setting. The scope of integration, Deaf or hearing, must be expanded beyond the limitations imposed by educators' and administrators' lack of knowledge about Deaf Studies and the confines of a classroom.

Conclusion

The literature contains extensive deliberations on various methods for including deaf students in the hearing mainstream of education, but little about the Deaf mainstream or about providing a variety of experiences in both Deaf and hearing environments. One purpose of all educational systems is to prepare students to become participating members of society, of which the Deaf community is one component. To accomplish that purpose, schools must create a sense of partnership between the Deaf and hearing segments of society.

Clearly, if hearing individuals wish to assume some of the responsibility of educating deaf children, then they must also assume the responsibility of learning about Deaf people. The institution of Deaf sport presents a readily available platform for educating both deaf and hearing persons about the outcomes of being Deaf in a predominantly hearing society.

For deaf individuals who have never been a part of the Deaf mainstream, for deafened individuals, and for hearing persons, Deaf sport is an optimal environment for integration. In school Deaf teams play hearing teams, and the differences in their academic achievements are of no relevance. Communication between deaf players and spectators and their hearing counterparts occurs through print, gestures, interpreters, speech, or whatever other mode is convenient. Efforts to communicate are mutual. Athletes come to compete, and spectators to watch; whether deaf or hearing, they are all able to participate without infringing on or succumbing to the social standards established within others' groups. Thus it is within this climate of social interaction that a real sense of partnership in society can be observed.

Within schools, a focus on Deaf sport and various Deaf cultural activities is a convenient vehicle for orienting deaf students to the beliefs and actions of the Deaf community. The activities of Deaf sport tend to occur more frequently than other cultural activities and therefore are more readily accessible. Nevertheless, deaf students in all types of educational settings should be aware of pageants, local versions of television game shows, cultural festivals, performances by local and traveling Deaf theater groups, and other events organized by Deaf people and located near their schools.

In addition to its benefits for Deaf integration, this new focus in educational programs for deaf students is a convenient means of educating hearing teachers, administrators, and parents. Hearing individuals who have close contact with Deaf individuals must take advantage of opportunities to explore the Deaf community. This way they will have a better chance of at least coming to some degree of understanding of a world that is in sharp contrast to their own.

CHAPTER 9

FUTURE DIRECTIONS
for Deaf Sport

Society is naive about the magnetic pull of the Deaf community. Most people are perplexed as to why Deaf people choose to maintain a distinct cultural identity that separates them from the hearing population. Despite their cultural differences, both Deaf and hearing people have a social responsibility to clarify the public's understanding of different groups of people in schools, workplaces, churches, and sports. The presence of a strong Deaf community goes a long way toward educating society about being Deaf and countering negative images of deaf persons that unfortunately continue to surface. Hence, a major goal for the Deaf population is to strengthen the organization and social effectiveness of the Deaf community at all levels. In the eyes of parents, educators, and all other individuals, deaf or hearing, involvement in the Deaf community must come to be recognized as one result of being deaf in a hearing world. Schools, in particular, have the responsibility of preparing their deaf students to be effective citizens inside and outside of the Deaf community.

The goals and actions of Deaf sport will have a direct impact on the strength of the Deaf community. In mapping out future directions for Deaf sport, one must consider historical influences in the development of Deaf sport organizations (for example, schools for deaf students) along with the challenge posed by changing demographics. This challenge arises mainly from the dispersement of fewer deaf students in more schools and the large number of deafened persons who use signs.

The push to integrate deaf students into the hearing mainstream of education over the past decade is the primary reason that deaf students are spread throughout the school system. Therefore, the pool of potential Deaf sport participants is no longer as concentrated as it once was, when residential schools were the primary educational setting for deaf students. Deaf sport associations must now expend extra effort to promote themselves among deaf persons across a broader geographical area.

With respect to deafened persons in the United States, it was estimated that in 1980 approximately 413,500 individuals who were deaf by the time they reached nineteen years of age used signs, whereas 135,000 adults deafened after the age of nineteen years were signers (Schein 1987). Hence, the population of deafened adults who use signs represents a potentially untapped resource for expanding the membership and thereby increasing the strength of Deaf sport. The recommendations for future directions in Deaf sport are set forth with these two demographic factors in mind.

Recommended Directions for Deaf Sport

Deaf sport has been a part of the Deaf community for many years, but only in recent years has an attempt been made to educate others about its prevalence and significance. As we learn more about Deaf sport, our understanding about Deaf people and their interactions inside and outside the Deaf community improves. Thus, interest and research in Deaf sport can serve to broaden our knowledge about the dynamics of being Deaf. Obviously, developing athletic skills, promoting a variety of competitions that will meet the range of skills found within the Deaf community, and developing and strengthening the overall effectiveness of an organization will continue to be global goals for all Deaf sport associations. In addition to these goals, a number of other areas of potential interest are identified here. The list is by no means inclusive. The information provided is intended to stimulate the reader's own thoughts about Deaf sport and delineate pertinent issues that will be critical to the growth of Deaf sport.

1. Increase efforts to introduce deaf children and youngsters to the activities of Deaf sport. The socialization value of Deaf sport should be impressed upon deaf students so that they will be more aware of the social options they will have as adults. To achieve this, Deaf sport associations should push for the incorporation of Deaf Studies into curricular materials for deaf students; provide in-service programs on Deaf sport activities for physical education teachers, teachers of deaf students, and other school personnel; have its members volunteer as sport mentors for deaf athletes in all types of educational settings; include educational programs for deaf people on their mailing lists so that these programs can be regularly updated on upcoming Deaf sport events; provide deaf students at the secondary level with free introductory memberships or even complimentary memberships until they have finished school; and, in conjunction with school districts, arrange sport festivals and recreational events for school-age deaf students. National and regional Deaf sport associations should explore the possibility of sponsoring summer games and camps for school-age students.

In addition, Deaf sport should be used for improving athletic skills. Some deaf children and youngsters might feel uncertain about competing on hearing teams because of their communication skills. Alternatively, competition in Deaf sport could be encouraged for the purposes of developing athletic skills and for boosting the self-esteem of deaf children and youngsters. Once their athletic skills have been developed, they will be better able to determine the type of sport they desire to play and the type of people with whom they wish to play. In Profile 4, the chairperson of the U.S. World Games for the Deaf Team Committee, Donalda Ammons, stresses the need to develop athletic skills at a young age. She suggests that deaf individuals would be in a better position to experience the pleasure of international competition if they had the opportunity to get involved in competitive sport while they are young.

Profile 4
Donalda Ammons, Ph.D.
Chairperson
United States
World Games for the Deaf
Team Committee

Donalda Ammons is chairperson for the United States World Games for the Deaf Team Committee. Like many other Deaf sport directors, she is a product of schools for deaf students but with an unusual twist. After graduating from the Maryland School for the Deaf, she got her bachelor's degree from Gallaudet University and her master's from Western Maryland College while studying foreign languages. She received her doctorate in foreign language education from Nova University and recently became director of Foreign Study Programs at Gallaudet University. Her interest in Deaf sport began at a young age, as both of her parents and her two sisters are Deaf. She excelled in basketball and swimming, but her academic interests and an injury prevented her from trying out for any U.S. team. Before holding her current positions with the U.S. World Games for the Deaf Team Committee she was its vice-chairperson and special assistant. She is also a representative for deaf athletes on the United States Olympic Committee (USOC).

Ammons addresses the importance of developing strong youth sport programs in the following comments:

"Sport is a highly visual event and is easily accessible to the Deaf. This was an important point that attracted me to sport when I was just six or seven years old. As a youngster I was fascinated with pictures of athletes, especially those related to sport articles written by Art Kruger in *The Deaf American*. Sports on TV was also an important influence because when I was growing up there was no captioning of television programs. Therefore, the TV programs I enjoyed when I was younger had to have lots of action, and sport shows fitted that requirement. This budding interest as a youngster soon developed into a driving desire to travel and compete in other parts of the world. When an ankle injury prevented me from competing, I turned my attention to helping the other Deaf athletes compete internationally.

"An important part of all international competition is the opportunity to meet and develop friendships with people from all over the world. Deaf athletes are not so much rivals fiercely competing for a prize as they are friends competing alongside and against one another. There are few words that can describe the sensations that arise from being at a table with twenty athletes and sport directors from many different countries. Our national sign languages are all different, and yet by using an international sign language, we communicate without any assistance from translators. We do not avoid one another simply because we may be playing against each other the next day. No matter what sign language we use or what country we are from, the urge to socialize with one another will always be there because we are Deaf first and athletes second.

"On the other hand, the athletic side of competition cannot be ignored. Deaf youngsters do not enjoy the same opportunities for involvement in community sports as do hearing youngsters because of difficulty in communication with hearing peers. Parents may feel uncertain about placing their deaf youngsters in community sports programs for this same reason. For many deaf youngsters involvement in competitive sport does not start until they are able to participate on teams in a school for deaf students. This is too late for many to become elite athletes. That is why it is so critical that the AAAD with support from USOC create effective development programs for deaf athletes. Training camps and coaching clinics are good examples of the type of programs needed to enhance the overall skills and competitiveness of our athletes. All deaf individuals should have opportunities to experience the thrills and rewards of international competition. If more of us can help to create some of these opportunities, then we will have made a valuable contribution to future generations of Deaf athletes."

2. Deaf sport associations must become more involved in educating parents about the benefits of their activities. As yet, the educational system cannot be relied upon to inform parents about the implications of the Deaf community for their deaf children. Until the educational system itself comes to accept these implications, Deaf adults must assume some of the responsibility for reaching out to the parents of deaf children while simultaneously educating schools about Deaf sport. With respect to parents, complimentary memberships to deaf children accompanied with information packages on Deaf sport is one possibility. Noncompetitive tournaments that bring deaf students and their parents together with Deaf adults could be sponsored as a means of introducing both to the social benefits of the Deaf community. Volleyball, bowling, slo-pitch, and broomball (on ice) are games that can be enjoyed without heavy emphasis on skills. During these tournaments Deaf adults should participate alongside students and parents to pave the way for social opportunities away from the games. Recreational and leisure activities should also be used as a backdrop for educating parents. Hiking, cross-country skiing, ice skating, roller skating, camping, games organized at picnics, and other activities can all be used to provide opportunities for Deaf adults to mingle with parents and their deaf children.

Communication should occur in whichever mode appears to be convenient for the parties involved, and interpreters should be available. Because many parents do not know how to sign, effort should be taken to ease them into the socialization process. In many situations where Deaf and hearing individuals are together, it is common to find both groups associating with their own kind. This even occurs in some schools for deaf students, where Deaf staff members would sit and chat among themselves while the hearing staff members do likewise. (This is a message that has been virtually ignored by educators trumpeting the benefits of integration while failing to practice it in their own schools, the most logical and convenient of all possible settings for integration.) Obviously, forced integration should not be the purpose of having Deaf and hearing individuals interact with each other. Still, for those who do wish this type of socialization, measures should be taken that facilitate communication. One way of doing this is for Deaf sport organizers to prepare some of their members to act as communication facilitators. Also, during both sport and recreation events a few basic signs could be taught to the parents and information provided about where they might go in their local communities to learn signs.

The recommendation that parents become more aware of the benefits of the Deaf community and allow their deaf children to experience some of these benefits does not mean that parents should be willing to relinquish their responsibility for supervising the activities of their children to other adults. Social interactions of children in the Deaf community with Deaf adults should never purposefully exclude the parents. Ideally, any activity that serves to enrich a child's life should be introduced, encouraged, supervised, and facilitated by parents. This condition holds for any child, deaf or hearing. Thus, in addition to their conduct as role models to deaf children, Deaf adults should act as a support system for parents who are willing to allow their children and themselves to explore the activities of the Deaf community.

The need to educate parents and educators is of special interest to Deaf sport because transportation, among other considerations, may be hindering deaf youngsters who rely on special transportation services to take them to and from school. If this is the case, then the potential pool of athletes available to try out for spots on a national Deaf team may be decreasing. In time, a decreasing pool of athletes might decrease the competitiveness of Canadian and United States teams, which must meet strong European Deaf teams.

Finally, it might be worthwhile for Deaf sport groups in North America to study the example of their counterparts elsewhere. For example, Deaf sport groups in Australia have initiated a public relations program in which representatives go into public schools and, to a lesser extent, residential schools, to make their case for involving deaf youngsters in sport. This strategy may soon be adopted in Canada, where the CDSA has recently created the position of a Youth/Recreation Director to oversee strategies for reaching out to all deaf youngsters.

Getting deaf students involved in Deaf sport is also the responsibility of parents and educators. Society must realize that a Deaf way of life is a distinct and desirable option for many deaf individuals. Obviously, the first step toward involving deaf students in Deaf sport is to expose them to the pleasures and physical benefits of sports participation. For me, this started with my dad's getting me into the neighborhood pick-up baseball games when I was just six years old and then later signing me up for lacrosse and hockey. For others, the start might come from enrollment in a community-based sport or recreational activity such as early motor skills programs, soccer, and bowling. In schools, teachers must ensure that deaf children are able to experience the full benefits of physical education and extracurricular programs.

Beyond this first step, and assuming that parents and educators have been informed about options in Deaf sport, they should then be prepared to contact Deaf sport organizations for assistance in exposing deaf youngsters to Deaf sport. In locations where there is no immediate access to a Deaf sport organization or other Deaf associations, it may be necessary to arrange for transportation to regional or national Deaf sport events. Parents and educators should also make an effort to obtain for deaf children and youngsters books, newsletters, magazines, and videos that report on Deaf sport activities.

3. Sport and recreation activities should aim to include older Deaf adults. The benefits of physical fitness should be translated into sport programs designed to fit the physical and social needs of specific age groups of Deaf adults. In hearing sport, Masters leagues (for instance, United States Masters Swimming) provide a model for age-group sport competitions. Currently, sports for older Deaf adults tend to be handled at a local level, with bowling easily the most popular sport among Deaf adults in the middle and older age groupings. The keen interest in bowling has spilled over to some regional associations like the Great Lakes Deaf Bowling Association, which hold tournaments for senior Deaf bowlers.

An example of action in this direction, is seen in the CDSA's sponsorship of the First Annual Canadian Deaf Senior Mixed Championship in curling, in 1989. The groundwork for this event was laid by Deaf sport directors who were also active in curling. It might be expected that as Deaf sport associations become more sophisticated and capable in their operations, they will pay increasing attention to the entire age range of sport participants. Sports that are likely to be emphasized for older adults include bowling, golf, darts, and slo-pitch. Because

Deaf sport directors usually have had extensive involvement in sport, they might well be the major impetus for initiating action in this direction as they themselves age.

Obviously, there will always tend to be many more recreational opportunities than sports available in any given locale, and the role of Deaf sport associations in coordinating recreational events for older adults must be thoughtfully determined with respect to the needs of each Deaf community. In particular, senior Deaf citizens would be deeply appreciative of recreational activities that will help them get out of their home environments and associate them with other adults and youngsters. Again, as the organization of Deaf sport associations improves and as Deaf sport directors and active Deaf athletes become older, attention to this often neglected population should increase.

4. The role of Deaf sport in the lives of deafened adults needs to be investigated. Adults, deafened at a later age, should be included in deliberations about sports for older Deaf adults. Loss of hearing during the adult years is a traumatic experience for many individuals. Those who come to terms with it may appreciate an environment for integrating among Deaf adults. This is a consideration of which rehabilitation agencies need to be cognizant. Deafened adults should be informed of the advantages that the Deaf community might hold for them.

On the other hand, it might be argued that the behavior of deafened adults is more in line with that of hard-of-hearing individuals because of their long-time reliance on speech as their main form of communication. However, there are many deafened adults who, although they have the ability to speak, are unable to speechread or use their residual hearing to any significant degree. They tend either to miss out on most of a conversation or to resort to using pencil and paper to converse with others. They may be told not to learn to sign until they have exhausted all efforts to maintain their capacity to communicate in the speech mode. Those who do make the transition to signing may need exposure to an environment that will facilitate optimal socialization. Although Deaf sport is one possible environment, its benefits for deafened adults requires investigation, and potential conflicts with the commitment of Deaf sport to the Deaf population must be determined. It may be that some

Deaf communities might resent the intrusion of deafened adults, whereas other communities might appreciate the infusion of more members.

5. The role of recreation needs to be conceptualized within the realm of Deaf sport. Although not everyone wishes to be involved in competitive or even noncompetitive sports, the Deaf community must be concerned about the physical and mental health of its members. If it is accepted that there is strength in organization and that the Deaf community is a vital force in the social well-being of Deaf adults, then the Deaf community has much to gain by increasing its emphasis on recreational activities. Recreation that appeals to a wide range of adults may be used as a means of expanding membership in a Deaf association or of making Deaf adults more active in the Deaf community. Examples of such recreational activities are noncompetitive games of tennis, volleyball, and other sports.

But recreation need not always focus on team sports. Fitness classes can meet the needs of many individuals, and they represent an area that has received little attention in the Deaf community. In this direction, the Aerobics and Fitness Training Institute of the Deaf (AFTID) at Gallaudet University provides information designed to train instructors and set up community-based exercise classes. Gina Oliva is the Deaf director of the AFTID; she views integrated fitness classes composed of Deaf and hearing persons as a forum for Deaf advocacy. These classes provide an opportunity for Deaf people to "educate hearing people about deafness and sign language" while urging "deaf people to explore what hearing culture has to offer them" (Oliva 1989, 51). Whatever the motive for establishing an exercise program for Deaf persons, raising the physical fitness level of all communities, Deaf and hearing, is a worthy goal.

Although within the Deaf community recreation is frequently arranged at a personal level among friends rather than on a community-wide basis, Deaf sport provides a convenient structure upon which recreational events can be organized. Its organizational structure connects it with others throughout all Deaf communities. This structure could be used to disseminate information related to recreation. Moreover, Deaf sport may have a more open-door policy than other organizations in the Deaf community and therefore would be more likely to attract a wider range of participants.

One organization that is solely devoted to recreational activities is the World Recreation Association of the Deaf (WRAD). The WRAD is relatively new (its founding club, the Southern California Recreation Association of the Deaf, was established in 1984) and may become a driving force of recreational activities in many Deaf communities. However, Deaf communities can be rather small, and there may be a shortage of Deaf leadership to promote recreational activities. In these areas it might be more resourceful to combine recreation and sport under a common umbrella association. Indeed, many local Deaf sport groups are already part of a community-wide Deaf association that responds to the social, cultural, political, sport, educational, and other needs of the Deaf population. Thus, joining sport and recreation interests may be an efficient means of using community resources.

Another factor that may favor having Deaf sport clubs assume responsibility for recreation is that the WRAD aims specifically to integrate deaf and hearing individuals (Gross 1987). Moreover, the WRAD bylaws clearly stipulate that each of its chapters must include a hearing person as a second vice-president. This stipulation is in line with the WRAD's purpose of integrating deaf and hearing cultures. The WRAD is a possible example for administering education of deaf persons; it will be interesting to observe how planned integration in the WRAD's executive structure influences integration in its recreational activities. It will also be interesting to see if having hearing members on the WRAD's executive committee creates a threat to the mechanism by which Deaf individuals determine their own cultural destiny.

6. Deaf sport must promote itself beyond the boundaries of the Deaf community. Deaf sport as a social institution is a critical player in educating the public about the enduring qualities of the Deaf community. Deaf sport is a prime example of the vitality of this community. Deaf sport clubs should make a point of submitting to local newspapers scores and reports of their league and tournament games. Reporters from local television stations and newspapers should be informed of upcoming tournaments, especially those that involve a large number of participants. Arrangements should be made to provide interpreters so as to facilitate communication, or at least to inform potential reporters that they should obtain one.

At all times, care should be taken to impress upon reporters that stories about Deaf athletes and games should be included in the sport section of the newspaper or newscast, not presented as a special or a human-interest item. Newspapers have wasted far too many trees with themes related to the silent games, the roar of signing, overcoming deafness, and other worn-out topics of "interest." We will know that the Deaf community has come of age when a television sport reporter from ESPN casually reports that Kalamazoo defeated St. Louis, 4 to 3, to wrap up the championship of another AAAD softball tournament.

Promotional events for the public are not always easy to arrange, given that the nature of Deaf sport is to promote the interaction of Deaf individuals among themselves. To get around this, the CDSA sponsors an annual Silent Walk that helps raise funds for Deaf sport and other Deaf associations across Canada. The press is informed of Silent Walk events as they occur in different cities, and the public is welcome to participate. Another example of promotional activities is seen in the CDSA's organization of a walk both ways across Canada by a Deaf man, Jim Terrion. Starting in Edmonton, Alberta, on February 5, 1990, Terrion's walk was designed to help the CDSA raise money and promote the World Winter Games for the Deaf held in Banff, Alberta, in 1991. By attending press conferences and being interviewed on local and national television across Canada, Terrion provided Deaf sport with a forum for reaching the public.

7. The legacy of Deaf sport must be preserved for future generations. The business of Deaf sport must include systematic documentation of events at all levels of organization. In the past, historical accounts of Deaf sport relied primarily on word of mouth, statistical reports of games, the private photograph collections of a few individuals, and a handful of newspaper articles. Today, this unorganized attention to the affairs of Deaf sport is no longer acceptable, given the ease of documentation through the use of videotape recorders, computer networks, home computers, photocopy machines, telefax machines, TDDs, high-quality automatic cameras, and increasing mass media reports of Deaf community events.

There is indication that some progress is already being made in this direction. Both the AAAD and the CDSA instituted sport halls of fame to recognize elite athletes and outstanding contributions of Deaf sport directors. The United States World Games for the Deaf Team Committee has slide shows, video-tapes, portable exhibits, and printed materials available for distribution. Many Deaf sport associations publish newsletters and bulletins to keep their members up-to-date. A book on the history of the CDSA is currently being prepared, and a book on the accomplishments of famous deaf athletes is also in the works (B. Strassler, personal communication, 1989).

However, there is more to Deaf sport than that represented by regional, national, and international associations. Local levels of Deaf sport should establish procedures that will ensure ongoing documentation of their own affairs and members. This effort should also include the social and political aspects of Deaf sport. With strong support at the local level, it would then be feasible to establish a clearinghouse for materials on Deaf sport from all Deaf communities. Future generations of Deaf individuals would then be more knowledgeable about their own Deaf heritage, which will strengthen the character and desirability of the Deaf community.

8. More research is needed in Deaf sport. The amount of research in this area is very small, despite the fact that Deaf sport is a microcosm of the Deaf community and the number of potential topics is vast. Various topics for research in Deaf sport are mentioned throughout this book. In addition, future researchers might explore the extent to which Deaf sport reproduces hearing sport and creates its own sport form or the extent to which Deaf sport is associated with racism, sexism, elitism, commercialism, authoritarianism, violence, and other aspects that have been widely researched in hearing sport. Examining the physical characteristics of deaf athletes is also a possibility. An example is found in the work of Bressler (1990), who compared the shoulder anatomy and sprinting strategies of deaf and hearing sprinters and noted differences that have implications for the way deaf sprinters are trained.

As discussed earlier, Deaf sport seems to have created a different value orientation with respect to winning. Thus, one research possibility would be to determine why it was able to do so. Was it because Deaf sport is not as commercialized as hearing sport? Or does Deaf sport seek to ensure continued participation over and above the promotion of excellence in sport?

It is important to note that studies in areas related to deafness pose unique challenges for researchers coming from outside the mainstream of research in deafness. Communication, the low incidence of deafness, the diversity of characteristics among the deaf population (for example, their knowledge of signs, degree of hearing loss, educational background, parents' and siblings' hearing status, age at onset of deafness, etiology), and researchers' naïveté about deafness and Deaf people are just some of the variables that may influence the type of research conducted.

One possible solution to these challenges is to involve Deaf individuals as investigators or consultants whenever possible. This is not to say that the presence of a Deaf person would necessarily ensure the best collection and interpretation of data. Instead, their importance lies in their experience and insights, which help offset a lack of support in the literature. Care must be taken to credit Deaf individuals for their contributions to our body of knowledge on deafness. Bitterness within the Deaf community is stirred when hearing researchers tap Deaf resources and then become instant experts.

9. The curriculum of physical education should be revised to better meet the needs and interests of deaf students. One focus of an investigation might be on the content of the curriculum. Knoppers (1988) criticized the present curriculum for its inequitable treatment of females and males. She noted that the "curriculum in content and intent is structured for boys, especially those who prize athletic skills and competition" (Knoppers 1988, 55). In addition, the curriculum does not attempt to address any needs that specifically relate to deaf youngsters. Alternatively, a desirable curriculum would take into consideration equity among all students regardless of gender, race, ethnicity, hearing status, and other demographic factors. It would also account for the stipulations of Public Law 95–606, the Amateur Sports Act, which promotes the need for athletic programs and competitions for athletes with disabilities (Seaman and De-Pauw 1989). Deaf sport operates its own games separate from disabled sport competitions, and the implication of PL 95–606 to the development of deaf athletes must be carefully explored.

10. Deaf sport should be used as a vehicle for preparing young Deaf leaders. The structure of Deaf sport is ideally suited for introducing individuals to the business of planning and managing its many activities. Deaf sport involves many different sports at various levels of organization, all of which depend on the organizational skills of volunteers. General meetings, team meetings, committee work, and boards of directors all provide newcomers with opportunities to learn organizational skills from experienced Deaf leaders. They also provide an introduction to the complexity of the tasks required to sponsor community activities. Leadership skills developed through interactions and responsibilities gained in Deaf sport can be transferred to other areas within the Deaf community.

There are several avenues for pursuing a leadership role in Deaf sport. Typically, experience as a Deaf athlete introduces the individual to the roles of Deaf sport directors. Personal contact is also a popular means of recruiting directors. Although some organizations rely on electing sport directors, many organizations hold elections for key positions, and then these officers are asked to select directors to assist them. This chairperson of the United States World Games for the Deaf Team Committee is elected by AAAD directors every four years. The chairperson then must select a committee of seven, which is subject to the approval by the AAAD administrative board (D. Ammons, personal communication, November 21, 1989). The same format is followed by the CDSA, which selects a chairperson for its World Games for the Deaf Organizing Committee once every four years at its Annual Congress.

Measures must also be taken for leadership training. Outside of schools for deaf students, the leadership skills of deaf persons are largely neglected. Deaf students do not normally compete with their hearing peers to be class president, gain a position on the student council, or become team captain of a sport team. Therefore, Deaf sport organizations must help their directors acquire knowledge and skills that will enable them to assume leadership in their communities. To this end, the CDSA sponsored the First National Deaf Sport Conference in Ottawa, June 2, 1989. Along with representatives from the CDSA, there were guest speakers from the CISS, AAAD, WRAD, and the CDIHF. There were also two research presentations on the motor-skills development of deaf children and youth, and on the characteristics of a Deaf sprinter. The audience consisted mainly of Deaf sport directors, who commented on the richness of the presentations and how their own understanding of the complex issues in Deaf sport was enhanced (Dummer and Stewart, in press).

In addition to conferences and workshops, Deaf sport organizations should encourage their members to keep abreast of developments in the field by subscribing to relevant journals (for example, *Palaestra*), magazines (for example, *The Deaf American, Deaf Life*), and newsletters (for example, the AAAD's *Spotlight,* the CDSA's *The Competitor,* the WRAD's *WRAD News*).

On and off the playing field coaches can exert much influence on the success of athletes and sport organizations. Both the AAAD and the CDSA organize workshops for Deaf individuals seeking coaching certification. The CDSA also conducts workshops for hearing coaches wishing to coach Deaf athletes. Finally, for those who desire to provide leadership on the playing field but not as an athlete, the AAAD sponsors workshops for officiating in different sports.

11. The institution of Deaf sport must always be committed to the development of its grassroots connections. Irrespective of level of competition, socialization is the overarching function of Deaf sport. Deaf sport is not an institution of elite Deaf athletes, although competition in the World Games for the Deaf may well be the ultimate goal of many of the athletes. Indeed, the skills required to be an elite athlete can also be obtained from competition among hearing athletes. The message that Deaf sport sends to society lies in its facilitation of togetherness among the Deaf, which has consequences for the evolution of the Deaf community. A single Deaf team playing among twenty-six hearing teams in a local bowling league is a powerful reminder to all of the cohesive forces that stem from the unique social needs of Deaf people.

Conclusion

Deaf sport fills a void within the larger realm of sport in society. It is not an alternative to participation in hearing sport but, rather, a parallel social institution with prescribed notions of social behavior and social values. Its directions in the future will depend on the extent to which its resources can be tapped to fulfill the needs of the Deaf community. Greater recognition of the role Deaf sport has in the lives of Deaf people will be advanced when it is understood that Deaf sport is not a subculture within the "world of jocks." As an institution Deaf sport symbolizes the social, political, and educational will of the Deaf community.

All communities, Deaf and hearing, can benefit from having well-organized sport and recreational programs for their members. To encourage the development of strong sport programs, hearing people, and especially parents and educators, must assume some of the responsibility for educating deaf children about their social opportunities within the Deaf community. Eventually, many of their children and students will come to treasure their Deaf identity. When the choice to be Deaf is fostered through fair exposure to the values of both Deaf and hearing communities, we will have achieved a higher standard of equity between the two communities.

Deaf sport allows Deaf people to be themselves. This central thesis illustrates the commitment of Deaf people to design and control the place that Deaf sport will always hold for them. Deaf sport will continue to serve as an equalizer that integrates deaf people from all backgrounds into the Deaf mainstream.

REFERENCES

Allen, J. C., and Allen, M. L. 1979. Discovering and accepting hearing impairment: Initial reaction of parents. *Volta Review* 81: 279–285.

Allison, M. 1987. Kaleidoscope and prism: The study of social change in play, sport, and leisure. *Sociology of Sport Journal* 4: 144–155.

———. 1982. Sport culture, and socialization. *International Review of Sport Sociology* 17: 11–37.

Ammons, D. 1990. Unique identity of the World Games for the Deaf. *Palaestra* 6 (Winter/Spring): 40–43.

———. 1986. World Games for the Deaf. In *Sport and disabled athletes,* ed. C. Sherrill, 65–72. Champaign, Ill.: Human Kinetics.

———. 1984. American Athletic Association of the Deaf. *Journal of Physical Education, Recreation, and Dance* 55: 36–37.

Auxter, D., and Pyfer, J. 1985. *Principles and methods of adapted physical education and recreation.* St. Louis: Times Mirror/Mosby College Publishing.

Bailey, C. S., ed. In press. *American Sign Language in Canada: A regional/bilingual approach.* Mississauga, Ont.: Copp Clark Pitman.

Baker, C., and Padden, C. 1978. *American Sign Language: A look at its history, structure, and community.* Silver Spring, Md.: T. J. Publishers.

Baker-Shenk, C. 1985. The facial behavior of Deaf signers: Evidence of a complex language. *American Annals of the Deaf* 130: 297–304.

Batson, T., and Bergman, E., eds. 1985. *Angels and outcasts: An anthology of deaf characters in literature.* Washington, D.C.: Gallaudet University Press.

Benderly, B. L. 1980. *Dancing without music: Deafness in America.* Garden City, N.Y.: Anchor Press/Doubleday.

Berges, S. A. 1969. The deaf student in physical education. *Journal of Health, Physical Education, and Recreation* 40: 69–70.

Bienvenu, M. J., and Colonomos, B. 1986. *An introduction to American Deaf culture, values and traditions* (film). Silver Spring, Md.: Sign Media.

———. 1985. *An introduction to American Deaf culture: rules of social interaction* (film). Silver Spring, Md.: Sign Media.

Biklen, D. 1987. Framed: Print journalism's treatment of disability issue. In *Images of the disabled, disabling images,* ed. A. Gartner and T. Joe, 79–95. New York: Praeger.

Blair, S. 1985. Professionalization of attitude toward play in children and adults. *Research Quarterly for Exercise and Sport* 56: 82–83.

Blumer, H. 1962. Society as symbolic interactionism. In *Human behavior and social processes: An interactionist approach,* ed. A. Rose. Boston: Houghton Mifflin.

Bornstein, H. 1973. A description of some current sign systems designed to represent English. *American Annals of the Deaf* 118: 454–463.

Bourcier, P., and Roy, J. 1985. *La Lanque des Signes (LSQ).* Montreal: Bourcier & Roy.

Bowe, F. 1986. *Changing the rules.* Silver Spring, Md.: T. J. Publishers.

Boyd, J. 1967. Comparison of motor behavior in deaf and hearing boys. *American Annals of the Deaf* 112: 598–605.

Brasel, K., and Quigley, S. 1977. The influence of certain language and communication environments in early childhood on the development of language in deaf individuals. *Journal of Speech and Hearing Research* 20: 95–107.

Bressler, H. 1990. The deaf sprinter: An analysis of starting techniques. *Palaestra* 6 (Summer): 32–37.

Brunt, D., and Broadhead, G. D. 1982. Motor proficiency traits of deaf children. *Research Quarterly for Exercise and Sport* 53: 236–238.

Butterfield, S. A. 1988. Deaf children in physical education. *Palaestra* 4 (Spring): 28–30, 52.

———. 1987. The influence of age, sex, hearing loss, etiology and balance ability on the fundamental motor skills of deaf children. In *International perspectives on adapted physical activity,* ed. M. E. Berridge and G. R. Ward, 43–51. Champaign, Ill.: Human Kinetics.

Butterfield, S. A., and Ersing, W. F. 1986. Influence of age, sex, etiology, and hearing loss on balance performance by deaf children. *Perceptual and Motor Skills* 62: 659–663.

Caccamise, F., Dirst, R., DeVries, R. D., Heil, J., Kirchner, C., Kirchner, S., Rinaldi, A. M., and Stangarone, J. 1980. *Introduction to interpreting.* Silver Spring, Md.: Registry of Interpreters for the Deaf.

Carver, R. 1987. An oppressive silence. *Canadian Journal of the Deaf* 1: 26–44.

Christiansen, J. B., and Barnartt, S. N. 1987. The silent minority: The socioeconomic status of deaf people. In *Understanding deafness socially,* ed. P. Higgins and J. Nash, 171–196. Springfield, Ill.: Charles C. Thomas.

Claiborne, R. 1983. *Our marvelous native tongue.* New York: Times Books.

Clarke, B., Leslie, P., Rogers, W., Booth, J., and Horvath, A. 1977. *Selected characteristics of hearing impaired school-age students, British Columbia: 1977.* Vancouver: University of British Columbia.

Coakely, J. 1982. *Sport in society: Issues and controversies.* Toronto: Mosby.

Cokely, D. 1986. A resource list: 772 college level programs teaching sign language or "manual communication." *Sign Language Studies* 50: 78–92.

———. 1983. When is a pidgin not a pidgin? An alternate analysis of the ASL-English contact situation. *Sign Language Studies* 38: 1–24.

Commission on the Education of the Deaf. 1988. *Toward equality: Education of the Deaf.* Washington, D.C.: Department of Education.

Condon, E. C., Peters, J. Y., and Sueiro-Ross, C. 1979. *Special education and the Hispanic child: Cultural perspectives.* Philadelphia: Temple University, Teacher Corps Mid-Atlantic Network.

Cratty, B. 1980. *Adapted physical education for handicapped children and youth.* Denver: Love Publishing.

Cratty, B., Cratty, I., and Cornell, S. 1986. Motor planning abilities in deaf and hearing children. *American Annals of the Deaf* 131: 281–284.

Crowley, M., Keane, K., and Needham, C. 1982. Fathers: The forgotten parents. *American Annals of the Deaf* 127: 38–40.

Deci, E. L. 1975. *Intrinsic motivation.* New York: Plenum.

Delgado, G., ed. 1984. *The Hispanic deaf.* Washington, D.C.: Gallaudet University Press.

DiPietro, L., Williams, P., and Kaplan, H. 1987. *Alerting and communication devices for hearing impaired people: What's available now?* National Information Center on Deafness/American-Speech-Language-Hearing Association serial publication. Washington, D.C.: Gallaudet University, National Information Center on Deafness.

Dummer, G., and Stewart, D. In press. A summary of the 1st National Deaf Sport Conference. *Palaestra.*

Dummer, G., Stewart, D., and Haubenstricker, J. 1988. Fundamental motor skills of deaf children and youth. Michigan State University, East Lansing. Typescript.

Dunn, L. 1990. Black Deaf students: Overlooked by two worlds. *Silent News,* February.

Edwards, H. 1973. *Sociology of sport.* Homewood, Ill.: Dorsey.

Effgen, S. K. 1981. Effect of an exercise program on the static balance of deaf children. *Physical Therapy* 6: 873–877.

Eichstaedt, C. B., and Seiler, P. J. 1978. Signing: Communicating with hearing impaired individuals in physical education. *Journal of Health, Physical Education, and Recreation* 49: 19–21.

Eitzen, D. S. 1973. The effect of group structure on the success of athletic teams. *International Review of Sport Sociology* 8: 7–17.

Eitzen, D., and Sage, G. 1986. *Sociology of North American sport.* 3d ed. Dubuque, Iowa: Wm. C. Brown.

———. 1982. *Sociology of North American sport.* 2d ed. Dubuque, Iowa: Wm. C. Brown.

Evans, A., and Falk, W. 1986. *Learning to be deaf.* New York: Mouton de Gruyter.

Falberg, R. 1971. Speech presented at the National Association of the Deaf, Communicative Skills Advisory Board Meeting, Tucson, Ariz.

Fine, M., and Asch, A., eds. 1988. *Women with disabilities.* Philadelphia: Temple University Press.

Fleischer, L. 1990. AAAD restructure committee report. *AAAD Bulletin,* September.

Freeman, R., Carbin, C., and Boese, R. 1981. *Can't your child hear?* Baltimore: University Park Press.

Freeman, R., Malkin, S., and Hastings, J. 1975. Psychosocial problems of deaf children and their families: A comparative study. *American Annals of the Deaf* 120: 391–401.

Gannon, J. 1981. *Deaf heritage: A narrative history of Deaf America.* Silver Spring, Md.: National Association of the Deaf.

Gill, D. L. 1986. *Psychological dynamics of sport.* Champaign, Ill.: Human Kinetics.

Gilligan, C. 1982. *In a different voice.* Cambridge, Mass.: Harvard University.

Gliedman, J., and Roth, W. 1980. *The unexpected minority: Handicapped children in America.* New York: Harcourt Brace Jovanovich.

Goffman, E. 1974. Stigma and social identity. In *The handicapped person in the community,* ed. D. M. Boswell and J. M. Wingrove, 79–92. London: Tavistock.

———. 1963. *Stigma: Notes on the management of spoiled identity.* Englewood Cliffs, N.J.: Prentice-Hall.

Gottlieb, B. 1985. Social support and the study of personal relationships. *Journal of Social and Personal Relationships* 2: 351–375.

Greenberg, M. 1983. Family stress and child competence: The effects of early intervention for families with deaf infants. *American Annals of the Deaf* 128: 407–417.

———. 1980. Hearing families with deaf children: Stress and functioning as related to communication method. *American Annals of the Deaf* 125: 1063–1071.

Greenberg, M., and Marvin, R. 1979. Attachment patterns in profoundly deaf preschool children. *Merrill-Palmer Quarterly* 25: 265–279.

Greendorfer, S. 1987. Gender bias in theoretical perspectives: The case of female socialization into sport. *Psychology of Women Quarterly* 11: 327–340.

Greendorfer, S., and Lewko, J. 1978. Role of family members in sport socialization of children. *Research Quarterly* 49: 146–152.

Gregory, S. 1976. *The deaf child and his family.* London: George Allen.

Gresham, F. 1982. Misguided mainstreaming: The case for social skills training with handicapped children. *Exceptional Children* 48: 422–433.

Gross, B. 1987. Mainstreaming as a new concept for recreation and leisure in the deaf community. Unpublished manuscript.

Hairston, E., and Smith, L. 1983. *Black and deaf in America: Are we that different?* Silver Spring, Md.: T. J. Publishers.

Higgins, P. 1980. *Outsiders in a hearing world: A sociology of deafness.* Beverly Hills, Calif.: Sage.

Hoemann, H. 1986. *Introduction to American Sign Language.* Bowling Green, Ohio: Bowling Green Press.

Hoijer, H. 1948. Linguistic and cultural change. *Language* 24: 335–345.

Holcomb, M., and Wood, S. 1988. *Deaf women: A parade through the decades.* Berkeley, Calif.: Dawn Sign Press.

Holcomb, R. 1985. *Silence is golden: Sometimes.* Berkeley, Calif.: Dawn Sign Press.

Hymes, D. 1971. *Pidginization and creolization of languages.* New York: Cambridge University Press.

Jacobs, L. 1980. *A Deaf adult speaks out.* 2d ed. Washington, D.C.: Gallaudet University Press.

———. 1974. *A Deaf adult speaks out.* Washington, D.C.: Gallaudet University Press.

Jordan, J. M. 1989. Speech given by CISS President J. M. Jordan. *Comité International des Sports des Sourds Bulletin,* October.

Kampfe, C. 1989. Parental reaction to a child's hearing impairment. *American Annals of the Deaf* 134: 255–259.

Kannapell, B. 1982. Inside the Deaf community. *Deaf American* 34: 23–26.

Kaufman, M., Gottlieb, J., Agard, J., and Kukie, M. 1975. Mainstreaming: Toward and explication of the construct. In *Alternatives for teaching exceptional children,* ed. E. L. Meyen, G. A. Vargason, and R. J. Whelan, 35–54. Denver: Love.

Kenyon, G., and McPherson, B. 1973. Becoming involved in physical activity and sport: A process of socialization. In *Physical activity—human growth and development,* ed. G. L. Rarick, 304–338. New York: Academic Press.

Kileny, P. 1985. Evaluation of vestibular function. In *Handbook of clinical psychology,* ed. J. Katz, 582–603. Baltimore, Md.: Williams & Wilkins.

Klima, E., and Bellugi, U. 1979. *The signs of language.* Cambridge, Mass.: Harvard University Press.

Knoppers, A. 1988. Equity for excellence in physical education. *Journal of Physical Education, Recreation, and Dance* 59(August): 54–58.

Knoppers, A., Schuiteman, J., and Love, R. 1986. Winning is not the only thing. *Sociology of Sport Journal* 3: 43–56.

Kruger, A. 1986. American Athletic Association of the Deaf. In *Gallaudet encyclopedia of deaf people and deafness: Volume I,* ed. J. V. Cleve, 17–19. New York: McGraw-Hill.

Lane, H. 1988. Is there a "Psychology of the Deaf"? *Exceptional Children* 55: 7–19.

———. 1984. *When the mind hears.* New York: Random House.

———. 1980. A chronology of the oppression of sign language in France and the United States. In *Recent perspectives on American Sign Language,* ed. H. Lane and F. Grosjean, 119–159. Hillsdale, N.J.: Lawrence Erlbaum.

Lane, H., and Grosjean, F., eds. 1980. *Recent perspectives on American Sign Language.* Hillsdale, N.J.: Lawrence Erlbaum.

Leigh, I. 1987. Parenting and the hearing impaired: Attachment and coping. *Volta Review* 89: 11–21.

Leonard, W. 1980. *A sociological perspective of sport.* Minneapolis, Minn.: Burgess.

Levesque, J. 1988. Real life incidents show true impact of Deaf President. *DCARA News,* April, p. 2.

Levine, E. 1981. *The ecology of early deafness: Guides to fashioning environments and psychological assessments.* New York: Columbia University Press.

Lewis, R., and Doorlag, D. 1987. *Teaching special students in the mainstream.* 2d ed. Columbus, Ohio: Merrill.

Lindsey, D., and O'Neal, J. 1976. Static and dynamic balance skills of eight year old deaf and hearing children. *American Annals of the Deaf* 121: 49–55.

Longmore, D. 1987. Screening stereotypes: Images of disabled people in television and motion pictures. In *Images of the disabled, disabling images,* ed. A. Gartner and T. Joe, 65–78. New York: Praeger.

Loy, J., Birrell, S., and Rose, D. 1976. Attitudes held toward agonetic activities as a function of selected social identities. *Quest* 26: 81–93.

Loy, J., McPherson, B., and Kenyon, G. S., eds. 1981. *Sport, cul-*

ture, and society: A reader on the sociology of sport. Philadelphia: Lea & Febiger.

Loy, J. W., McPherson, B. D., and Kenyon, G. S. 1978. *Sport and social systems: A guide to the analysis, problems, and literature.* Reading, Mass.: Addison-Wesley.

Luterman, D. 1979. *Counseling parents of hearing-impaired children.* Boston: Little, Brown.

McCartney, B. 1986. An investigation of the factors contributing to the ability of hearing impaired children to communicate orally as perceived by oral deaf adults and parents and teachers of the hearing impaired. *Volta Review* 88: 133–143.

McPherson, B. D. 1976. The black athlete: An overview and analysis. In *Social problems in athletes,* ed. D. Landers. Urbana, Ill.: University of Illinois Press.

Maestas y Moores, J. 1980. Early linguistic environments. *Sign Language Studies* 26: 1–13.

Maloney, T., and Petrie, B. 1972. Professionalization of attitude toward play among Canadian school pupils as a function of sex, grade, and athletic participation. *Journal of Leisure Research* 4: 184–195.

Markowicz, H. 1977. *American Sign Language: Fact and fancy.* Washington, D.C.: Gallaudet University.

Markowicz, H., and Woodward, J. 1978. Language and the maintenance of ethnic boundaries in the Deaf community. *Communication and Cognition* 11: 29–38.

Maslow, A. 1954. *Motivation and personality.* New York: Harper & Row.

Masters, L., Mori, A., and Lange, E. 1983. *Adapted physical education: A practitioner's guide.* Rockville, Md.: Aspen Systems.

Meadow, K. 1972. Sociolinguistics, sign language, and deaf subculture. In *Psycholinguistics and total communication: The state of the art,* ed. T. J. O'Rourke, 19–32. Washington, D.C.: American Annals of the Deaf.

Meadow, K., Greenberg, M., Erting, C., and Carmichael, H. 1981. Interactions of deaf mothers and deaf preschool children. *American Annals of the Deaf* 124: 454–468.

Mindel, E., and Vernon, M. 1971. *They grow in silence.* Silver Spring, Md.: National Association of the Deaf.

Moores, D. 1989. School for deaf builds tradition on football field. *USA Today,* November 8.

Moores, D. F. 1987. *Educating the deaf: Psychology, principles, and practices.* 3d ed. Boston: Houghton Mifflin.

Moores, D. F., and Oden, C. 1978. Educational needs of black deaf children. *American Annals of the Deaf* 122: 313–318.

Morgan, C., King, R., and Robinson, N. 1979. *Introduction to psychology.* 6th ed. New York: McGraw-Hill.

Morsh, J. 1936. Motor performance of the deaf. *Comparative Psychology Monographs* 13: 1–51.

Myklebust, H. 1946. Significance of etiology in motor performance of deaf children with special reference to meningitis. *American Journal of Psychology* 59: 249–258.

Nash, J. E., and Nash, A. 1981. *Deafness in society.* Lexington, Mass.: Heath.

Newman, B. 1987. A true Jet fighter. *Sports Illustrated,* October 12, pp. 109–112.

Newman, S. 1985. A quiet Olympics. *Los Angeles Times,* July 11.

Northern, J., and Downs, M. 1984. *Hearing in children.* 3d ed. Baltimore: Williams & Wilkins.

Ogden, P. W., and Lipsett, S. 1982. *The silent garden: Understanding the hearing impaired child.* New York: St. Martin's.

Oliva, G. 1989. Advocacy: Evolution or revolution. *Palaestra* 6: 49–51, 59.

Orlick, T. 1980. *In pursuit of excellence.* Champaign, Ill.: Human Kinetics.

Orlick, T., and Mosher, R. 1978. Extrinsic rewards and participant motivation in a sport-related task. *International Journal of Sport Psychology* 9: 27–39.

Padden, C. 1980. The Deaf community and culture of deaf people. In *Sign language and the Deaf community: Essays in honor of William Stokoe,* ed. C. Baker and R. Battison, 89–103. Silver Spring, Md.: National Association of the Deaf.

Padden, C., and Humphries, T. 1988. *Deaf in America: Voices from a culture.* Cambridge, Mass.: Harvard University.

Padden, C., and Markowicz, H. 1976. Cultural conflicts between hearing and Deaf communities. In *Proceedings of the Seventh World Congress of the World Federation of the Deaf.* Silver Spring, Md.: T. J. Publishers.

Panara, R., and Panara, J. 1983. *Great deaf Americans.* Silver Spring, Md.: T. J. Publishers.

Pannella, L. 1974. XII World Games for the Deaf. *Journal of Health, Physical Education, and Recreation* 45: 12–14.

Paul, P., and Quigley, S. 1990. *Education and deafness.* New York: Longman.

Pepper, F. 1976. Teaching the American Indian child in mainstream settings. In *Mainstreaming and the minority child,* ed. R. L. Jones, 133–158. Reston, Va.: Council for Exceptional Children.

Popenoe, D. 1983. *Sociology.* 5th ed. Englewood Cliffs, N.J.: Prentice-Hall.

Potter, C., and Silverman, L. 1984. Characteristics of vestibular function and static balance skills in deaf children. *Physical Therapy* 64: 1071–1075.

Robinson, J. 1989. The relationship of Deaf sport and disabled sport. Paper presented at the First National Deaf Sport Conference, Ottawa, Ontario, June 2.

Robinson, J., and Stewart, D., eds. 1987. *Coaching deaf athletes.* Ottawa: Canadian Deaf Sports Association.

Rodriguez, R., Cole, J., Stile, S., and Gallegos, R. 1979. Bilingualism and biculturalism for the special education classroom. *Teacher Education and Special Education* 4: 175–177.

Rogers, C. 1987. The employment dilemma for disabled persons. In *Images of the disabled, disabling images,* ed. A. Gartner and T. Joe, 117–127. New York: Praeger.

Ryan, E. 1980. Attribution, intrinsic motivation, and athletics: A replication and extension. In *Psychology of motor behavior and sport—1979,* ed. C. Nadeau, W. Halliwell, K. Newell, and G. Roberts, Champaign, Ill.: Human Kinetics.

Ryan, R., Vallerand, R., and Deci, E. 1984. Intrinsic motivation in sport: A cognitive evaluation theory interpretation. In *Cognitive sport psychology,* ed. W. Straub and J. Williams, 231–242. Lansing, N.Y.: Sport Science Associates.

Sabornie, E. 1985. Social mainstreaming of handicapped students: Facing an unpleasant reality. *Remedial and Special Education* 6(March/April): 12–16.

Sacks, O. 1988. The revolution of the Deaf. *New York Review of Books,* June 2, pp. 23–28.

Sage, G. 1986. Social development. In *Physical activity & wellbeing,* ed. C. Seefeldt, 343–371. Reston, Va.: American Alliance for Health, Physical Education, Recreation, and Dance.

———. 1980. *Sport and American society: Selected readings.* Don Mills, Ont.: Addison-Wesley.

Saur, R., Layne, C., Hurley, E., and Opton, K. 1986. Dimensions of mainstreaming. *American Annals of the Deaf* 131: 325–330.

Schafer, W. 1971. Sport, socialization and the school. Paper presented at the Third International Symposium on the Sociology of Sport, Waterloo, Ont., August 22–28.

Schappell, L. 1986. American Hearing Impaired Hockey Association. *Palaestra* 2(Summer): 33–35, 47.

Schein, J. D. 1987. The demography of deafness. In *Understanding deafness socially,* ed. P. Higgins and J. Nash, 3–27. Springfield, Ill.: Charles C. Thomas.

Schlesinger, H., and Meadow, K. 1972. *Sound and sign: Childhood deafness and mental health.* Berkeley: University of California Press.

Schmidt, S. 1985. Hearing impaired students in physical education. *Adapted Physical Activity Quarterly* 2: 300–306.

Schmidt, S., and Dunn, J. 1980. Physical education of the hearing impaired: A system of movement symbols. *Teaching Exceptional Children* 12: 99–102.

Schmitt, R., and Leonard, W. 1986. Immortalizing the self through sport. *American Journal of Sociology* 91: 1088–1111.

Schuetz, K. 1988. Recreation: Bringing the deaf back together. *People,* July 27, pp. B7, B8.

Schultz, J., and Turnbull, A. 1983. *Mainstreaming handicapped students.* 2d ed. Boston: Allyn & Bacon.

Seaman, J., and DePauw, K. 1989. *The new adapted physical education: A developmental approach.* 2d ed. Mountain View, Calif.: Mayfield.

Sherrill, C. 1981. *Adapted physical education and recreation: A multidisciplinary approach.* Dubuque, Iowa: Wm. C. Brown.

Snyder, E., and Spreitzer, E. 1978. *Social aspects of sport.* Englewood Cliffs, N.J.: Prentice-Hall.

Sofranko, A., and Nolan, M. 1972. *Early life experiences and adult sport participation.* Urbana, Ill.: University of Illinois Press.

Solow, S. 1981. *Sign language interpreting: A basic resource book.* Silver Spring, Md.: National Association of the Deaf.

Somers, M. 1987. Parenting in the 1980's: Programming perspectives and issues. *Volta Review* 89: 68–77.

Spradley, T., and Spradley, J. 1978. *Deaf like me.* New York: Random House.

Stern, R. 1989. Recruitment and development of athletes and

coaches. Paper presented at the First National Deaf Sport Conference, Ottawa, Ontario, June 2.

Stewart, D. In press. Game orientations of deaf adults: A preliminary investigation. *Palaestra.*

———. 1987. Social factors influencing participation in Deaf sport. *Palaestra* 3(Summer): 22–28, 50.

———. 1986. Deaf sport in the community. *Journal of Community Psychology* 14: 196–205.

———. 1984a. The hearing impaired student in P.E.: Some considerations. *Palaestra* 1(Fall): 35–37.

———. 1984b. Mainstreaming deaf children: A different perspective. *ACEHI Journal* 10: 91–104.

———. 1982. The opinions of the adult deaf community towards methods of communication in the education of deaf children. Masters' thesis, University of British Columbia.

Stewart, D., and Akamatsu, C. 1988. The coming of age of American Sign Language. *Anthropology and Education Quarterly* 19: 235–252.

Stewart, D., and Benson, G. 1988. Dual cultural negligence: The education of black deaf children. *Journal of Multicultural Counseling and Development* 16: 98–109.

Stewart, D., Benson, G., and Lindsey, J. 1987. A unit plan for siblings of handicapped children. *Teaching Exceptional Children* 19: 24–28.

Stewart, D., and Donald, M. 1984. Deaf teachers to teach deaf children. *Education Canada* 24: 16–21.

Stewart, D., Dummer, G., and Haubenstricker, J. 1990. Review of administration procedures used to assess the motor skills of deaf children and youth. *Adapted Physical Activity Quarterly,* 7: 231–239.

Stewart, D., McCarthy, D., and Robinson, J. 1988. Participation in Deaf sport: Characteristics of Deaf sport directors. *Adapted Physical Activity Quarterly* 5: 233–244.

Stewart, D., Robinson, J., and McCarthy, D. In press. Participation in Deaf sport: Characteristics of elite Deaf athletes. *Adapted Physical Activity Quarterly.*

Stewart, L. 1985. Program focuses on a special group of athletes. *Los Angeles Times,* July 5, p. 3.

Stokoe, W. 1978. Sign language versus spoken language. *Sign Language Studies* 18: 69–90.

———. 1960. *Sign language structure: An outline of the visual commu-*

nication of the American Deaf. Studies in Linguistics: Occasional Papers No. 8. Buffalo, N.Y.: University of Buffalo.

Stokoe, W., Casterline, D., and Croneberg, C. 1976. *A dictionary of American sign on linguistic principles.* New ed. Silver Spring, Md.: Linstok.

Strain, P., Odom, S., and McConnell, S. 1984. Promotion of social reciprocity of exceptional children: Identification, target behavior selection, and intervention. *Remedial and Special Education* 5: 21–28.

Strassler, B. 1988. The Western States Basketball Classic story. *NAD Broadcaster,* May, p. 26.

———. 1976. Deaf athletes and the handicap of deafness. *Silent News,* February.

Streng, A., Kretschmer, R., and Kretschmer, L. 1978. *Language, learning, & deafness: Theory, application, and classroom management.* New York: Grune & Stratton.

Stuckless, E., and Birch, J. 1966. The influence of early manual communication on the linguistic development of deaf children. *American Annals of the Deaf* 111: 425–460, 499–504.

Thomas, J. R., and Thomas, K. T. 1986. The relation of movement and cognitive function. In *Physical activity & well-being,* ed. V. Seefeldt, 443–452. Reston, Va.: American Alliance for Health, Physical Education, Recreation, and Dance.

Vernon, M., and Andrews, J. 1990. *The psychology of deafness: Understanding deaf and hard-of-hearing people.* New York: Longman.

Vernon, M., and Makowsky, B. 1969. Deafness and minority group dynamics. *Deaf American* 21: 3–6.

Vogel, P. 1986. Effects of physical education programs on children. In *Physical activity & well-being,* ed. V. Seefeldt, 455–509. Reston, Va.: American Alliance for Health, Physical Education, Recreation, and Dance.

Webb, H. 1969. Professionalization of attitudes toward play among adolescents. In *Aspects of contemporary sport sociology,* ed. G. Kenyon, 161–178. Chicago: Athletic Institute.

Wiegersma, P., and Van der Velde, A. 1983. Motor development of deaf children. *Journal of Psychology and Psychiatry* 24: 103–111.

Wilbur, R. 1987. *American Sign Language: Linguistic and applied dimensions.* 2d ed. Boston: Little, Brown.

Williams, L. College for deaf is shut by protest over president. *New York Times,* March 8.

Wilson, D. 1988. Deaf actress's use of speech proves divisive among peers. *New York Times,* April 13.

Wiseman, D. C. 1982. *A practical approach to adapted physical education.* Reading, Mass.: Addison-Wesley.

Wolk, S., and Allen, T. 1984. A 5-year follow-up reading-comprehension achievement of hearing-impaired students in special education programs. *Journal of Special Education* 18: 161–176.

Wood, D., Wood, H., Griffiths, A., and Howarth, I. 1986. *Teaching and talking with deaf children.* New York: John Wiley & Sons.

Woodward, J. 1982. *How you gonna get to heaven if you can't talk with Jesus: On depathologizing deafness.* Silver Spring, Md.: T. J. Publishers.

———. 1978. Historical bases of American Sign Language. In *Understanding language through sign language research,* ed. P. Siple, 333–347. New York: Academic Press.

———. 1976. Black southern signing. *Language in Society* 5: 211–218.

———. 1973. Some characteristics of pidgin sign English. *Sign Language Studies* 3: 39–46.

Woodward, J., and Erting, C. 1975. Synchronic variation and historical change in ASL. *Language Science* 37: 9–12.

Wylie, R. C. 1989. *Measures of self-concept.* Lincoln: University of Nebraska Press.

APPENDIX
National Deaf Sport Organizations

The following list provides a quick reference to selected national sport organizations serving the sport and/or recreational interests of Deaf communities in Canada and the United States. Most organizations are run by volunteers and the names and addresses of their contact persons are subject to change, usually at the annual meetings of each organization. Therefore, only the names of the organizations are given below; the reader is advised to contact the National Association of the Deaf (814 Thayer Avenue, Silver Spring, MD 20910) or the Athletic Department at Gallaudet University (800 Florida Avenue NE, Washington, DC 20002) for addresses of current contact persons in the United States. In Canada, information regarding contacts for Deaf sport organizations can be obtained from Fitness and Amateur Sport, 365 West Laurier Avenue, Ottawa, Ontario, K1A-0X6. In both countries, information about Deaf sport organizations can also be obtained from local Deaf clubs and schools for deaf children.

American Athletic Association of the Deaf—AAAD

Founded in 1945, the AAAD is the major Deaf sport governing body in the United States. It regulates competition among member clubs and sponsors annual basketball and softball tournaments. The AAAD promotes the development of various sport programs, public relations activities, and research in Deaf sport. In addition, the AAAD sponsors training camps for various sports and promotes the develvment of athletic skills in deaf youths. The U.S. Deaf Team Committee is a standing committee of the AAAD and is responsible for U.S. participation in international Deaf sport competitions and the World Games for the Deaf (WGD).

The work of the AAAD is facilitated through the activities of its eight regional affiliates. One becomes a member of the AAAD by joining a local Deaf club that is a member of one of the eight regional affiliates:

> Central Athletic Association of the Deaf
> Eastern Athletic Association of the Deaf
> Farwest Athletic Association of the Deaf
> Midwest Athletic Association of the Deaf
> New England Athletic Association of the Deaf
> Northwest Athletic Association of the Deaf
> Southeast Athletic Association of the Deaf
> Southwest Athletic Association of the Deaf

(See chapter one for further information about the AAAD.)

Canadian Deaf Sports Association—CDSA

The CDSA was incorporated in 1964 and is primarily responsible for regulating national and interprovincial competitions in Canada, as well as for promoting public relation activities and research programs. The CDSA promotes physical fitness and participation in sports and recreation among deaf people of all ages. The CDSA's WGD Organizing Committee selects and trains athletes for national and international competitions. The CDSA's Non-Olympic Sports Committee facilitates competition in sports not included in the WGD, which include slo-pitch, curling, and darts.

Membership in CDSA is achieved by joining a local Deaf club that is affiliated with one of the following ten provincial Deaf sport associations:

Alberta Deaf Sports Association
British Columbia Deaf Sports Federation
Féderation Sportive des Sourds du Québec
Manitoba Deaf Sports Association
New Brunswick Deaf Sports Association
Newfoundland Deaf Sports Association
Nova Scotia Deaf Sports Association
Ontario Deaf Sports Association
Prince Edward Island Deaf Sports Association
Saskatchewan Deaf Sports Association

(See chapter one for further information about the CDSA.)

American Deaf Volleyball Association—ADVBA

The ADVBA was established in 1986 and has a membership of around 500 individuals. The purposes of the ADVBA are to promote local, zone, and national volleyball competitions among deaf individuals; to select players to represent the United States in international volleyball competitions and in the World Summer Games for the Deaf; to sponsor an annual volleyball tournament; and to advance the performance of deaf players through volleyball clinics and camps.

American Hearing Impaired Hockey Association— AHIHA

The AHIHA was established in 1973 to promote the development of hockey skills in deaf children and deaf teenagers. Much of AHIHA's work is devoted to running summer hockey camps that train young deaf hockey players from all over the United States. In addition, the AHIHA selects and trains hockey players to represent the United States in international competitions and in the World Winter Games for the Deaf.

Canadian Deaf Curling Championship—CDCC

Although the CDCC is not an organization, it is mentioned here because it is a popular annual event in Canada and there is no national Deaf sport organization that is only for curling. Competition in the CDCC is open to men, women, and seniors mixed teams representing their respective provincial Deaf sport association. Sanctioned by the Canadian Sports Association, the CDCC is hosted by local Deaf clubs or provincial Deaf sport associations. The first CDCC was held in 1979. There are approximately 500 deaf curlers throughout Canada.

Canadian Deaf Ice Hockey Federation—CDIHF

The CDIHF was established in 1984 with the dual purposes of developing fundamental skills in young deaf hockey players and organizing competition for adult deaf hockey teams. In addition, the CDIHF is responsible for selecting and training players to represent Canada in international tournaments and in the World Winter Games for the Deaf. The selection process is accomplished through training camps. As part of its fundraising efforts, the CDIHF regularly selects a team of deaf players to compete against the National Hockey League Oldtimers.

Canadian Hearing Impaired Hockey Association— CHIHA

Incorporated in 1984, the goals of the CHIHA are to provide a forum for deaf boys and girls to socialize, gain life skills, and develop expertise in hockey and to promote the development of leadership skills among deaf youngsters. The CHIHA conducts an annual summer hockey school and many of its graduates move on to play for the Canadian Deaf Hockey Team.

Deaf Athletic Federation of the United States—DAFUS

The DAFUS was founded in 1987 and has about 200 members. Its purpose is to conduct and coordinate the participation of deaf athletes in regional, national, and international athletic competitions. Through its affiliation with the AAAD, DAFUS is responsible for recruiting and helping prepare deaf athletes in track and field events to represent the U.S. Deaf Team at the WGD, as well as for selecting coaches, trainers, and team directors.

National Deaf Bowling Association—NDBA

The NDBA was established in 1963 and is primarily responsible for promoting a recreational and competitive interest in bowling among deaf bowlers in the United States. With upwards of 1000 members, the NDBA helps regulate the participation of deaf bowlers in regional and national bowling tournaments. Bowling was recently added to the WGD and it is likely that the NDBA will assume some responsibility for recruiting and preparing bowlers for this type of competition.

National Racquetball Association of the Deaf— NRAD

The NRAD was founded in 1983 and has 125 individual members. The purposes of the NRAD are to foster interest and participation in racquetball among deaf people in the United States, to sponsor an annual national racquetball tournament, and to support the efforts of Deaf communities in promoting racquetball activities and hosting local racquetball tournaments.

United States Aquatic Association of the Deaf— USAAD

The USAAD was established in 1990 to promote aquatic sports such as swimming, diving, and water polo among deaf people in the United States. With a membership of 50, the USAAD provides year-round training and development programs; selects athletes, coaches, trainers, and officials for national and international competitions; and supports research, development, and dissemination of information regarding deaf aquatic athletes.

United States Deaf Skiers Association—USDSA

Established in 1968, the USDSA promotes recreational and competitive downhill and cross-country skiing. Through its affiliation with the AAAD, the USDSA is responsible for selecting and preparing skiers for international competitions and for the World Winter Games for the Deaf and for selecting coaches, trainers, and team directors. The USDSA has 420 individual members.

United States Deaf Tennis Association—USDTA

The USDTA was established in 1985 and has a membership of around 50 players. The purposes of the USDTA are to encourage participation in tennis; to recruit young deaf tennis players; to develop tennis skills through competitions, tournaments, and tennis camps; and to help select and train players for international competitions and the World Summer Games for the Deaf.

World Recreation Association of the Deaf— WRAD

The WRAD was incorporated in 1985 and has 1300 individual members, mostly in the United States. The primary purpose of the WRAD is to provide a range of recreational activities in the general community for both deaf and hearing individuals. A sampling of some of WRAD's activities are skiing, camping, scuba diving, white water rafting, hiking, roller skating, beach parties, bicycling, and paint pistol war games. WRAD also provides tours of educational and cultural institutions.

INDEX

A

AAAD. *See* American Athletic Association of the Deaf (AAAD)
Adapted physical education, 172–173
Aerobics and Fitness Training Institute of the Deaf (AFTID), 196
Age-group competitions, 194
Alcohol abuse, 8
Alerting devices, 27, 44
Amateur Sports Act, 200–201
American Athletic Association of the Deaf (AAAD), 11–14, 218–219; board, 12; *Bulletin,* 12; communication with local clubs, 117, 118; federal support, 11–12; formation, 12, 182; goals, 12; hearing people in, 11, 32, 71–72; national affiliates, 115; officiating workshops, 202; regional associations, 12, 13, 115, 219; tournaments, 12, 115, 117; women administrators and officers, 4
American Athletic Union of the Deaf, former name of AAAD, 12
American Deaf Volleyball Association, 220
American Hearing Impaired Hockey Association (AHIHA), 113, 220; clinics, 130
American Sign Language (ASL), 20, 28–36; acceptance, 30–31, 35; aesthetics, 32; bonding, 29; cultural value, 30; as distinguishing feature, 31, 143; efficiency, 32; English lexicon and grammar incorporated, 67–68; evolution, 32–33, 68; facial expressions, 89; hearing people learning, 31–32, 35–36; instruction in, 16, 31, 35, 176–177, 184; legal recognition, 109–110; linguistics, 28, 29; manual alphabet incorporated, 28, 68; motivation to learn, 30–34; oppression of, 34–35; role modeling, 162; schools using, 3, 155, 184; socialization tool, 30, 33, 67; sport, use in, 32–34, 67, 68, 128, 129, 155
Ammons, Donalda: profile, 189, 190–191
Amplification. *See* Hearing aids
Arkansas School for the Deaf wrestling team, 160
ASL. *See* American Sign Language (ASL)
Assimilation. *See* Social identification; Socialization through Deaf sport
Athletes, Deaf, 76–79, 160–161; bonding, 78, 143–145; communication and interaction preferences, 129–130; development programs, 189, 191, 194; extrinsic rewards, 76–77, 183; on hearing teams/leagues, 78–79, 114, 121–132, 136–137,

141–144, 147–148; intrinsic
motivation, 77–79, 85, 142,
183; media portrayals, 123–
124; parental influence, 132–
141; qualifying standards, 22–
24, 37; recruiting, 115–118,
152, 163, 166–167; as role
models, 8, 72, 79, 178–179,
181; senior athletes, 194–196;
soliloquies, 38–39, 40–42;
symbolic behavior, 90; value
orientation, 125–126
Athletes, hearing: on Deaf teams,
131, 142–143, 145; interactions with Deaf athletes, 123
Attraction of sport, 5, 8–9, 10–
11, 119–121, 151

B

Badminton, 9, 113
Balancing skills, 166
Baseball, 10; umpire signals, 161
Basketball, 9, 10, 117, 168; AAAD
tournaments, 12, 115, 117;
North Carolina School for the
Deaf Negroes team, 161; re-
gional tournaments, 13, 117;
Western States Basketball
Classic (WSBC), 163
Because It's Time Network (BIT-
NET), 27
Bell, Alexander Graham, 152
Belsky, Martin: profile, 115, 116–
117
BITnet, 27
Black Deaf persons, 69–70, 91;
North Carolina School for the
Deaf Negroes basketball team,
161; sport clubs, 3–4
Bonding: ASL fostering, 29; Deaf
athletes, 78, 143–145. _See also_
Social identification

Bove, Linda, 104
Bowling, 9; CDSA tournaments,
115; Deaf athletes in hearing
leagues, 127; senior tournaments, 194
British Columbia Deaf Sports
Federation (BCDSF), 13, 114,
220
Bulletin, of AAAD, 12
Business of Deaf sport, 9–11;
documentation of sport
events, 198–199; TDD usage,
26. _See also_ Funding of Deaf
sport; Organization of Deaf
sport

C

Canadian Deaf Curling Championships, 221
Canadian Deaf Ice Hockey Federation (CDIHF), 113, 221;
clinics, 130
Canadian Deaf Sports Association (CDSA), 4, 11–14, 114–
115, 219; board, 14, 115; coaching workshops, 79, 202; committees, 14; _Competitor, The,_ 12,
184; federal support, 11–12;
First National Deaf Sport Conference, 201–202; formation,
13, 113; French-speaking director, 14, 28; goals, 13–14, 115;
hearing people in, 11, 32, 71–
72, 115; provincial associations, 13, 114–115, 220; Silent
Walk, 198; tournaments, 4,
112, 115; World Games for the
Deaf Organizing Committee,
201; Youth/Recreation Director, 163, 193
Canadian Hearing Impaired

Hockey Association (CHIHA), 113, 221

Captioned television, 18, 27, 28, 44, 110

CDSA. *See* Canadian Deaf Sports Association (CDSA)

Children of a Lesser God, 98, 104

CISS. *See* Comité International des Sports des Sourds (CISS)

Clerc, Laurent, 32

Coaches, Deaf, 76–79; lack of, 162; workshops, 79, 202

Coaches, hearing, 78–79, 81; judgments about Deaf athletes, 123, 148

Cochlear implants, 103–104

Colleges. *See* Universities and colleges

Comité International des Sports des Sourds (CISS), 5, 115; goals, 7; motto, 24; qualifying standards for athletes, 22–23; women administrators, 7. *See also* World Games for the Deaf

Communication technologies for the deaf, 25–28, 44, 110

Community values, transmission. *See* Socialization through Deaf sport

Competitions. *See* Tournaments

Competitor, The, 12, 184

Computer networking, 26–27

Conformity, 87, 156

Council on Education of the Deaf: report on improving educational standards, 102–103

Cultural values: Deaf community, 66–67, 107–109, 128; diversity, 106–107; transmission (*see* Socialization through Deaf sport)

Curling, 9, 113; CDSA tournaments, 14, 115; senior tournaments, 194

D

Darts: CDSA tournaments, 115

Deaf American, The, 37

Deaf Athletic Federation of the United States, 222

Deaf consciousness, 65–66, 161

Deaf equity. *See* Equity for the deaf

Deaf integration, 19, 175–186, 192, 197; definition, 178–180; principles, 180–185. *See also* Equity for the Deaf

"Deaf Mosaic, The," television program, 16, 79

Deafness: acceptance of, 55–59, 75, 134, 136; adjustments to, 21, 44; as disability, 94–99, 134, 147–148; ecology of, 93–94; media portrayals, 103–106, 123–125, 153, 197–198; misconceptions about, 20, 44, 100–101, 103, 148; redefining, 20–43; societal attitudes toward, 14–18, 38–39, 75, 89, 94–101, 122–123 (*see also* Ethnocentrism); stereotypes of (*see* Stereotypes of deafness); stigma of (*see* Stigma of deafness)

Deaf Studies, 176, 184, 189

DEAFTEK, 27

Demographic factors in Deaf sport, 9, 78, 114, 122, 130–131

Disability: deafness viewed as, 94–99, 134, 147–148; media portrayals, 105–106

Disability Information Services of Canada (DISC), 27

Disabled sport groups, 5, 7, 95–96

Discovery of self, 73–76

Documentation of Deaf sport, 198–199

Drug abuse, 8

E

Ecology of deafness, 93–94
Economics of Deaf sport. *See* Funding of Deaf sport
Education for All Handicapped Children Act (Public Law 94–142), 146, 162, 176
Education of the deaf, 3, 155–174; ASL used in, 35, 155, 184; central school model, 159; Council on Education of the Deaf report, 102–103; curriculum, 184–185; discontent of students, 156; Education for All Handicapped Children Act affecting, 146, 162, 176; hearing people involved in, 60–62, 155, 185; integration policies and practices, 177, 179–181, 184–186; mainstreaming, 135, 146, 176, 177, 188; methodologies, 157–162; oral training, 52, 54, 94, 152, 156–162, 176; paternalism in, 60–61; physical education (*see* Physical education); sport programs, 146–149, 152, 167–168, 173–174, 181; total communication, 157–160, 162, 176. *See also* Schools for the deaf; Teachers; Universities and colleges
Education of the Deaf Act: amendment, 103
Emotional value of sport, 11, 49–50. *See also* Psychological dimensions of Deaf sport
Endogamous marriage, 66, 152
Equity for the deaf, 101–110; cultural pluralism, 106–110; media as tool, 103–105, 125; political strategies, 102–103. *See also* Deaf integration

Eskimo Sign Language, 28
Ethnocentrism, 15, 44–45, 86–87, 94–101, 152–153; abilities of Deaf athletes, 123; researchers, 93, 146. *See also* Stereotypes of deafness
Eye gazing, 31

F

Family influence. *See* Home environment
Fans. *See* Spectators
FAX use by sport directors, 27
Federal support of Deaf sport, 11–12
Federation of Silent Sports of Canada, former name of CDSA, 13
Fingerspelling: ASL incorporating, 28, 68
Fitness programs, 196
Float, Jeff, 108–109, 123, 178
Football, 10, 117; Gallaudet University team, 124, 161
Four-wheel drive clubs, 9
French Canadians, Deaf, 4, 14, 28; sport clubs, 68
French Sign Language (FSL): ASL evolving from, 32–33
Funding of Deaf sport, 198; competition for funds, 2, 96; federal support, 11–12
Future of Deaf sport, 187–203

G

Gallaudet, Thomas Hopkins, 32
Gallaudet University, 103; Aerobics and Fitness Training Institute of the Deaf (AFTID), 196; first Deaf president, 104,

140, 176; football team, 124,
161; student rebellion, 16, 45,
59–62; wrestling team, 160
Gender issues in Deaf sport, 4, 8,
69, 170
Geographic factors in Deaf
sport, 9, 78, 118
Greater Vancouver Association
for the Deaf (GVAD), 9, 114,
131
Great Lakes Deaf Bowling Association, 194

H

Hall of Fame for Deaf Sport, 79,
199
Hearing aids, 24–25, 27–28, 94;
benefit of, 18; stigma of, 103
Hearing community: interaction
with Deaf community, 16–18,
38–39, 89, 101–102, 196; learning ASL, 31–32, 35–36; perspective on deafness (*see* Deafness: societal attitudes toward;
Ethnocentrism); sign language
used by, 51–53, 59–62, 173;
World Games supported by,
36
Hearing sport: Deaf athletes participating in (*see* Athletes,
Deaf: on hearing teams/
leagues); Deaf sport directors
participating in, 126, 128–129;
separation from Deaf sport,
1–2, 9, 19, 107, 203
Hockey, 9, 10, 113, 115, 130–131
Home environment, 45, 46–59;
acceptance of deafness, 55–
59, 134, 136; communication
methods, 48–56, 133; cultural
education in, 51, 56, 139; deaf
parents of deaf child, 55, 138–

140; deaf siblings' influence,
138–139; emotional barriers,
49–50, 52–54, 133; hearing
parents of deaf child, 46–59,
133–138; language development in, 48, 50–51, 139; self-
help groups, 48–49; sport socialization affected by, 132–
141
Hoy, Dummy, 161

I

Integration. *See* Deaf integration
Intellectual value of sport, 11,
165
International competition. *See*
World Games for the Deaf
Interpreters, 18, 173, 198

J

Jordan, Jerald M., 95; profile, 5,
6–7

K

Kruger, Art: profile, 181, 182–
183
Kyte, Jim: magazine article
about, 123

L

La Langue des Signes Québécois
(LSQ), 28
Language: assimilation by, 10; facial expressions in, 89; home
environment influencing, 48,
50–51, 139. *See also* American

Sign Language (ASL); Sign language
Leadership development, 60, 201–202

M

Mainstreaming deaf students, 135, 146, 176, 177, 188
Manual alphabet: ASL incorporating, 28, 68
Manually coded English systems (MCE), 33, 36–37
Manual signs: umpires using, 10
Maritimes Sign Language (MSL), 28
Marriage, endogamous, 66, 152
Matlin, Marlee, 104
McCarthy, Donald, 90; profile, 40–42
Meagher, J. Frederick, 160
Media portrayals of deafness, 103–106, 123–125, 153, 197–198
Mentors, sport, 189
Message-relay centers, 18, 26, 28
Michigan School for the Deaf track team, 160
Minority Deaf persons, 3–4, 8, 69. *See also* Black Deaf persons; French Canadians, Deaf
Misconceptions about deafness, 20, 44, 100–101, 103, 148
Motivation in Deaf sport, 75–79, 85
Motor performance, 164–166
Muscular development, 165

N

NAD Broadcaster, The, 37, 184
National Deaf Bowling Association, 222

National Racquetball Association of the Deaf, 222
National Technical Institute for the Deaf, 103
Newsletters for Deaf sport, 12, 37, 71, 184, 199, 202
Newspaper portrayals of deafness, 103–104, 106, 123–124
North American Deaf Sports Association (NADSA), 12
North Carolina School for the Deaf Negroes basketball team, 161

O

Officials, sport. *See* Referees and umpires
Olympics, 6–7; 1984 boycott, 4–5
Oral training, 52, 54, 94, 152, 157–162, 176
Organization of Deaf sport, 11–14, 71–72, 95; communication facilitators, 192–193; goals, 188–189; hearing people in, 32, 71–72, 115; purpose, 112–113; student memberships, 189. *See also* American Athletic Association of the Deaf (AAAD); Canadian Deaf Sports Association (CDSA); Comité International des Sports des Sourds (CISS); Sport clubs, Deaf

P

Pagers, 27
Paralympics, 7
Parents. *See* Home environment
Paternalism in education of the deaf, 60–61

Peer influence, 134–135, 141–146; deaf peers, 143–145, 157; hearing peers, 141–143

Physical education, 164–174, 184, 200–201; adapted physical education, 172–173; goals, 164–165, 173–174; personal/social effects, 166–167; physical effects, 166; public schools, 170–174; schools for the deaf, 168–169

Pidgin Sign English, 33, 36–37

Political issues in Deaf sport, 4–5, 11, 95; combatting inequity, 102–103; media reports, 125, 153

Promotion of Deaf sport, 151–154, 188–189, 198; by schools, 167–169, 173–174, 181

Provincial associations of CDSA, 13, 220–221

Psychological dimensions of Deaf sport, 2–3, 11, 64–85; discovery of self, 73–76; motivation, 75–79, 85; nonathletic participants, 80–84, 163; self-determination, 2, 19, 91, 111–112; self-esteem, 81–82, 183, 189. *See also* Socialization through Deaf sport

Psychology of the deaf, 44–63; Gallaudet student rebellion, 59–62; Home environment influencing, 46–59 (*see also* Home environment); self-actualization, 57, 73–74; self-image, 2, 61, 65–66, 74–75. *See also* Self-determination; Self-esteem

R

Racial issues in Deaf sport, 3–4, 8, 69

Racquetball, 115

Reagan, Ronald: hearing loss, 103

Recreational programs, 8, 196–197

Redefining deafness, 20–43

Referees and umpires, 80–84; manual signs, 10; workshops, 202

Regional affiliates of AAAD, 12, 219

Regional Postsecondary Education Programs for the Deaf, 103

Research on Deaf sport, 199–200; ethnocentrism of researchers, 93, 146

Ritual in sport, 8

Roberts, Earl, 160

Role models, 75, 83, 162, 181, 193; athletes as, 8, 72, 79, 178–179, 181

Rules of Deaf sport, 9–10, 174

S

Sacks, Oliver: article on Gallaudet student rebellion, 61

Scholarships: effect on motivation, 77

Schools for the deaf, 3, 152; declining enrollment, 116, 148, 162–163, 178; educational practices, 160–164; physical education courses, 168–169; sport programs, 149–150, 160–161, 162–163. *See also* Education of the deaf; Gallaudet University

Self-actualization, 57, 73–74

Self-determination, 60, 63, 77; through Deaf sport, 2, 19, 91, 111–112

Self-discovery, 73–76
Self-esteem, 74–75, 81–83, 97; physical education affecting, 165–166; sport promoting, 81–82, 183, 189
Self-help groups: parent-child relations, 48–49
Self-image, 2, 61, 65–66, 74–75
Senior deaf athletes, 194–196
Separation of Deaf and hearing sport, 1–2, 9, 19, 107, 203
"Sesame Street," 104
Siblings, deaf: influence of, 138–139
Sign language, 28, 33, 36–37, 188; hearing people using, 51–53, 59–62, 173; international, 66, 191; media portrayals, 104–105, 124; in sport activities, 10, 34, 42, 66, 178, 191; stigmatization, 100, 110, 151, 157; total communication promoting, 159. *See also* American Sign Language (ASL)
Silent News, 37
Silent Walk of CDSA, 198
Skiing, 9, 113, 115
Slo-pitch, 9, 113, 168; AAAD tournaments, 115; CDSA tournaments, 14, 112, 115; manual signs by umpires, 10
Smith, Rohan, 69–70
Soccer, 9, 117; signal calls, 10
Social identification, 157, 193; through Deaf sport, 1, 2, 78, 88, 91–92, 143–145, 158, 161, 163, 179, 185, 191; with hearing world, 10, 122, 134–137. *See also* Bonding
Social interactions, 87–92; in Deaf sport, 118–120, 128–129, 151–152; deaf students in public schools, 147; symbolic interactionism, 89–92 (*see also* Symbolic interactionism)
Socialization through Deaf sport, 8–9, 11, 19, 37, 65–72, 108, 111–154, 189, 202; ASL role in, 30, 33, 67; Deaf consciousness, 65–66; empowerment, 71–72; ethnic integration, 68–70; family influence, 132–141 (*see also* Home environment); peer influence, 134–135, 141–146; school influence, 146–150. *See also* Role models
"Socially Deaf" as criterion for athletic competition, 23
Societal attitudes toward deafness. *See* Deafness: societal attitudes toward; Ethnocentrism
Softball: AAAD tournaments, 12, 117; regional tournaments, 13, 117
Spectators, 8, 80, 84, 88; school games, 163
Speechreading. *See* Oral training
Speech training. *See* Oral training
Sport clubs, Deaf, 13, 114–115, 117, 192, 193; Black, 3–4; French Canadian, 68; press releases, 197–198
Sport directors, Deaf, 201–202; communication and interaction preferences, 128–129; computer networking, 26; FAX machines, 27; female, 4; Greater Vancouver Association for the Deaf, 114; in hearing sport programs, 126, 128–129; introduction to Deaf sport, 166–167; lack of, 78; motivation, 83–84; values, 108, 125–126; workshops, 202
Sport festivals, 116–117, 118, 189

Sport mentors, 189
Sport officials. *See* Referees and umpires
Spotlight, 184
Stereotypes of deafness, 30, 44–45, 59, 61, 62, 88; athletes, 123; in Deaf community, 3; internalization, 97; professional abilities, 181; students encountering, 156; teachers having, 172–173. *See also* Ethnocentrism
Stern, Ron, 162
Stigma of deafness, 99–101, 140, 152; hearing aids, 103; sign language, 100, 110, 151, 157; sports participation affected by, 122–123
Students. *See* Education of the deaf; Schools for the deaf
Summer camps, 189
Support system. *See* Social identification
Swimming, 144; lights to start, 10
Symbolic interactionism, 89–92; in Deaf sport, 89–90; language, 89; social definitions, 97–98; stigmatization, 99–100

T

Table tennis, 9; World Games competition, 7
Teachers, 3, 81; in-service training, 189; physical education teachers, 168, 169, 171–172, 174; qualifications to teach the deaf, 61, 156–157, 167. *See also* Education of the deaf
Telecommunication devices for the Deaf (TDD), 25–26, 28, 44, 110. *See also* Message-relay centers

Television: captioned (*See* Captioned television); portrayals of deafness, 16, 79, 104, 105
Tennis, 9, 113, 115; World Games competition, 7
Terrion, Jim, 198
Total communication training, 157–160, 162, 176
Tournaments: AAAD, 12, 115, 117; age-group events, 194; CDSA, 14, 112, 115; hearing and deaf teams, 90–91; media coverage, 197–198; noncompetitive, 192; regional, 13, 117; student events, 164. *See also* World Games for the Deaf
Track: lights to start, 10; Michigan School for the Deaf team, 160
Transportation factors in Deaf sport, 159–160, 162, 193
Tuttle, Marvin, 161

U

Umpires. *See* Referees and umpires
United States Aquatics Association of the Deaf, 222–223
United States Deaf Skiers Association (USDSA), 113, 223
United States Deaf Tennis Association, 223
United States Olympic Committee: Committee on Sports for Disabled, 126
United States World Games for the Deaf Committee, 13, 126, 201; *Spotlight,* 184
Universities and colleges: Regional Postsecondary Education Programs for the Deaf, 103; sign language courses,

35. *See also* Gallaudet University

V

Value orientation in Deaf sport, 107–108, 125–126, 128–130, 137–138
Values of Deaf culture, 66–67, 107–109, 128; influence on choice of sport, 121
Vibrotactile skills, 157
Videotapes, captioned, 27
Volleyball, 9, 113, 168; AAAD tournaments, 12, 115; regional tournaments, 13; signal calls, 10

W

Western States Basketball Classic (WSBC), 163
Women: sport association administrators and officers, 4, 7.

See also Gender issues in Deaf sport
Workshops in Deaf sport, 202; coaches, 79, 202; students, 117
World Games for the Deaf, 6–7, 115, 182–183; AAAD hosting, 13; boycott, 4–5; CDSA Organizing Committee, 201; community support, 36; hearing aids prohibited, 24–25; hearing tests, 22; location, 118; media reports, 124, 153; number of participants, 118, 119; sign language used in, 34, 66; United States committee, 13, 126, 201
World Recreation Association of the Deaf (WRAD), 17, 197, 223–224
Wrestling, 10; Arkansas School for the Deaf team, 160; Gallaudet College team, 160

Z

Zimble, Nathan, 160